AP® ENGLISH LANGUAGE AND COMPOSITION CRASH COURSE®

Dawn Hogue, M.A.

T0371754

Research & Education Association

www.rea.com

Research & Education Association
1325 Franklin Ave., Suite 250
Garden City, NY 11530
Email: info@rea.com

AP® ENGLISH LANGUAGE AND COMPOSITION CRASH COURSE® 4th Edition

Printed in the United States of America

Library of Congress Control Number 2024947565

ISBN-13: 978-0-7386-1291-1
ISBN-10: 0-7386-1291-X

AP® English Language and Composition Crash Course
TABLE OF CONTENTS

About Our Book v
About Our Author vi

PART I   Introduction

Chapter 1   Keys for Success on the AP® English Language
             and Composition Exam 3

Chapter 2   The Student's Tools: What You Can Do to
             Ensure Success 9

Chapter 3   Classifying Nonfiction: Genres, Patterns,
             and Purposes..13

Chapter 4   Representative Authors and Texts 25

PART II   Elements of Argument, Style, and Rhetoric

Chapter 5   Key Terms 49

Chapter 6   Rhetoric and Rhetorical Strategies 59

Chapter 7   Logical Fallacies...81

Chapter 8   Style–The Writer's Choices: Diction, Tone,
             Structure, Imagery, and Figurative Language.............85

Chapter 9   Style–Syntax: Sentence Construction and
             Word Order..97

Chapter 10   Grammar Basics 105

PART III   Analytical Reading and Thinking

Chapter 11   Engaged and Active Reading 125

Chapter 12   Enhancing Vocabulary 135

Chapter 13   Point of View, Perspective, and Position 145

Chapter 14   The World of Ideas: Philosophies, Concepts,
and Literary Themes 155

Chapter 15   Irony and Satire: Reading Between the Lines 163

PART IV   Research and Composition

Chapter 16   Free-Response Questions 181

Chapter 17   Developing an Argument: Creating Excellence
Through Structure, Style, and Voice 189

Chapter 18   Citing and Documenting Sources Effectively 217

Chapter 19   Free-Response Question 1: The Synthesis Essay 227

Chapter 20   Free-Response Question 2: Rhetorical Analysis 249

Chapter 21   Free-Response Question 3: The Argument Essay 261

Chapter 22   Aim High: Tips and Tools for Success 271

Chapter 23   Rubric Analysis for Essays 277

PART V   Mastering the Multiple-Choice Section

Chapter 24   General Test-Taking Strategies 287

Chapter 25   Types of Questions in the
Multiple-Choice Section 291

Chapter 26   Practice Multiple-Choice Questions 297

Chapter 27   Reiteration: Advice Worth Restating 319

References 323

Practice Exam .... *www.rea.com/studycenter*

ABOUT OUR BOOK

REA's *AP® English Language and Composition Crash Course®* is designed for the last-minute studier or any student who wants a quick refresher on the AP® course. This *Crash Course* is based on the latest changes to the AP® English Language and Composition course and exam and focuses only on the topics tested, so you can make the most of your study time.

Written by a veteran AP® English Language and Composition test expert, our *Crash Course* gives you a concise review of the major concepts and important topics tested on today's AP® digital exam.

- **Part I** offers you our **Keys for Success**, so you can tackle the exam with confidence. It also explains the different genres of literature and offers a list of representative authors and texts to strengthen your awareness of potential arguments included on the exam.

- **Part II** covers **Elements of Argument, Style, and Rhetoric** and includes information on elements of language, logical fallacies, and syntax and grammar basics, among other topics.

- **Part III** examines **Analytical Reading and Thinking** and gives advice on practicing engaged and active reading, enhancing your vocabulary, as well as improving your understanding of irony and satire.

- **Part IV** presents **Research and Composition** topics. It covers essay-writing basics, citing sources, and specific approaches for answering the exam's free-response questions.

- **Part V** is devoted to **Mastering the Multiple-Choice Section** of the exam. Test-taking strategies, along with AP®-style practice test questions that reflect the latest four-answer choice format prepare you for what you'll see on test day.

ABOUT OUR ONLINE PRACTICE EXAM

How ready are you for the AP® English Language and Composition exam? Find out by taking **REA's online practice exam** available at *www.rea.com/studycenter*. This test features automatic scoring, detailed explanations of all answers, and diagnostic score reporting that will help you identify your strengths and weaknesses so you'll be ready on exam day.

Whether you use this book throughout the school year or as a refresher in the final weeks before the exam, REA's *Crash Course* will show you how to study efficiently and strategically, so you can boost your score.

Good luck on your AP® English Language and Composition exam!

ABOUT OUR AUTHOR

Dawn Hogue taught all levels of high school English and AP® English for the Sheboygan Falls School District, Sheboygan Falls, Wisconsin. She has earned numerous awards and other recognition for her role in the classroom.

Ms. Hogue received her B.A. in English, graduating summa cum laude, from Lakeland University, Sheboygan, Wisconsin. She also earned her M.A. in Education from Lakeland University and her M.S. in Educational Leadership from Cardinal Stritch University, Milwaukee, Wisconsin.

She is interested in promoting technology and web resources in the classroom, and maintains a website (*www.mshogue.com*) for that purpose. Ms. Hogue was an adjunct faculty member at Johns Hopkins University's Center for Talented Youth, where she worked in digital spaces to help gifted students improve their writing skills.

Ms. Hogue is also the author of REA's *AP® English Literature and Composition Crash Course.*

ABOUT REA

Founded in 1959, Research & Education Association (REA) is dedicated to publishing the finest and most effective educational materials—including study guides and test preps—for students of all ages.

Today, REA's wide-ranging catalog is a leading resource for students, teachers, and other professionals. Visit *www.rea.com* to see our complete catalog.

ACKNOWLEDGMENTS

We would like to thank Larry B. Kling, Editorial Director, for his overall guidance; Pam Weston, Publisher, for setting the quality standards for production integrity and managing the publication to completion; Heidi Gagnon for digital content prep; and Jennifer Calhoun for processing content revisions and preflighting the book file.

We also extend our special thanks to Jason Webb for ensuring the book's technical accuracy; John Kupetz for copyediting; Ellen Gong for proofreading; and Kathy Caratozzolo of Caragraphics for typesetting.

PART I

INTRODUCTION

Keys for Success
on the AP® English Language and Composition Exam

There are no secrets to success. It is the result of preparation, hard work, and learning from failure.—Colin Powell

OVERVIEW

Congratulations! You have chosen to enhance your AP® English Language and Composition study with the help of this *Crash Course.* You are a person who wants to know more and go further. That speaks well of your intent to do what it takes to succeed. In the chapters that follow, you will get content-specific help, tips for success, and general insight about what you need to know to be successful on the AP® English Language and Composition exam. This chapter gives you a glimpse into the structure and scoring of the exam.

COURSE AND EXAM CONTENT

The AP® English Language and Composition exam is based on an instructional framework that seeks to express the essential knowledge and skills gained and demonstrated in an AP® English Language and Composition course. This framework covers four foundational areas, or big ideas, with which you should acquaint yourself.

BIG IDEAS AND ENDURING UNDERSTANDINGS

The phrase "big ideas and enduring understandings" refers to the core knowledge teachers want students to have, not just in their class, but also beyond high school. The information that follows comes directly from the College Board's 2024 *AP® English Language and Composition Course and*

Exam Description. These four foundational areas represent a boiled-down view of what you should know and be able to demonstrate on the exam.

BIG IDEA 1: RHETORICAL SITUATION (RHS)

Enduring Understanding RHS–1: Individuals write within a particular situation and make strategic writing choices based on that situation.

BIG IDEA 2: CLAIMS AND EVIDENCE (CLE)

Enduring Understanding CLE–1: Writers make claims about subjects, rely on evidence that supports the reasoning that justifies the claim, and often acknowledge or respond to other, possibly opposing, arguments.

BIG IDEA 3: REASONING AND ORGANIZATION (REO)

Enduring Understanding REO–1: Writers guide understanding of a text's lines of reasoning and claims through that text's organization and integration of evidence.

BIG IDEA 4: STYLE (STL)

Enduring Understanding STL–1: The rhetorical situation informs the stylistic choices that writers make.

GETTING A FEEL FOR THE EXAM

The English Language exam is delivered digitally. As with traditional paper-based exams, it allows you to go back within a section or part to review or complete previous questions. The College Board offers additional testing options for students with approved accommodations.

The exam asks questions in two main areas: reading and writing.

The reading questions ask students to read, comprehend, and analyze—as a reader—the various rhetorical choices writers make and the function or effect of those choices. There are approximately 23–25 reading questions.

The writing questions will shift the focus to you—as a writer. In these questions, you'll be asked to choose options that would represent written arguments best, such as the ideal style, organization, rhetorical strategy, and best claims and use of evidence. There will be approximately 20–22 writing questions.

The division of the two question types is nearly equal. However, according to the College Board, three of the five prose passages are devoted to the reading questions.

EXAM FOCUS

The following skill categories cover the four Big Ideas and are assessed in the multiple-choice section of the exam.

Skill Category	Exam Weighting
1: Rhetorical Situation—Reading	11%–14%
2: Rhetorical Situation—Writing	11%–14%
3: Claims and Evidence—Reading	13%–16%
4: Claims and Evidence—Writing	11%–14%
5: Reasoning and Organization—Reading	13%–16%
6: Reasoning and Organization—Writing	11%–14%
7: Style—Reading	11%–14%
8: Style—Writing	11%–14%

Source: College Board, 2024

STRUCTURE OF THE EXAM

Section I: Multiple-Choice Questions—There are typically five passages to read and 45 multiple-choice questions to answer in 60 minutes. Each item presents four answer choices. This section represents 45 percent of your total score.

Section II: Free-Response Questions—You are given 135 minutes to read materials, prep for writing, and compose three essays: a synthesis essay, a rhetorical analysis essay, and an argument essay. Note that 15 minutes is set aside as a reading period. This section represents 55 percent of your total score.

Test proctors will give a ten-minute break between Section I and Section II.

SCORING THE EXAM

The multiple-choice section of the exam is scored by machine. Scores on the multiple-choice section are based only on the number of questions answered correctly. Points are not deducted for incorrect answers and no points are awarded for unanswered questions.

The three essays are scored by College Board readers in early June. Readers include college professors and experienced AP® English teachers. These readers score essays using rubrics created by the College Board's test development committee for this exam. Your essay is not identified by name or geographical location. Essays are also criterion-referenced, which means you earn points for how well you meet defined criteria. You are not measured against the work done by other students.

The scores from Section I and Section II are combined to create a composite score. Scores are reported to you and your designated colleges in July.

AP® SCORE SCALE

AP® Score	Credit Recommendation	College Grade Equivalent
5	Extremely well qualified	A
4	Well qualified	A−, B+, B
3	Qualified	B−, C+, C
2	Possibly qualified	n/a
1	No recommendation	n/a

Qualification means you may receive college credit or advanced placement at colleges and universities in the United States and many international institutions as well.

In 2024, the College Board reported that 54 percent of all students who took the exam scored a 3 or higher. And while only 9 percent of students scored a 5, which says something about the difficulty of the exam, you can take heart at the high number of test-takers who passed. Passing generally equates with a score of 3, 4, or 5. These scores will commonly earn you college credits or placement, but always check with your intended colleges for their AP® credit policy.

PREPARE FOR YOUR DIGITAL EXAM

To get ready for this all-digital exam, download the College Board's Bluebook app and practice using it. This way, you won't be facing the program for the first time on exam day. The practice function is free to use. Be sure as well to consult College Board exam-day policies beforehand. The Bluebook app is available at *https://bluebook.collegeboard.org/students/download-bluebook.*

The Student's Tools:
What You Can
Do to Ensure Success

Diligence is the mother of good luck.—Benjamin Franklin

OVERVIEW

Any study text is useless if you don't pair it with your best intentions. This brief chapter outlines what you can do to enhance your own success.

A MATTER OF TIME

You may have heard the saying, "What's worth doing, is worth doing well." This is so true for your preparation for the AP® English Language and Composition exam. Even though this is a *Crash Course*, be realistic about the extent to which you can cram. The information and tips you get in this book will help you no matter how much time you have to prepare, but you will optimize your prep if you start early enough (and use this book to track your progress during your year-long course!) to learn what you need to know. Except for some literary and rhetorical terms, little in this text can be memorized. Instead, you need focus on developing your reading, writing, and thinking skills.

Ideally you should give yourself at least six to nine months to prepare for the exam. Keep this book at your side or in your backpack throughout your course as a way to check your progress. If that is not possible, then a few weeks of serious review with this book will still help you earn a higher score on the exam.

SUGGESTED STRATEGIES FOR USING THIS BOOK

1. Read this entire book, making notes about which chapters are important for you to study. New research shows that handwritten

notes (versus digital or e-notes) are better at helping us remember information. Focus on what you need to know instead of what you already know.

2. Make a goal sheet, listing specific tasks for the upcoming months. Examples of these tasks might be:

   • Read and study several texts, maybe two books and four articles. (See Chapter 4 for a list of authors and texts.)

   • Practice annotating all the texts you read.

3. Good goals have time limits, so be sure to state when you plan to meet your goals.

4. Re-read this book as often as necessary to reinforce ideas. Most people will not remember everything they read the first time.

5. Make a short list of the five most important skills you need to improve before test time, such as reading complex texts or understanding satire. Find ways to practice those skills.

6. Form a study team with friends who are also taking the exam. Learn from each other. Here are some reasons to form a study team:

   • Quizzing each other on terms can help you remember them.

   • You can share your essays with your group. Peer review can help you see strengths and weaknesses in your writing, and by reading others' work, you can learn from them as well.

   • If you all read the same books, you can discuss them, which will help you to understand a text more completely.

7. If you get frustrated, try these strategies:

   • Analyze the reason for your frustration. Why are you frustrated? What can you do to alleviate or minimize your negative feelings?

   • Take a short break to refocus: Go for a walk without headphones. Let nature (or the city) help you get out of yourself for a bit.

   • Talk to your study group and vent, but then find ways together to get back on track.

   • Ask your teacher for help.

MORE TIPS

- Because the AP® English Language and Composition exam is delivered digitally, your typing skills are critical to optimize your success. If you are slow on the keyboard, it can have an impact on the time you have to express your ideas. If needed, work now to improve your keyboarding speed and accuracy.

- Your attitude may be more important than you think—it influences everything, even your physical well-being. A positive attitude will give you energy and confidence. A negative attitude will:

  — Limit your ability to read carefully (you'll want to rush, skim, or get it over with);

  — Lead to frustration and fatigue;

  — Keep you from having an open mind;

  — Possibly infect others, giving them doubt about their own abilities.

- Study hard and take the exam seriously. Remember, however, that this is just one test of what you know at this point in your life. It is not the most important thing you will ever do. Try to keep it all in perspective. Try to have fun with all of this.

PREPARING YOURSELF

1. Eat well in the weeks prior to the exam. The AP® English Language exam is generally scheduled in the morning, so get used to eating breakfast so that you can eat a good breakfast on exam day. A good breakfast for your brain consists of fruit, lean protein, and complex carbohydrates. Also, drink water instead of sugared drinks. Energy drinks are notoriously loaded with sugar and should be avoided.

2. Get enough sleep and not just the night before the exam. Establish good sleep patterns in the weeks prior to the exam. High school students typically do not get enough sleep. Aim for 8–9 hours a night.

3. Wake up early enough to be fully awake and ready to go on exam day. Set your alarm so you don't oversleep. You don't want to be groggy!

4. Caffeine may help you be more alert, but overdoing it can make you jittery and make it difficult for you to focus. If you are not accustomed to caffeine, don't have any on exam day.

5. Wear comfortable clothes and shoes on the day of the exam. Prepare for fluctuations in room temperature by wearing layers that you can adjust.

Don't take my word for it. Research the effect of health and wellness on academic performance. You'll enhance your informed and active reading skills by doing this research.

Classifying Nonfiction:
Genres, Patterns, and Purposes

Writing is writing, and stories are stories. Perhaps the only true genres are fiction and nonfiction. And even there, who can be sure?—Tanith Lee

OVERVIEW

The word **genre** means "type." There are many and diverse types of literature in the nonfiction realm, which seems to change daily, especially with Web platforms like Facebook and TikTok. Are profile updates or video clips considered genres? Some of you have probably read multi-genre or graphic novels and have seen how authors weave nontraditional forms with more traditional narratives to create interesting and new types of fictional texts.

Nonfiction authors have also blurred the line between fiction and nonfiction in the latter part of the twentieth century, blending the elements of fiction (imagery, figurative language, suspense, and even dialogue) with nonfiction prose. In general, this blend is called Creative Nonfiction.

The essay itself is said to have originated with French writer Michel de Montaigne, whose short, topic-focused essays set the standard for what followed. For Montaigne, the act of writing the essay was the act of discovering knowledge. He was writing to know. This may also be your essay experience on the AP® English Language and Composition exam, as you will be pondering and writing about topics that you may not normally think about in your daily life. You will be writing to know.

To that end, the exam presents you with many engaging texts to read and analyze. It is impossible to predict the actual genres of the texts you'll encounter on your exam, as the field is so rich and diverse.

However, according to the College Board, students can expect to encounter a variety of genres on a variety of subjects, such as "essays, journalism, political writing, science writing, nature writing, autobiographies/biographies, diaries, history, and criticism."

Additionally, it is vital that you expand your selection of reading to include images—from print (cartoons, photographs, charts, graphs, and other infographics) to video (video, film, any broadcast live image)—used rhetorically. Several visual texts are typically included in the sources provided for the synthesis essay.

Texts that you will encounter on the exam will share some common attributes. They will be challenging and may require more than one reading—college-level texts, in other words. But each passage on the exam (usually an excerpt from a full text) will present a clear rhetorical situation and purpose. As far as the age of the texts you will encounter, you should see a mix of contemporary and historical texts whose writers grapple with issues that continue to confront us as human beings.

Chapter 4 includes an analysis organizer that can help you break down the important components of any text.

Depending on how much time you have, try to read a few books to deepen your overall knowledge, which will help you in more than one way on this exam. If your sense of history is lacking depth, you could read a biography, which would help you expand your knowledge not just of a person, but more importantly, his or her impact on events. Choose biographies of historically impactful people over those of celebrities. If your time is limited, it may be best to read more short works, such as essays included in an anthology of model arguments. It is likely that you have been issued such a book in school. Go beyond what your teacher assigns to strengthen your knowledge base.

This chapter also details the specific patterns of exposition that you are likely to encounter in your reading. You should be able to use these patterns in your own writing.

GENRE LIST

The following list is not complete, but does include all of the print genres that could appear on the exam based on a study of released exams. No matter what the genre, the writer's purposes can be layered and often are. A diary can provide information, chronicle a life, and also describe and persuade. The letters John and Abigail Adams wrote to each other tell us more than details of their lives; these letters are also important historical documents.

Genre	Attributes and Notes
Advertising	Whether video, audio (e.g., radio) or print, all advertisements have a rhetorical goal: to sell a product or service. Advertisers often embed a variety of rhetorical elements—particularly appeals—to reach audiences.
Advice Column	This popular culture genre is written (or recorded) by someone who is an expert in an area. Such columnists have a variety of intentions, from altruistic to mercenary.
Allegory	Allegory tells a literal story by using another story, a figurative one, to create ambiguity. Jonathan Swift's *Gulliver's Travels* is social criticism and satire veiled as a fantastical tale of strange lands and peoples.
Autobiography	An author's story of his or her own life; written in first person. Varies from memoir in that it generally reads less like a novel (as memoirs often do) and more like a chronological account, though there are no rules for either.
Biography	A third-person account of another's life.
Blog Post (or Weblog Post)	An entry on a personal or professional website called a blog; can be on any topic, from any point of view, and written for various audiences and various purposes. Truly a democratic genre; anyone can write a blog.

Continued →

Genre	Attributes and Notes
Commentary	An opinion piece, written or televised. A commentator is often an experienced voice whose ethos has been developed over time. A newspaper column is a type of commentary.
Creative Nonfiction	A relatively new genre, creative nonfiction tells true stories using the tools fiction writers use, such as plot, narratives, imagery, dialogue, and more. Topics are diverse, from personal narratives to travelogues, and more.
Critique (Criticism)	Similar to a review, a critique points out the strengths and weaknesses of a work (art, literature, speech, performance, etc.).
Debate	A traditional debate is a spoken event in which participants (two opposing teams) argue (with supporting details) a controversial issue. Political debates feature candidates (sometimes only two, sometimes many) who give their own point of view on current topics.
Diary (journal, log)	An account that is kept daily, or almost daily, by an individual to record events of his/her life and to express his/her views.
Documentary Film	Documentary films use images to explore topics. The written counterpart is a trade book or extended text.
Editorial	Written by the editor of a newspaper, it traditionally expresses the view of the editor or the editorial board on an issue prominent in the news. An editorial is typically short (300–350 words) and generally persuasive.
Essay	Essays are considered the principal genre in the realm of rhetoric. The writing you will do on your AP® English Language and Composition exam is an essay. You'll get a deep explanation of essays throughout this book.

Genre	Attributes and Notes
Excerpt	A short portion of a larger text meant to stand on its own. You may be asked to infer the broader context of an excerpt, such as from what genre it was excerpted or the identity of the intended audience.
Extended Texts	The College Board uses this term to refer to longer works written in the past that still retain relevant value. Some extended texts are thought to be seminal texts, which means they are texts that stand as iconic works in a subject.
Eyewitness Account	A first-person report (primary source) of a witness to an important event. As each person's point of view is affected by a wide variety of limiting factors, more than one account is desired for a more objective view of reality.
Fable	A narrative meant to teach a lesson in which the characters are sometimes animal representatives of human types or specific human beings, especially if used for satirical purposes.
History/ Historical Commentary or Criticism	A history is a factual account of an event or period in time. A historical commentary is one person's view of that event, so opinion is based on research, fact, or observation.
Homily	A sermon or a lecture, generally narrative in style, with a moralizing (didactic) purpose.
Image	Graph, chart, or other infographic. Could also be a photograph, editorial cartoon, or other type of visual image.
Imaginative Texts	At times writers of poetry, short stories, novels, or plays are moved to express an argument within their particular genre. The 1906 novel *The Jungle* by Upton Sinclair is considered a searing exposé of the harsh treatment of immigrant workers in the meat-packing industry. The novel led to important reforms.

Continued →

Genre	Attributes and Notes
Interview	Whether televised or in print, an interview can accomplish a variety of purposes, from entertainment to persuasion. Also, TV (or radio) talk show.
Letter (epistle)	Letters can take various forms, from business letters to personal correspondence. The genre now seems nearly obsolete due to email, but historically letters were preserved. Letters from writers, politicians, artists, and others are viewed as historical documents or even as literary works. Letters are also written for a wide variety of purposes: to inform, persuade, entertain, satirize, criticize, and more. The term *epistolary style* means "in letter form."
Literary Criticism	Beyond a review, a literary criticism measures a work of literature against current standards; an analysis of a work that investigates a certain aspect of the work, such as symbolism or irony. Literary criticism may also discuss the work as seen through a specific literary theory, such as feminist, Freudian, or Marxist.
Memoir	A personal narrative that reflects upon one's own life experiences. May be less chronological and encompassing than a typical autobiography.
Monologue	One voice, generally first-person, narrates a train of thought or consciousness on one topic. Typically spoken, as on the stage, for an audience.
Personal Reminiscence	First-person account of a particular event in time.
Political Cartoon	Generally a one-celled comic, the political cartoon is primarily satire that seeks to point out inadequacies or corruption in the political sphere.

Genre	Attributes and Notes
Propaganda	Less a genre, and more of a rhetorical goal, propaganda is meant to undermine a dominant hegemony. Learn more about propaganda in Chapter 6.
Review	Gives the writer's informed opinion about the quality of literary works, movies or other visual media, art, music, even restaurants. Reviewers are called critics.
Satire	The satirist seeks to improve society by revealing its faults through irony and humor, either with a friendly nudge or sharp-edged jabs. See Chapter 15 for more on satire.
Sermon	A speech given by the clergy to the congregation, typically didactic in nature.
Social Criticism	Various subgenres (satire, essay, speech, etc.) meant to criticize current social trends, philosophies, standards, mores, etc.
Speech	Oral essay, commentary; there is a wide variety of types of speeches. The important distinction is that a speech is spoken to an intended audience, which impacts word choice, etc.
TED Talks	This relatively new genre is a video lecture series that features compelling speakers with a message for contemporary audiences. Each speaker's expertise is based on his/her experiences. TED Talks speakers are people of all ages and backgrounds.
Trade Book	A Trade Book explores a particular topic at length or presents an extended argument. Investigative journalism is sometimes presented in a trade book.
Travelogue/ Place Essay	The setting provides the basis for the writing; the author recognizes something significant in the setting.

Continued ➔

Genre	Attributes and Notes
Treatise	A formal and systematic exposition in writing of the principles of a subject, generally longer and more detailed than an essay.
Video	Surely you know what a video is. This wide-reaching genre has a multitude of purposes from entertainment to instruction. A vlog is a subgenre.

Test Tip

If you are given an excerpt on the exam, you may be asked to infer the broader context, such as from what genre it was likely excerpted or the probable identity of the intended audience.

PURPOSES OF ESSAYS (OF WRITING IN GENERAL)

While writers may have one main purpose in mind, they may achieve more than one simultaneously. You will be asked to determine the writer's purpose on the exam and should choose the author's main or dominant reason for writing.

Inform	To give information, clearly and objectively.
Persuade	To convince another to adopt a point of view or engage in an action.
Entertain	To provide humor or a pleasant escape.
Satirize	To point out flaws in people or institutions with the intent of making positive change.
Inspire	Through one's own experiences or observations, provide models that guide or give hope to others.
Reflect	To think back upon, to put into perspective. Reflection is typically personal, but considers the self in relation to others, to history, or to events in time.
Document	To mark in time, to record the significance of some event or action.

TYPES (PATTERNS) OF ESSAYS

Often a writer will use one of the following patterns briefly in a larger, more general argument. But sometimes the entire goal of the essay is to explore cause-and-effect or to define a term or concept.

Pattern	Purpose
Analogy	To explain something abstract or complex by showing its similarity to something simpler and more concrete. For the analogy to be effective, the writer should assume that the reader is familiar with the subject. The main purpose of the analogy is to explain.
Cause and Effect	The writer wishes to explain *why.* Types of causes are the *immediate* causes, which are encountered first, and the *ultimate* causes, which are the basic, underlying factors that explain the more apparent causes. Example: Mom was late for work today because she overslept (immediate cause). She didn't sleep well because she was worrying about her annual employment review and hoped her boss would not bring up the obvious dip in quarterly sales, which she was prepared to explain was due more to the economic recession than her ad campaign (ultimate cause). In writing a logical cause-and-effect essay, the writer must consider all possible relevant factors. There must be evidence for all assertions and attention to objectivity.
Classification	The author divides the subject into categories or other systems to analyze the material, such as types, sizes, number, appearance, prevalence, etc. The system needs to be logical and consistent throughout the essay.
Comparison and Contrast	When we show, in writing, the similarities and differences between two subjects, we are asking readers to look more closely at each. Sometimes the writer looks only to suggest how two things are alike (for example, how Iraqis are similar to Americans, which brings understanding). Or, she may want to show the superiority of one thing over another (such as contrasting the nutritional value of eggs from free-range chickens with those cooped up in large commercial poultry farms). See Chapter 17 for more on comparison and contrast.

Continued →

Pattern	Purpose
Definition	When terms need clarification because they are ambiguous, abstract, unusual, or otherwise not generally understood, the writer will seek to define them for the reader, especially if the overall explanation relies on an understanding of these terms. There are several ways to define. One is through exclusion or differentiation, which shows what is not meant by the term, also called clarification by negation. Writers can also give examples to illustrate the definition. This type of essay, or extended definition, will most likely do more than simply define. The writer seeks also to bring about a greater sense of understanding on an important topic or issue. For example, an essay defining the word "nerd" might be funny and informative, but could also challenge basic stereotypes.
Description	Description is either objective (factual, not an impression or opinion) or subjective (filtered through the writer's perspective and his/her opinion). Subjective description begins in fact. Careful description helps readers see things more clearly, understand abstract concepts more simply, and appreciate ideas and events in a more personal way. Imagery and sensory language nearly always engage the reader emotionally. In such an essay, the writer hopes to present a single, dominant impression.
Exemplification (Illustrating by use of examples)	Uses examples to put abstract or complex ideas into a simpler, more concrete form. To support an argument, a writer must choose a clearly typical example or present several examples that represent the situation fairly. Examples must be relevant or pertinent to the argument.
Hypothesis/ Support	The writer presents a hypothesis or theory and provides details and examples to support or refute it.

Pattern	Purpose
Narration	A narrative essay tells a story and uses the tools of fiction: the selection of important, telling details; logical sequencing of events (such as those in a plot), which may or may not add an element of suspense; transitions to mark time and events; a narrative point of view, which affects how readers view events; and even dialogue. These essays, while non-fiction, may read like short stories, but the characters and events are derived from real life. The overall purpose is to illuminate or explain.
Process Analysis	There are two kinds of processes: a set of directions, that is, how to do something; and an information process, which explains how something is done or how it works or operates. A process analysis essay can be written in chronological order, that is, the order of the steps in the process (first, next, after that, finally). Some processes are more complicated and require a different approach. For example, a historian who writes about how civil rights activists helped register voters would not necessarily follow a chronology of events.

Representative Authors and Texts

*Rarely do we find men who willingly engage in hard, solid thinking.
There is an almost universal quest for easy answers and
half-baked solutions. Nothing pains some people more
than having to think.*—Martin Luther King, Jr.

OVERVIEW

The purpose of this chapter is to give you a sense of the diversity of literature you will encounter on the AP® English Language and Composition exam. In preparing for the exam, commit to reading a variety of texts, even if you only read partial texts. Many of the older works are in the public domain and can be found online. If you have an e-reader, you can download them easily. And don't overlook the fact that a public library is still an amazing place. I am sure that even the smallest local library is going to have many works by these writers on its shelves. In searching for contemporary works (extended texts or investigative journalism), *The New York Times Nonfiction Best Sellers* list is a helpful resource.

ABOUT THE LITERATURE

Most of the selections you will read will be nonfiction, but as that overall genre has changed dramatically over the years, a diverse spectrum indeed awaits you. This is not to say that you will *never* see a poem or a fictional selection on the exam. You might. But it would not be typical. See the previous chapter about how imaginative texts often have a rhetorical purpose.

So, what should you read to prepare yourself for the exam? You could not possibly study all authors and their works. What you should do instead is select a few names from each major category in the list included in this chapter. Read some old, some new. Read a variety of topics. For example, if you are interested in ecology and the environment, find authors who share that interest. But if you only read these authors and their works, you will be limiting your scope.

If you are enrolled in an AP® English Language and Composition course at your school, you most likely have been provided with an anthology-style textbook. If you're like my students, you read only what the teacher assigns. Course anthologies contain selections chosen purposefully for AP® English Language students. Not only should you consider your classroom anthology to be a free resource of great material, but depending on your time, you should read and study as many of the selections as possible. Strive to read diversely: various viewpoints, various styles, and various genres.

Nonfiction is, or can be, just as entertaining to read as fiction or drama. You won't find characters that are embroiled in complex plots, but real life is full of conflict and drama, and the real people who walk across the stage of life are just as interesting, if not more so.

As you read, think about the authors' ideas, but more importantly, the rhetorical strategies and techniques they use to get their point across to their reader. Study how effectively they present their arguments.

REPRESENTATIVE AUTHORS

While many of the writers listed on the next few pages are known for more than what is shown in representative works, I have chosen to list those works that seem most suited to the exam or what is generally thought to be that writer's most accomplished or famous work. For example, Oscar Wilde is best known for his plays, but he is also known for his literary criticism and his involvement with the aesthetic movement, which embraced the idea of art for art's sake.

There may be many writers on this list who are familiar to you for one reason or another. If you've seen some of these people interviewed on television or if you've read about them in your history class, you may be motivated to read more of what they have to say.

The following list is by no means inclusive of all the great writers you could potentially encounter on the AP® English Language exam. However, the list includes names that the College Board has published in their latest Course and Exam Description. Ask your teacher for help in selecting texts to study.

PRE-TWENTIETH-CENTURY AUTHORS

Writer	Representative Work(s)
Joseph Addison (1672–1719) English essayist, poet, playwright and politician	Founded *The Spectator* magazine with Richard Steele
Francis Bacon (1561–1626) English philosopher, statesman, scientist, lawyer, jurist and author	*The Advancement of Learning; Novum Organum*
James Boswell (1740–1795) Scottish lawyer, diarist, author	*The Life of Samuel Johnson*, a biography, and his journals
Thomas Carlyle (1795–1881) Scottish satirist, essayist, and historian	*Sartor Resartus; Signs of the Times*
Samuel Taylor Coleridge (1722–1834) English poet, literary critic, and philosopher	*Biographia Literaria*
Charles Darwin (1809–1882) English naturalist	*On the Origin of Species*
Frederick Douglass (circa 1818–1895) American abolitionist, editor, orator, author, and statesman	*A Narrative of the Life of Frederick Douglass, an American Slave; My Bondage and My Freedom; Life and Times of Frederick Douglass*
Ralph Waldo Emerson (1803–1882) American philosopher, essayist, and poet	Various essays can be found at *http://www.rwe.org/*
Benjamin Franklin (1706–1790) one of the Founding Fathers of the United States; also a leading author and printer, satirist, political theorist, politician, and diplomat	*The Autobiography of Benjamin Franklin*
Margaret Fuller (1810–1850) American journalist, critic, and women's rights advocate	*Woman in the Nineteenth Century*
Edward Gibbon (1737–1794) English historian and member of Parliament	*The History of the Decline and Fall of the Roman Empire*
Thomas Hobbes (1588–1679) English political philosopher	*Leviathan*
Harriet Jacobs (Linda Brent) (1813–1897) American writer, abolitionist speaker, and reformer	*Incidents in the Life of a Slave Girl*

Continued ➜

Writer	Representative Work(s)
Thomas Jefferson (1743–1826) third President of the United States, philosopher, and writer (among numerous other things)	Primary author of the *Declaration of Independence*; *Declaration of the Causes and Necessity of Taking Up Arms*
Samuel Johnson (1709–1784) British author, poet, essayist, literary critic, biographer, and editor	*Dictionary of the English Language*; *Lives of the Most Eminent English Poets*
Chief Joseph (Hin-mah-too-yah-lat-kekt, which means Thunder Rolling Down the Mountain) (1840–1904) Leader of the Wal-lam-wat-kain (Wallowa) band of Nez Perce, a Native American tribe of the interior Pacific Northwest region of the United States	Known primarily for his pacifist beliefs. Search online for his compelling speeches.
Charles Lamb (1775–1834) English essayist	*Specimens of English Dramatic Poets who Lived About the Time of Shakespeare*; *Essays of Elia*
Abraham Lincoln (1809–1865, assassinated) American lawyer, politician, and president	Known for the emancipation of American slaves and striving during the Civil War to keep the union whole. Seek out his speeches and debates
John Locke (1632–1704) English philosopher	*An Essay Concerning Human Understanding*
Niccolò Machiavelli (1469–1527) Italian philosopher and writer; considered one of the main founders of modern political science	*The Prince*
John Stuart Mill (1806–1873) British philosopher	His collected works are easily accessed online: *http://www.gutenberg.org/browse/authors/m#a1705*
John Milton (1608–1674) English poet, author	*Areopagitica*; *Paradise Lost*
Michel de Montaigne (1533–1592) French writer, essayist	His collected essays (Montaigne is considered to be the father of the modern essay.)

Writer	Representative Work(s)
Thomas More (1478–1535) English lawyer, social philosopher, author, and statesman	*Utopia*
Thomas Paine (1737–1809) American author, pamphleteer, radical, intellectual, revolutionary; one of the Founding Fathers of the United States	*Common Sense; The American Crisis; The Rights of Man*
Francis Parkman (1823–1893) American historian	*The Oregon Trail: Sketches of Prairie and Rocky-Mountain Life; France and England in North America*
Walter Pater (1839–1894) English essayist, critic, and fiction writer	*The Renaissance,* especially *The Conclusion*
George Bernard Shaw (1856–1950) Irish playwright, critic, journalist; Nobel Prize in Literature	*The Intelligent Woman's Guide to Socialism and Capitalism; Treatise on Parents and Children; Pygmalion*
Richard Steele (1672–1729) Irish writer and politician; remembered as co-founder, with his friend Joseph Addison, of the magazine *The Spectator*	*The Tatler; The Spectator*
Jonathan Swift (1667–1745) Anglo-Irish satirist, essayist	*Gulliver's Travels; A Modest Proposal; A Tale of a Tub; Drapier's Letters*
Henry David Thoreau (1817–1862) American author, naturalist, critic	*Walden; Civil Disobedience*
Alexis de Tocqueville (1805–1859) French political thinker and historian	*Democracy in America; The Old Regime and the Revolution*
Sojourner Truth (1797–1883) born Isabella [Belle] Baumfree; an African-American abolitionist and women's rights activist	Look for her speeches, most notably *Ain't I a Woman.*
Oscar Wilde (1854–1900) Irish writer, poet, and playwright	*Intentions; De Profundis*
Mary Wollstonecraft (1759–1797) British writer, philosopher, and feminist	*A Vindication of the Rights of Woman*

AUTHORS OF THE 20TH CENTURY TO THE PRESENT

Writer	Representative Work(s)
Edward Abbey (1927–1989) American author and essayist noted for his advocacy of environmental issues and criticism of public land policies	*The Monkey Wrench Gang; Desert Solitaire*
Diane Ackerman (1948–) American author, poet, and naturalist	*A Natural History of the Senses*
Paula Gunn Allen (1939–2008) Native American poet, literary critic, lesbian activist, and novelist	*The Sacred Hoop: Recovering the Feminine in American Indian Traditions*
Natalie Angier (1958–) American nonfiction writer and a science journalist for the *New York Times*; also a contributor to *Time* magazine	*Natural Obsessions*
Margaret Atwood (1939–) Canadian author, poet, critic, essayist, feminist, and social campaigner	*Writing with Intent: Essays, Reviews, Personal Prose—1983–2005; Second Words: Selected Critical Prose*
James Baldwin (1924–1987) American novelist, writer, playwright, poet, essayist, and civil rights activist	*Notes of a Native Son; The Fire Next Time; No Name in the Street; The Devil Finds Work; The Evidence of Things Not Seen; The Price of the Ticket*
Dave Barry (1947–) Pulitzer Prize-winning American author and columnist; humorist	*The World According to Dave Barry; Dave Barry is NOT Making This Up*
Melba Patillo Beals (1941–) American journalist and member of the Little Rock Nine, a group of African-American students who were the first to integrate Central High in Little Rock, Arkansas	*Warriors Don't Cry; White is a State of Mind*
Simone de Beauvoir (1908–1986) French existentialist philosopher and writer	*The Ethics of Ambiguity; The Second Sex*
Lerone Bennett, Jr. (1928–2018) American scholar, author, and social historian	*When the Wind Blows; History of Us*
Wendell Berry (1934–) American writer, fiction, nonfiction, and poetry	Essay collections: *Citizenship Papers; The Way of Ignorance*
Susan Bordo (1947–) modern feminist philosopher and writer	*Unbearable Weight: Feminism, Western Culture, and the Body*

Writer	Representative Work(s)
Jacob Bronowski (1908–1974) British mathematician and biologist	*The Ascent of Man; A Sense of the Future; Magic Science & Civilization; The Origins of Knowledge and Imagination*
William F. Buckley (1925–2008) American author, commentator, editor	See *https://cumulus.hillsdale.edu/ Buckley*
Judith Butler (1956–) American feminist, philosopher, and writer	*Gender Trouble: Feminism and the Subversion of Identity*
Nicholas Carr (1959–) American writer; according to his website, Carr "is an acclaimed writer on technology, economics, and culture"	*The Shallows: What the Internet Is Doing to Our Brains*
Rachel Carson (1907–1964) American marine biologist and nature writer	*Silent Spring*
G.K. Chesterton (1874–1936) British journalist, novelist, and essayist	*Eugenics and Other Evils*
Winston Churchill (1874–1965) British Prime Minister, historian, and writer	*The Second World War; A History of the English-Speaking Peoples*
Judith Ortiz Cofer (1952–2016) Puerto Rican author	*Sleeping with One Eye Open: Women Writers and the Art of Survival; The Myth of the Latin Woman*
Richard Dawkins (1941–) British ethologist, evolutionary biologist, and popular science author	*The Selfish Gene*
Joan Didion (1934–2021) American novelist, essayist, and memoir writer	*Slouching Towards Bethlehem; The Year of Magical Thinking*
Annie Dillard (1945–) Pulitzer Prize-winning American author and artist, best known for her narrative nonfiction	*Pilgrim at Tinker Creek*
Maureen Dowd (1952–) columnist for the *New York Times* and best-selling author	*Are Men Necessary?: When Sexes Collide;* also see current and archived columns in the *New York Times*

Continued ➡

Writer	Representative Work(s)
Elizabeth Drew (1935–) American political journalist and author	Washington Journal: *The Events of 1973–74; Portrait of an Election: The 1980 Presidential Campaign; On the Edge: The Clinton Presidency; Citizen McCain; George W. Bush's Washington*
W.E.B. Du Bois (1868–1963) American civil rights activist, historian, and author	*The Souls of Black Folk* and much more
Dave Eggers (1970–) American writer, editor, and publisher	*A Heartbreaking Work of Staggering Genius; The Circle; The Monk of Mokha; What is the What; A Hologram for the King;* and *The Lifters.*
Richard Ellmann (1918–1987) American literary critic and biographer	*Four Dubliners: Wilde, Yeats, Joyce, and Beckett*
Nora Ephron (1941–2012) American film director, producer, screenwriter, novelist, and journalist	Various screenplays: *Silkwood; When Harry Met Sally; Julie and Julia*
Timothy Ferris (1944–) American science writer	*The Science of Liberty; Coming of Age in the Milky Way*
M.F.K. Fisher (1908–1992) American writer	*Map of Another Town: A Memoir of Provence; To Begin Again: Stories and Memoirs*
Frances FitzGerald (1940–) American journalist and author, known for her journalistic account of the Vietnam War	*America Revised; Cities on a Hill; Way Out There in the Blue: Reagan, Star Wars and the End of the Cold War; Rewriting American History,* a short article in *The Norton Reader;* and *Vietnam: Spirits of the Earth*
Tim Flannery (1956–) Australian paleontologist and environmental activist	*The Weather Makers: The History & Future Impact of Climate Change*
Jonathan Safran Foer (1977–) American writer	*Extremely Loud & Incredibly Close* (2005); Foer's first book of non-fiction, *Eating Animals* (2009), addresses ethical problems associated with industrial production of meat.

Writer	Representative Work(s)
Shelby Foote (1916–2005) American novelist and historian of the American Civil War	*The Civil War: A Narrative*
John Hope Franklin (1915–2009) United States historian	*Racial Equality in America; My Life and an Era: The Autobiography of Buck Colbert Franklin; Runaway Slaves: Rebels on the Plantation; Mirror to America: The Autobiography of John Hope Franklin*
Antonia Fraser (1932–) Anglo-Irish author	*The Weaker Vessel: Woman's Lot in Seventeenth-Century England; The Warrior Queens: Boadicea's Chariot; The Gunpowder Plot*
Thomas L. Friedman (1953–) American journalist, columnist, and Pulitzer Prize-winning author	*The Lexus and the Olive Tree; The World Is Flat; Longitudes and Attitudes*
Paul Fussell (1924–2012) American cultural and literary historian, professor of literature	*The Great War and Modern Memory; Thank God for the Atom Bomb and Other Essays*
John Kenneth Galbraith (1908–2006) Canadian-American economist, writer	*A Life in Our Times*
Henry Louis Gates, Jr. (1950–) American literary critic, educator, scholar, writer, and editor	*Colored People; Tradition and the Black Atlantic: Critical Theory in the African Diaspora; Personal History: Family Matters*
Indira Ghandi (1917–1984) Indian politician and India's third prime minister, serving from 1966 until 1984, when she was assassinated.	Search for her political speeches and writings online or in anthologies.
Malcolm Gladwell (1963–) Canadian writer, journalist, public speaker; staff writer for *The New Yorker* since 1996.	*The Tipping Point: How Little Things Can Make a Big Difference* (2000); *Blink: The Power of Thinking Without Thinking* (2005)

Continued →

Writer	Representative Work(s)
Jane Goodall (1934–) English primatologist and anthropologist	Well known for her work with primates (primarily chimpanzees) in Tanzania. Her research and opinions are available across genres, from extended topic books, personal commentaries and memoirs, to television and film.
Ellen Goodman (1941–) American journalist and Pulitzer Prize-winning syndicated columnist	*Making Sense; Value Judgments; Paper Trail*
Nadine Gordimer (1923–2014) South African writer, political activist, and Nobel laureate	*The Conservationist; The Pickup; The Essential Gesture: Writing, Politics and Places*
Stephanie Elizondo Griest (1974–) Chicana author and activist from South Texas	*Around the Bloc: My Life in Moscow, Beijing, and Havana; 100 Places Every Woman Should Go*
David Halberstam (1934–2007) American Pulitzer Prize-winning journalist and author; known for his early work on the Vietnam War	*Summer of '49; The Next Century; The Fifties; October 1964*
Elizabeth Hardwick (1916–2007) American literary critic, novelist, and short-story writer	*A View of My Own* (1962); *Seduction and Betrayal* (1974); *Bartleby in Manhattan* (1983); and *Sight-Readings* (1998).
Elva Trevino Hart (1949–) Mexican-American writer	*Barefoot Heart: Stories of a Migrant Child* (memoir)
John Hersey (1914–1993) Pulitzer Prize-winning American writer and journalist	*Hiroshima*
Edward Hoagland (1932–) American author best known for nature and travel writing	*Compass Points; Hoagland on Nature; Early in the Season*, plus numerous essays
Richard Holmes (1945–) British biographer	*Shelley: The Pursuit; Coleridge: Early Visions*
bell hooks* (1952–2021) American author, feminist, and social activist	*Ain't I a Woman?: Black Women and Feminism; Yearning: Race, Gender, and Cultural Politics*

---

* bell hooks lowercased her name to place the focus on her work rather than herself.

Writer	Representative Work(s)
Zora Neale Hurston (1891–1960) American folklorist, anthropologist, and author	*Mules and Men; Their Eyes Were Watching God*
Evelyn Fox Keller (1936–2023) American author and physicist	*The Century of the Gene, Making Sense of Life: Explaining Biological Development with Models, Metaphors, and Machines*
Helen Keller (1880–1968) American author and lecturer	*The Story of My Life*
Robert F. Kennedy (1925–1968) American politician and lawyer, U.S. Attorney General (1961–1964), senator from New York (1965–1968, when he was assassinated)	Well known for his civil rights work, his ideas and commentary can be found online and in anthologies. Search for his speeches and essays.
Martin Luther King, Jr. (1929–1968) American clergyman and political leader	various speeches, letters, and essays
Barbara Kingsolver (1955–) American novelist and author	*Animal, Vegetable, Miracle; Small Wonder: Essays, High Tide in Tucson*
Maxine Hong Kingston (1940–) Asian American author	*The Woman Warrior*
Paul Krugman (1953–) American columnist, author, and Nobel Prize-winning economist	Op-ed columns for the *New York Times*; various books and articles
Alex Kuczynski (1967–) American author and reporter for the *New York Times*, columnist for the *New York Times Magazine*	*Beauty Junkies*
Lewis H. Lapham (1935–) American author and journalist	*Waiting for the Barbarians; Theater of War; Gag Rule; and Pretensions to Empire*
T.E. Lawrence (1888–1935) British army officer, known also as Lawrence of Arabia	*Seven Pillars of Wisdom; Revolt in the Desert*
Gerda Lerner (1920–2013) American historian and author	*Why History Matters; The Creation of Feminist Consciousness; Fireweed: A Political Autobiography*

Continued ➞

Writer	Representative Work(s)
Phillip Lopate (1943–) American author and media critic	*Waterfront: A Walk Around Manhattan; Against Joie de Vivre*
Barry Lopez (1945–2020) American environmental author and social critic	*Home Ground: Language for an American Landscape*
Norman Mailer (1923–2007) American writer, co-founder of "new journalism"	*The Executioner's Song; The Big Empty: Dialogues on Politics, Sex, God, Boxing, Morality, Myth, Poker and Bad Conscience in America*
Nancy Mairs (1943–2016) American author, writes about her experiences with multiple sclerosis	*Waist High in the World*
Peter Matthiessen (1927–2014) American writer and environmental activist	*In the Spirit of Crazy Horse; Travelin' Man; Shadow Country*
Mary McCarthy (1912–1989) American author and political activist	*Memories of a Catholic School Girl; Vietnam; Ideas and the Novel*
Frank McCourt (1930–2009) Irish-American writer	*Angela's Ashes*
Bill McKibben (1960–) American environmentalist and writer	*The Bill McKibben Reader: Pieces from an Active Life; Eaarth: Making a Life on a Tough New Planet*
John McPhee (1931–) American writer and pioneer of creative nonfiction	*Annuls of the Former World; Encounters with the Archdruid; Silk Parachute*
Margaret Mead (1901–1978) American anthropologist	*Sex and Temperament in Three Primitive Societies; Male and Female*
Jan Morris (1926–2020) Welsh historian and travel writer	*Locations; O Canada!; Contact! A Book of Glimpses*
John Muir (1838–1914) Scottish-born American naturalist, author, and early advocate of preservation of wilderness in the United States, co-founder of the Sierra Club	*The Story of My Boyhood and Youth*
Donald M. Murray (1923–2006) American journalist and teacher	*My Twice-Lived Life: A Memoir, The Lively Shadow: Living with the Death of a Child*
V.S. Naipaul (1932–2018) Trinidadian novelist and essayist, awarded the Nobel Prize in literature in 2001 for his life's work	*The Writer and the World: Essays,* or anything by this writer

Writer	Representative Work(s)
Joyce Carol Oates (1938–) American novelist and essayist	*Where I've Been, And Where I'm Going: Essays, Reviews, and Prose*
Barack Obama (1961–) 44th President of the United States, president of *Harvard Law Review*	Keynote address at the Democratic National Convention in 2004; *The Audacity of Hope*
George Orwell (1903–1950) English author and journalist	*Politics and the English Language; 1984*
Cynthia Ozick (1928–) Jewish American writer	*Fame & Folly: Essays; Quarrel & Quandary; The Din in the Head: Essays*
Francine Prose (1947–) American writer	*Blue Angel; The Lives of the Muses: Nine Women & the Artists They Inspired*
David Quammen (1948–) award-winning science, nature, and travel writer	*Monster of God: The Man-Eating Predator in the Jungles of History and the Mind*
Arnold Rampersad (1941–) biographer and literary critic, born in Trinidad	*Days of Grace: A Memoir; Jackie Robinson: A Biography*
Ishmael Reed (1938–) American poet, essayist, and novelist	*Barack Obama and the Jim Crow Media: The Return of the "Nigger Breakers;" Mixing It Up: Taking on the Media Bullies and Other Reflections*
David Remnick (1958–) American journalist and Pulitzer Prize-winning writer	*Lenin's Tomb: The Last Days of the Soviet Empire*
Mordecai Richler (1931–2001) Canadian author, screenwriter, and essayist	*Oh Canada! Oh Quebec! Requiem for a Divided Country; Dispatches from the Sporting Life*
Sharman Apt Russell (1954–) American nature and science writer	*An Obsession with Butterflies: Our Long Love Affair with a Singular Insect; Anatomy of a Rose: Exploring the Secret Life of Flowers*
Carl Sagan (1934–1996) American astronomer, astrophysicist, and author	*Pale Blue Dot: A Vision of the Human Future in Space; Cosmos*

Continued →

Writer	Representative Work(s)
Edward Said (1935–2003) Palestinian-American literary theorist	*Out of Place*
George Santayana (1863–1952) Spanish-American philosopher and author	*The Sense of Beauty; The Life of Reason*
Arthur M. Schlesinger (1917–2007) Pulitzer Prize-winning American historian and social critic	*A Thousand Days: John F. Kennedy in the White House; The Disuniting of America: Reflections on a Multicultural Society, A Life in the 20th Century, Innocent Beginnings, 1917–1950*
David Sedaris (1956–) American humorist and writer	*Naked; Holidays on Ice; Me Talk Pretty One Day; Dress Your Family in Corduroy and Denim*
Richard Selzer (1928–2016) American surgeon and author	*The Exact Location of the Soul: New and Selected Essays; Raising the Dead: A Doctor's Encounter with His Own Mortality*
Leslie Marmon Silko (1948–) Native American author	*Yellow Woman and a Beauty of the Spirit: Essays on Native American Life Today*
Rebecca Skloot (1972–) American science writer	*The Immortal Life of Henrietta Lacks* (2010)
Peter Singer (1946–) Australian moral philosopher and Ira W. DeCamp Professor of Bioethics at Princeton University.	His books and articles examine what it means to live an ethical life. Search for his work online.
Barbara Smith (1946–) American lecturer, author, and lesbian feminist	*Writings on Race, Gender and Freedom: The Truth That Never Hurts*
Red Smith (1905–1982) American sportswriter	*Views of Sport; Out of the Red*
Susan Sontag (1933–2004) American writer, filmmaker, and political activist	*At the Same Time: Essays & Speeches* (2007), edited by Paolo Dilonardo and Anne Jump.
Shelby Steele (1946–) American author and documentary filmmaker, specializing in the study of race relations	*The Content of Our Character*

Writer	Representative Work(s)
Lincoln Steffens (1866–1936) American journalist, lecturer, and political philosopher; a famous muckraker	*The Shame of the Cities*
Ronald Takaki (1939–2009) American author	*Debating Diversity: Clashing Perspectives on Race and Ethnicity in America*
Lewis Thomas (1913–1993) American physician, researcher, and writer	*The Lives of a Cell: Notes of a Biology Watcher*
Barbara Tuchman (1912–1989) American historian and Pulitzer Prize-winning author	*The Guns of August*
Cynthia Tucker (1955–) American journalist and Pulitzer Prize-winning columnist	Her blog can be found at *http://blogs.ajc.com/cynthia-tucker/*
Laurel Thatcher Ulrich (1938–) Harvard University professor and women's historian	*Good Wives: Image and Reality in the Lives of Women in Northern New England, 1650–1750; A Midwife's Tale: The Life of Martha Ballard based on her diary, 1785–1812*
John Updike (1932–2009) American novelist and critic	*The Clarity of Things: What's American About American Art?; Due Considerations: Essays and Criticism; Still Looking: Essays on American Art*
Gore Vidal (1925–2012) American author and political activist	*Gore Vidal: Snapshots in History's Glare; Imperial America: Reflections on the United States of Amnesia*
Alice Walker (1944–) American author	*In Search of Our Mothers' Gardens: Womanist Prose; We Are the Ones We Have Been Waiting For*
Jonathan Weiner (1953–) American journalist, science writer	*Long For This World; The Next One Hundred Years: Shaping the Fate of Our Living Earth; The Beak of the Finch: A Story of Evolution in Our Time* (Pulitzer Prize)

Continued →

Writer	Representative Work(s)
Cornel West (1953–) African American philosopher, author, and civil rights activist	*The African-American Century: How Black Americans Have Shaped Our Century; Restoring Hope: Conversations on the Future of Black America; The War Against Parents: What We Can Do For America's Beleaguered Moms and Dads*
E.B. White (1899–1985) American writer	Essays of E.B. White
George Will (1941–) U.S. newspaper columnist, journalist, author, and baseball fan	Will has published numerous books, but search online for his editorials and columns in *Newsweek, The Washington Post*, and ABC News. He is syndicated across the nation.
Terry Tempest Williams (1955–) American author, naturalist, and environmental activist	*Mosaic: Finding Beauty in a Broken World*
Garry Wills (1934–) American historian and Pulitzer Prize-winning author	*Lincoln at Gettysburg: The Words That Remade America; Inventing America: Jefferson's Declaration of Independence*
E.O. Wilson (1929–2021) American biologist, researcher, and Pulitzer Prize-winning author, specializing in the study of ants	*On Human Nature, The Ants, The Future of Life*
Edmund Wilson (1895–1972) American writer, literary and social critic	*The American Earthquake: A Documentary of the Twenties and Thirties, The Bit Between My Teeth: A Literary Chronicle of 1950–1965*
Tom Wolfe (1930–2018) American author and journalist, one of the founders of the New Journalism movement	*The Electric Kool-Aid Acid Test, The Right Stuff*, and 35th Jefferson Lecture in the Humanities titled "The Human Beast"
Virginia Woolf (1882–1941) English author	*A Room of One's Own, Women And Writing, Collected Essays*

Writer	Representative Work(s)
Richard Wright (1908–1960) American author	*American Hunger, Black Boy*
Malcolm X (1925–1965) African-American Muslim minister, public speaker, and human-rights activist	*The Speeches of Malcolm X at Harvard; The Autobiography of Malcolm X*
Anzia Yezierska (circa 1880–1970) Polish-American novelist	*Red Ribbon on a White Horse; Bread Givers*

Have you seen Lin-Manuel Miranda's *Hamilton* or listened to the soundtrack? If so, then you know that Alexander Hamilton, James Monroe, and John Jay wrote "The Federalist Papers," which set out the tenets and guiding principles of the new republic they helped create. You can find these documents online at *www.congress.gov/resources/display/content/The+Federalist+Papers*.

Why not pretend you were "in the room where it happen[ed]" and read a few of these important documents?

AN ANALYSIS ORGANIZER: E-T-C-E-A-S

The following graphic organizer will help you isolate the basic elements of any argument, represented by the acronym E-T-C-E-A-S, which stands for **Exigence, Thesis, Claims and Evidence, Appeals,** and **Style.**

Author _____ Year _____

Title _____

Exigence: Describe the author's urgent need. What does he/she want us to care about or take action on? If possible, explain the cultural context that led to or engendered this need. Who's the primary audience for this message?

_____
_____
_____
_____
_____
_____
_____
_____
_____

Thesis: Paraphrase the author's thesis.

_____
_____
_____
_____

Claims and Evidence: How does this author defend his/her thesis? List 2–3 major claims and summarize the source of and type of evidence given for each claim.

_____
_____
_____
_____
_____
_____
_____
_____

Appeals: Identify and explain one or more primary appeals used in the argument.

_____

_____

_____

_____

_____

_____

_____

_____

_____

(Rhetorical) Style: Briefly describe the function of one or two dominant elements of style evident in the work.

Diction | Tone | Syntax | Imagery | Figurative Language | Structure or Organization

_____

_____

_____

_____

_____

_____

_____

_____

_____

ESSENTIAL READING

Although the College Board does not provide a list of required texts, there are classic arguments AP® English teachers use year after year in their courses that prove effective in preparing students for the exam. If you have time to read nothing else prior to May, the list[†] below will serve you well. Everything listed here is a short text, either an essay or a speech. They're listed in alphabetical order (by author name).

Keep in mind that it is not enough to just read these texts. It is crucial that you read analytically, always with your eye on the speaker's thesis and how and why he or she creates the desired effect.

You will find many of these texts in your anthology textbook for your AP® class. If such a book is not available to you, visit your local public library.

1. "On Women's Right to Vote," Susan B. Anthony

2. "What to the Slave is the Fourth of July," Frederick Douglass

3. "Self-Reliance," Ralph Waldo Emerson

4. "Letter from Birmingham Jail," Martin Luther King, Jr.

5. From *The Prince*, "The Qualities of the Prince," Niccolò Machiavelli

6. "Shooting an Elephant," George Orwell

7. "Allegory of the Cave," Plato

8. "1999 Commencement Speech," Anna Quindlen

9. "Affirmative Action: The Price of Preference," Shelby Steele

10. "A Modest Proposal," Jonathan Swift

11. "I Want a Wife," Judy Brady Syfers

12. "Ain't I a Woman?" Sojourner Truth

13. "Corn-Pone Opinions," Mark Twain

14. "This Awful Slaughter," Ida B. Wells

15. "Death of a Pig," E.B. White

[†] Collated from an informal survey of college and AP® English Language and Composition teachers.

Also included in this *Crash Course* are several other great examples: "*Woman in the Nineteenth Century*," by Margaret Fuller; "Advice to Youth," by Mark Twain; and "Should We Ban Cigarettes?," by Peter Singer. Samples of each are annotated or analyzed in later chapters.

Test Tip

Read the texts included in this book and learn from the accompanying annotations or analysis. Then use what you learn to deepen your analytical reading skills.

PART II

ELEMENTS OF ARGUMENT, STYLE, AND RHETORIC

Key Terms

Learning never exhausts the mind.—Leonardo da Vinci

OVERVIEW

Every enterprise has its own vocabulary. As you emerge into the world of work, you'll realize how specialized language can become. The purpose of this chapter is to help you recognize and understand the basic terms used in persuasive writing, in all its various modes and styles.

TERMS LIST

In the past, you would have been expected to identify the meaning of certain terms for the AP® English Language and Composition exam. However, the new way of thinking is that you should already have a working knowledge of these terms. According to the College Board, the exam "evolved to emphasize the appropriate application of such terminology in students' analyses of texts." In other words, you need to have a functional knowledge of the uses and effects of these terms. It is hard to imagine you'll be highly successful if you're not comfortable in their use.

Some of these terms are defined elsewhere in this book but are here as well, in a condensed glossary, to make their reference easier.

Test Tip

Choose two unfamiliar terms to teach to someone else each day for several months. We tend to remember an idea better when we teach it. Involve your parents. They will be impressed with how smart you are and be happy to help you study.

1. **abstraction:** a concept or idea without a specific example; idealized generalizations.

2. **abstract noun:** ideas or things that can mean many things to many people, such as peace, honor, etc.

3. **allegory:** a narrative or description with a secondary or symbolic meaning underlying the literal meaning. Satirists sometimes use allegory because it allows them a way to indirectly attack their satirical target. Swift's *Gulliver's Travels* is an example.

4. **alliteration:** repetition, at close intervals, of beginning sounds.

5. **allusion (allude to):** a reference to something in culture, history, or literature that expands the depth of the text if the reader makes the connection.

6. **allusion, classical:** a reference to classical (especially Greek or Roman) myth, literature, or culture.

7. **analogy:** compares two things that are similar in several respects in order to prove a point or clarify an idea.

8. **anecdote:** a short narrative of an amusing, unusual, revealing, or interesting event. Usually, the anecdote is combined with other material such as expository essays or arguments to clarify abstract points or to create a memorable image. **Anecdotal:** evidence that relies on observations, presented in narrative.

9. **antecedent:** that which comes before; the antecedent of a pronoun is the noun to which the pronoun refers.

10. **anticlimax, anticlimactic:** an event or experience that causes disappointment because it is less exciting than was expected or because it happens immediately after a much more interesting or exciting event.

11. **antithesis:** the opposite of an idea used to emphasize a point; the juxtaposition of contrasting words or ideas. Hope is the antithesis of despair.

12. **antithesis, balanced:** a figure of speech in which sharply contrasting ideas are juxtaposed in a balanced or parallel phrase or grammatical structure, as in *To err is human; to forgive, divine.*

13. **apostrophe:** a speaker directly addresses something or someone not living, that cannot answer back.

14. **appeal to authority:** one of several appeals strategies; in appealing to authority, the writer refers to expert opinion. (See Chapter 6 for more rhetorical strategies.)

15. **assertion:** the claim or point the author is making.

16. **axiom, axiomatic:** a statement generally accepted as true (in no need of debate); we describe a self-evident truth as axiomatic.

17. **bias:** a preference or an inclination, especially one that inhibits impartial judgment.

18. **burlesque:** a comic tool of satire, the writer uses ridiculous exaggeration and distortion.

19. **cadence:** the rhythm of phrases or sentences created through repetitive elements. (See *syntax*.)

20. **candor:** open and honest communication; truthfulness.

21. **catalog (list):** a list of details that reinforces a concept. Inductive arguments build to a conclusion based on the collective impression of lists (facts, observations).

22. **cause and effect:** essay pattern in which the writer shows the immediate and underlying causes that led to an event or situation.

23. **circular reasoning:** type of faulty reasoning in which the writer attempts to support a statement by simply repeating the statement in different or stronger terms.

24. **circumlocution:** to write around a subject; to write evasively; to say nothing.

25. **claim:** a statement presented for argument that will be proven by evidence; see Chapter 6 for more about types of claims.

26. **coherence:** a quality of writing that refers to overall unity, clarity, and logic. To put it in the vernacular, "easy-to-follow."

27. **colloquial:** common or regional language or behavior; referring to local custom or sayings.

28. **commentary:** the aspect of an argument where the writer explains the connection or the relationship between his or her thesis (and subordinate claims) and supportive evidence. Commentary is where the writer's ethos is verified.

29. **concession:** acknowledgment of the validity of an opposing view.

30. **concrete versus abstract:** concrete is observable, measurable, easily perceived versus abstract, which is vague and not easily defined. An example of a concrete noun is *chair*. While there are many types of chairs, they have one basic purpose. An example of an abstract noun is *patriot*. There are many ways to define a patriot.

31. **connotation:** The emotional or cultural meaning or associative properties of a word that imbues the word with a secondary meaning.

32. **counterargument:** opposing argument that weakens the author's point.

33. **counterexample:** an exception to a proposed general rule.

34. **damn with faint praise:** accolades with words that effectively condemn by seeming to offer praise which is too moderate or marginal to be considered praise at all.

35. **deductive reasoning:** a logical method where we arrive at a truth by beginning with other related truths. We say if this is true and this is true, it is reasonable to know this is true. See Chapter 6 for more about deductive reasoning.

36. **denotation:** the base or literal meaning of a word.

37. **diatribe:** in contemporary terms, a rant. An explosion of harsh language that typically vilifies or condemns an idea.

38. **diction, concrete:** language that is concrete, quantifiable, based on facts, easily accepted by the reader, and generally understood. It is the opposite of abstract diction.

39. **digress, digression:** to move off the point, to veer off.

40. **dilemma:** basically an either/or situation, typically a moral decision.

41. **dilemma, false:** simplifying a complex problem into an either/or dichotomy.

42. **discretion:** refined taste; tact or the ability to avoid embarrassment or distress.

43. **double entendre:** a phrase or saying that has two meanings, one generally being sexual or provocative in nature.

44. **ellipsis (plural: ellipses):** a mark or series of marks (. . .) used in writing to indicate an omission, especially of a number of words. Plural is ellipses.

45. **empirical, empiricism:** knowledge based on experience or observation; the view that experience, especially of the senses, is the only source of knowledge.

46. **epigram:** a short quotation or verse that precedes text that sets a tone, provides a setting, or gives some other context for the text.

47. **episodic:** appearing in episodes, a long string of short, individual scenes, stories, or sections, rather than focusing on the sustained development of a single plot.

48. **epithet:** 1. a short, poetic nickname—often in the form of an adjective or adjectival phrase—attached to the normal name. Example: Grey-eyed Athena (Homer); 2. a term used as a descriptive substitute for the name or title of a person, such as "The Great Emancipator" for Abraham Lincoln; 3. an abusive or contemptuous word or phrase, commonly a slur.

49. **ethos:** a speaker's or writer's credibility; his or her character, honesty, commitment to the writing.

50. **euphemism:** a kinder, gentler, less crude, or harsh word or phrase to replace one that seems imprudent to use in a particular situation; also a word or phrase that dilutes the meaning of or evades responsibility for a more precise word or phrase (such as "assessment" for "test," "casualties" for "deaths").

51. **exemplar:** an example, especially one that is a model to emulate or particularly apt for the situation.

52. **exigence:** the situation that serves as a catalyst for writing; the writer's sense of urgency or need to argue a claim.

53. **explicit:** expressly stated; made obvious or evident; clear.

54. **fact versus fiction:** facts can be verified; fiction is supposed or imagined, and while it may possess truthful elements, fiction is not actual and cannot be verified.

55. **fallacy, fallacious claim:** an error of reasoning based on faulty use of evidence or incorrect inference.

56. **figurative language:** language that is not meant to be taken literally; in general: metaphor; specifically: metaphor, simile, personification, metonymy, and more.

57. **footnote:** an explanatory or documenting reference at the bottom of a page of text.

58. **hyperbole:** an exaggeration or overstatement—saying more than is warranted by the situation in order to expose reality by comparison; also, one of the main techniques in satire. (See Chapter 15 for more on satire.)

59. **hypothetical examples:** examples based on supposition or uncertainty.

60. **hypothetical situation (scenario):** a "what if" or imagined situation that serves an argument by engaging logical imagination; hypothetical situations or scenarios serve to emphasize or underscore.

61. **idealism:** the act or practice of envisioning things in an ideal form; seeing things as they could be or as you wish they were.

62. **idiom, idiomatic:** a figure of speech; a manner of speaking that is natural to native speakers of a language. (Example: Madder than a wet hen.)

63. **imagery:** language (descriptions) that evoke the senses.

64. **imagery, concrete:** imagery that relies on concrete language. Example: Describe the moon as full and orange instead of ominous, which can be interpreted in a variety of ways. Most people have an understanding of what a full moon is and of the color orange.

65. **implicit:** something that is implied.

66. **induction:** reasoning by which a general statement or conclusion is reached on the basis of particular examples.

67. **inference:** an interpretation of the facts based on available details, drawing conclusions.

68. **ironic commentary:** the commentator or opinion writer does not mean what she writes. The writer's point is meant to be taken ironically.

69. **juxtapose (juxtaposition):** to place side by side in order to show similarities or differences. The placement often reveals irony.

70. **list or enumeration:** a list of examples that illustrate a point.

71. **logic:** Logic is a writer's reasoned argument, shown in coherent sets of claims, evidence, and appeals. Commentary makes logic accessible to readers.

72. **logos:** Greek (part of Aristotle's Rhetorical Triangle, see Chapter 6) for "reason." Logos is a writer's appeal to logic.

73. **maxim:** a saying or expression that proposes to teach or tell a truth.

74. **metaphor:** a comparison of two unlike things in order to show one more clearly or in a new way.

75. **metaphor, extended:** the metaphor extends throughout the work or passage, even forming the basis for the entire work. The key to identifying an extended metaphor is length.

76. **mock (mockery):** to make fun of, to treat with ridicule or derision. A tool of satire. Also, a lesser, ignoble form of hero, epic, etc. A mock hero is all that a real hero is not.

77. **musing:** quiet reflection upon a topic; pondering.

78. **naïveté:** innocence in perception, lack of worldly knowledge.

79. **negation(s):** a negative statement; a statement that is a refusal or denial of some other statement, or a proposition that is true if, and only if, another proposition is false.

80. **neutrality:** not taking a position, staying out of an argument.

81. **onomatopoeia:** words whose sounds mimic their meaning.

82. **overgeneralization (also known as hasty generalization):** drawing conclusions from insufficient evidence. Example: All teenagers are sullen and argumentative.

83. **oxymoron:** a figure of speech in which two contradictory elements are combined for effect, such as "deafening silence" or "random order."

84. **paradox:** the juxtaposition of incongruous or conflicting ideas that reveals a truth or insight.

85. **parallel structure/syntax:** the use of parallel elements in sentences or in the structure of an essay or prose passage. Examples: A sentence with successive prepositional phrases uses parallelism. An essay that has four parts, each beginning with a question followed by an answer.

86. **parody:** a humorous imitation of an original text meant to ridicule; used as a technique in satire.

87. **pathos:** the quality in literature that appeals to the audience's emotion.

88. **personification:** to give human attributes or qualities to something nonliving or nonhuman.

89. **propaganda:** information that is spread for the purpose of promoting some cause; information, especially of a biased or misleading nature, used to promote a political cause or point of view.

90. **qualifying a claim/statement:** "to qualify" means to show how a claim can be true in some ways, but not true in other ways. In other words, a conditional claim clarifies the circumstances under which a claim or statement may or may not be true.

91. **rebut, rebutting, rebuttal:** to give an opposing point of view or to dismantle an opponent's argument, showing its flaws.

92. **refutation:** an attack on an opposing view to weaken, invalidate, or make it less credible.

93. **repetition:** any of a variety of devices that emphasize through repetition. One example of a repetition device is anaphora, which is the repetition of the same word or words at the beginning of successive phrases, clauses, or sentences. (See Chapter 9 on syntax for more of these patterns.)

94. **rhetorical question:** a figure of speech in the form of a question posed for its persuasive effect without the expectation of a reply.

95. **rhetorical situation:** The College Board says the rhetorical situation of a text "collectively refers to the exigence, purpose, audience, writer, context, and message." See Chapter 4 for a graphic organizer that can help you record the rhetorical situation (and more) for any argument.

96. **rhetorical strategy:** various strategies and appeals that writers use to persuade. (See Chapter 6 for more details.)

97. **satire (satirize):** a type of literature (or a rhetorical strategy) that exposes idiocy, corruption, or other human folly through humor, exaggeration, and irony. (See Chapter 15 for a more complete explanation of satire.)

98. **semantics:** the study of the logical aspects of words and their meanings.

99. **simile:** a metaphor using *like, than,* or *as* in the comparison.

100. **simile, extended:** the simile progresses throughout the passage or work and may provide the basis for the work in itself.

101. **specious:** attractive but false; on the surface, an argument that looks or seems true, but on close inspection is wrong.

102. **staccato phrases:** phrases composed of a series of short, sharp sounds or words.

103. **style:** the collective choices a writer makes in constructing an argument that includes word choice (diction), syntax, use of other elements of language, as well as types of appeals. See Chapter 8 for a list of terms to describe style.

104. **suspense:** an aspect of plot or narrative in which the author withholds information creating an urgent need to know in the reader.

105. **syllogism:** a formula of deductive argument that consists of three propositions: a major premise, a minor premise, and a conclusion.

106. **symbol:** a thing, idea, or person that stands for something else.

107. **syntax:** the order of words in a sentence; also the types and structures of sentences. (See more about syntax in Chapter 9.)

108. **synthesis:** to combine or integrate evidence from more than one source to defend a single claim.

109. **testimony:** a statement from a witness or an expert who attests to the truth as they see it. Testimony is only as valid as the sources themselves.

110. **thesis:** the main idea of the essay; what the writer hopes to prove is true.

111. **tone:** the speaker's (author's, narrator's) attitude toward a person, place, idea, or thing; the emotional quality of a phrase or passage.

112. **tongue-in-cheek:** humorous or ironic statement not meant to be taken literally.

113. **truism:** a statement that is obviously true and says nothing new or interesting.

114. **typography:** techniques in print (type) used for emphasis: italicizing, bold font, variation in font, etc.

115. **understatement:** saying less than is warranted by the situation in order to emphasize reality.

116. **verb phrase:** the verb and its object and modifiers.

117. **vernacular:** the ordinary, everyday speech of a region.

118. **wit:** clever use of language to amuse the reader, but more to make a point.

Test Tip

Look for these terms in everything you see and read. If you think of this list as merely terms you have to memorize, you will not really integrate them into your thought processes. Instead, apply what you know to how you think about everything you "read," even when you watch a movie or listen to a song.

Rhetoric and
Rhetorical Strategies

Rhetoric is the art of ruling the minds of men.—Plato

OVERVIEW

Rhetoric is the art of persuasion, whether spoken or written. The AP® English Language and Composition exam is a true measure of your ability to write persuasively, as well as to identify and analyze the rhetorical techniques effective writers use. The purpose of this chapter is to give you an overview of the most common elements of rhetoric, both as an aid in analyzing in the texts you are given on the exam and to help you employ them to strengthen your own writing.

A primary goal set for you by the College Board is stated this way: "Students will analyze what makes others' arguments convincing or confusing, engaging or dull, persuasive or powerless." Beyond that, you will be expected to apply your informed analysis to your own arguments, using rhetorical tools effectively.

RHETORIC, ARGUMENT, AND PERSUASION

To **persuade** is to convince someone else to believe something or to do something. The genres one can use to persuade are many, from a simple letter or note to a speech in front of thousands of people. Any instance of the use of persuasion is called an **argument**. The overall realm of argument is called **rhetoric**. Such terms are often used interchangeably. It is not wise to become befuddled by minor distinctions in meaning, or semantics.

This chapter summarizes the main tools that writers and speakers use to persuade.

You need to know that for the AP® English Language and Composition exam there are two main ways to consider argument:

1. As the work you create based on your own exigent goal, whether that exigence is driven by a native or internal catalyst (your own authentic need to express an idea) or by a supplied prompt and ensuing task. (Example: Any persuasive document you write on your own and your essays for Questions 1 and 3 on the exam.)

2. As an analytical assessment in which you argue how, why, and how well another writer achieves his or her own exigent goal. (Example: The rhetorical analysis essay; this view also relates to the analytical thinking required for correct answers in the multiple-choice section of the exam.)

Regardless of the rhetorical situation, all the writing on the AP® English Language exam will require you to put forth a claim and defend it using evidence and commentary.

THE RHETORICAL SITUATION

The rhetorical situation consists of a range of influences on an argument: exigence, audience, writer, purpose, context, and message.

Exigence: Exigence is the situation (experience) that moves a writer to express an opinion. It's the motivating factor. If you see a wrong and wish to right it, you might be moved to present a convincing argument and make a difference.

Audience: Who is the recipient of an argument? While many famous arguments are meant for a general audience, sometimes the writer or speaker has a particular audience in mind. An audience can be characterized by its perceived tendency to agree with you. We use the phrase "preaching to the choir" for situations when we're arguing a point of view that our audience already agrees with. Such arguments can be fun, but do not require much skill. The most difficult persuasive task is when we attempt to convince an audience hostile to our claim not only to accept it, but also to take action in defense of that claim. Always keep the audience in mind when considering the purpose and effect of the intended message.

The writer: Each of us has a voice and if we care to, we can add to ongoing conversations about issues that affect us all. I think of the exigency of the students from Parkland, Florida, who were motivated by their tragedy in 2018 to speak out. Their age and situation has made their voices particularly poignant.

Purpose: The purpose of an argument is what the writer or speaker hopes to accomplish. The highest rhetorical purpose is to compel an audience to take action that will improve life for everyone. Not all writers or speakers have such idealistic goals and may simply wish to expose an issue or topic to a wider public for consideration or inspection, or to add to an ongoing discussion of an important debate.

Context: Context refers to the set of circumstances surrounding an issue or event that often needs to be referenced for a full understanding. Think of these circumstances as the "who," "what," "when," "why," and "how" of any issue or event. Keep in mind historical context can also change over time.

Take this women's rights issue, for example. Prior to August 18, 1920, when the 19th Amendment was ratified, women across the United States argued for their right to vote. Once the law was passed, the context for women's rights changed. Think of what women fight for now. What about others whose rights are often infringed?

Message: The message can be thought of as the construction of the argument itself: its thesis, subordinate claims, evidence, appeals, and commentary.

Try it out: As an exercise, analyze the rhetorical situation for each of the examples below:

- Convincing your dad to let you use his car for a date.

- Convincing your principal that prom court is an antiquated idea based on popularity and should be abolished.

- Arguing that the prom king and queen paradigm is a cisgender construct that excludes transgender individuals.

THE RHETORICAL TRIANGLE

Aristotle defined qualities of argument centuries ago. We still use his language. Be sure you understand how these aspects of rhetoric apply both to texts you're analyzing on the exam as well as your own arguments in the free-response section.

- **Ethos**: The trustworthiness or credibility of the writer. You have to write what you know, what you believe, and support it well. Your essay will be voiceless and powerless if you don't believe in what you are saying.

  — An important element in ethos is **tone**. The tone of the prose must match the intent of the writer. For example, a condescending tone does not equal a willingness to foster positive change. You will not convince your audience if you talk down to them.

- **Logos**: Using reason and logic to persuade. You must have a point to argue and know how to do it. A good argument is based on solid facts to support a reasonable and well-founded claim.

- **Pathos**: Appeals to emotion or the emotional quality of the work.

  — Tone is critical here as well, especially for subtle appeals. Some writers make overt appeals to emotion, such as fear, doubt, etc.

THREE STRUCTURES FOR ARGUMENTS

A. Classic Argument

Developed by Greek philosophers, a classic argument has five basic parts. Note that the following list does not represent paragraphs, but *parts*. Some of these parts will require more than one paragraph.

1. The **introduction**, which establishes ethos and presents the general theme of the message and the thesis.

2. The **narration**, which is a summary of important background material and/or defines other aspects of the issue the audience needs to know, such a defining terms or clarifying a dilemma.

3. The **confirmation**, where the writer proves his or her thesis by presenting supporting claims, evidence, and commentary.

4. The **counterargument**, in which the writer acknowledges an opposing opinion and either refutes (proves is incorrect), rebuts, argues against, or concedes (admits has merit).

5. The **summation** (or conclusion) which ties up the argument and presents an impactful close; something readers (listeners) will remember.

B. Rogerian Argument

The Rogerian argument is based on the work of Carl Rogers, an American psychologist with a humanistic approach. Perhaps best used in arguing a problem-solution issue, Rogers' structure is as follows:

1. Introduce the problem.

2. Acknowledge the other side.

3. Bring the two sides together.

4. Remind the audience of a balanced perspective or that a mutually satisfying solution is desirable.

C. Toulmin Argument

Philosopher Stephen Toulmin developed his style of argumentation, for which the most fundamental components are the claim, the grounds, and the warrant. A full Toulmin argument has six parts: claim, grounds, warrant, qualifier, rebuttal, and backing. Unfamiliar terms are defined below.

- Grounds: Evidence and facts that support a claim.

- Warrant: A warrant links the grounds to the claim and can be either implied (assumed as self-evident) or explicit (purposefully explained). A warrant is a generally accepted premise or truth.

- Qualifier: *To qualify* means to let readers know that a claim may not be universally true in all circumstances. Words like "presumably," "some," "somewhat," and "many" show that the claim is not absolute.

- Backing: Additional support for the warrant—examples that further illustrate the truth of the warrant.

TWO STRUCTURES OF REASONING

A. Deductive Reasoning: Deductive reasoning is essentially a logical method based on a syllogism, which is a formula that includes a major premise (a general statement) and a minor premise (specific statement).

If one accepts these premises to be true, then one can extrapolate a logical deduction. The classic example follows:

Major Premise: All humans are mortal.

Minor Premise: All Greeks are human.

Logical Deduction: All Greeks are mortal.

B. **Inductive Reasoning:** *Induction* means to draw a conclusion from a set of specific instances or examples. Such a conclusion may later be used as a premise for an argument.

For example:

Observations: I noted over many months that each day the sun rose in the east.

Conclusion: Each day the sun rises in the east, and it will continue to each day.

THREE KINDS OF CLAIMS

A claim is a statement you are trying to prove. It requires evidence. It is your proposition or thesis. There are three basic types of claims.

1. CLAIM OF FACT

When you make a **claim of fact**, you are stating something is true and you want your audience to believe you. Example: Daylight Saving Time benefits leisure industries. Claims of fact can be countered by opposing or alternate claims of fact.

About Facts

A **fact** is a statement that can be verified in a variety of ways:

- It is published in credible references;
- It can be known by experience or observation;
- It is measurable or quantifiable.

Facts can also change over time. For example, the fact that the United States is comprised of 13 states has not been true for a while.

Facts may be true, but are not always true. For example: A high school diploma is necessary for success in life. This is generally true, but there are cases of highly successful people who did not earn a high school diploma.

Facts can be "qualified" using words such as "generally," "probably," or "typically." In this case, "qualified" means "not always."

2.   CLAIM OF VALUE

When you make a **claim of value** you are making a judgment or evaluation. Example: Reality TV will rot your brain.

Ways to Evaluate:

- Right or wrong

- Good or bad

- Approve or disapprove

- Beautiful or ugly

- Worth your time or a waste of time

Two Areas of Value:

1. Aesthetics (what is pleasing, beautiful, artistic)

2. Morality (what is moral, right, good)

Sometimes value judgments are actually matters of taste or preference. For example, you prefer straight-leg jeans and your friend prefers boot-cut jeans. In each case, the value lies within the person, not in the thing itself. There is nothing automatically better about either style, and presenting an argument about the superiority of boot-cut jeans is perhaps a waste of time. On the other hand, ads in fashion magazines are essentially arguments for exactly that; clothing manufacturers want you to value one style over another this year, so that you will buy what they are selling. Trends and fads are, to some degree, based on our need to feel beautiful and to fit in (belonging and esteem needs). What we approve of or disapprove of in fashion seems almost capricious—our likes are certainly not based on logic or reason. Don't worry. You will not be arguing about fashion on the exam, but you might be presented with a question a bit weightier, such as whether or not something is moral or right.

Morality judgments can be tricky, as people's views of morality can be conditional and based on culture, religion, ethnic tradition, etc. However, there are universal truths that nearly all cultures uphold. Most societies believe that lying, stealing, cheating, and killing are wrong.

It is likely you will need to provide definitions to ensure that your reader understands exactly what you mean. Not everyone defines "honor," for example, in the same way. By defining what you mean by "honor," you will create a more credible frame for your moral argument.

3. CLAIM OF POLICY

A **claim of policy** is when you argue that certain conditions or situations should exist or be changed. Example: All high school students should pass mandatory minimum proficiency tests before earning a diploma.

Argue a claim of policy if a problem exists for which a change in policy is warranted. You might need to refer to relevant values that support your opinion. Not everyone will agree that your proposal is the correct way to solve the problem, so you need to support your claim with appropriate data, examples, and testimony.

SUPPORT FOR CLAIMS

Two basic types of support:

1. evidence

2. basic appeals (appeals to needs and values)

1. EVIDENCE

A. Factual Evidence

Types of Factual Evidence:

- Examples

- Statistics
- Expert Opinion

Evaluating Factual Evidence:

- Is it up-to-date?
- Is it sufficient; is it enough?
- Is it relevant?
- Is it consistent with the audience's experience?

Evaluating Statistics:

- Are the statistics from a reliable source? Is the source objective or associated with a particular group or point of view that would create bias?
- Are the terms clearly defined?
- Are comparisons valid? Is the writer comparing things that can be compared?
- Has any pertinent information been omitted?

B. Expert or Qualified Opinions (experts, witnesses, qualified observers)

Observers and experts interpret facts and their testimony or opinion can support claims of fact.

Evaluating Opinions:

- Is the source credible or otherwise qualified to give the opinion?
- Does the source harbor any obvious biases?
- Can the source's opinion be verified by fact?

2. BASIC APPEALS

A writer can appeal to readers'

- **needs** (see details below);
- sense of **tradition** (we've always done it this way);
- **ethics** (sense of fairness, right or wrong);

- **emotions** (pull at the heartstrings);
- **logic/reason** (suggest what is logical and support it with a reasoned argument).

There are also appeals to

- **authority** (stating facts, expert opinion, statistics);
- accepted or shared **values** (success, freedom, equality, etc.).

According to psychologist Abraham Maslow, human beings are motivated in their behavior based on their response to whether or not certain basic needs have been met. Maslow arranged his list of needs in a hierarchy. He believed that we need to satisfy needs in a particular order, beginning with physiological and concluding with self-fulfillment.

- **Physiological Needs**: food, drink, air, health;
- **Safety Needs**: security, shelter, order;
- **Belonging Needs**: love from family and friends, belonging to a social group or community;
- **Esteem Needs**: recognition from others; self-esteem that comes from success and achievement;
- **Self-Actualization Needs**: the need to realize our potential, to become what we hope and dream we can become.

Many advertisements and arguments assume that our physiological needs are met, and sell to us based on other needs. Can you find ads that target safety needs, belonging needs, esteem needs? What about self-actualization needs? Your analysis of television commercials or print ads is actually an analysis of rhetorical strategies.

THE IMPORTANCE OF LANGUAGE

No doubt your English teachers have talked to you about how important word choice is for a writer. It's actually much more important than you realize. Words are powerful persuasion tools when the right person wields them for his or her purposes. In this section, I want to reiterate a few basic aspects of language about which you need to be aware, not only for your analyses of texts, but also to help you be a powerful "wielder of words" yourself.

Be aware that language can be used in many ways, ethical and not so ethical. It is important for you to adopt a skeptical stance regarding language. It's almost never a good idea to take words and phrases at face value. What else is there? What connotations exist? What equivocal meanings are apparent? Learn to read, as they say, "between the lines."

Terms and Definitions	Notes
Emotive language is that which expresses emotion or appeals to emotion in the reader.	Emotive language can be abusive, if the writer manipulates emotions for false claims or to gain power or control. Emotional appeals are very common in advertising, in political speeches, and in persuasive texts. It's important to recognize emotional appeals and to look at them for what they are instead of being swept up in the moment.
	A recent ad campaign for a particular smartphone tells consumers nothing about the quality of the product, what it can do, or why they should buy it. Instead, the advertiser presents a variety of emotion-filled vignettes to draw in consumers. One of these narratives is about a wife telling her husband that after a long wait, she's finally pregnant and another has a son showing his father a picture of his newborn son. These obvious appeals to emotion are effective. Empathy connects us in a visceral way. Tears, whether joyful or compassionate, are powerful persuaders.

Continued ➜

Terms and Definitions	Notes
Connotation is the emotional or social meaning of a word or phrase.	Connotations have positive or negative associations and can change over time. Connotations are also culturally anchored. That is, a word can mean one thing in one culture but something else in another. Writers consciously choose certain words over others based on the emotional associations they make with readers. Consider the different connotative meanings in the following pairs of words: "inquisitive" versus "nosy"; "youthful" versus "childish"; "assertive" versus "pushy." In each pair, is one word more positive? Why? Consider why one of the words in each pair is derogatory. Learn to look at why writers choose particular words to make their point.
Euphemisms are words or phrases that are used instead of harsher or uglier words or phrases to lessen or soften the effect.	A common euphemism is to say "passed away" instead of "died" when we report someone's death. It is often quite difficult to learn that someone has died, so a gentle term, we think, makes the news easier to take. The main danger with euphemisms is that they're evasive, sometimes abstract, and generally too ambiguous for clear communication. If a euphemism is used to cover up a truth, then that is an abuse of language equal to a lie.

Terms and Definitions	Notes
Slanted language presents a particular view or is in line with a particular interest. In other words, it is biased or prejudiced language that favors a particular group or point of view.	A good example of slanted language can be heard in almost every current political campaign. Listen for the phrase "career politician." The connotation is negative. The speaker expects the audience to automatically think of any incumbent as a bad politician, simply because he or she has had the job for a while. The term becomes almost a slogan that we should rally around, but why? Where's the evidence?
	Can you think of any other ways the term "career politician" is rhetorically unsound? Hint: Review logical fallacies in Chapter 7.
	Journalists are cautioned to be objective and neutral in their reporting, but this is a difficult task for human beings. Instead, writers who want to be fair will strive to report both sides of an issue, or at least acknowledge that the other side exists. **Loaded words** sympathize with one side only.
	For example, saying that more than a thousand tree-huggers showed up in their Birkenstocks to protest a new mine entails the use of slanted language. The loaded words "tree-huggers" and "Birkenstocks" pander to those who think that it's somehow wrong to want to protect the environment and those who do are crazy hippies (connotation of "Birkenstock," a brand of sandals that became popular with flower children in the U.S.). You can see how some people could be insulted by such slanted language, which for Birkenstock has also involved stereotyping.

Continued →

Terms and Definitions	Notes
Slang, colloquial expressions, and idioms **Slang** refers to informal language considered nonstandard or not acceptable in formal situations. Examples: "sketchy" for something suspect or potentially illegal; "lit" for cool, fun, or trendy; "bet" stands in for "you bet." **Colloquial expressions** are figures of speech that are regional and often anchored in time. Sometimes **colloquialisms** are simply one word. An example can be found with soft drinks, which can be called "soda" or "pop," depending on the region. An apartment may be called a "pad" or a "flat." **Idioms** are colloquial metaphors and are typically particular to a region. Two examples are: "Hotter 'n a fly on a griddle" or "Time to hit the hay."	These elements of vernacular can help one to bond with an audience, by speaking the language of the people. They also have an effect on an author's style. A memoir full of colloquial expressions has a down-home, honest feel to it. A serious, scholarly treatise would not include casual language, however. When you write your own persuasive essays for the exam, you will want to avoid casual language. Rather than try to memorize the subtle differences between these uses of language, simply remember casual versus formal or standard versus nonstandard. A person trying to connect with an audience might make use of the vernacular in order to seem "down-home" or "hip." However, such a tactic could backfire if a speaker is seen as inauthentic. For example, your grandpa trying to use teen-speak might seem inauthentic.

Terms and Definitions	Notes
Clichés and Slogans A **cliché** is a phrase or expression that has been used so often that it has lost its value. A **slogan** is a phrase or statement meant to represent an idea, a movement, a campaign, or even an organization. No doubt your school has a slogan. How does it represent you? Does it have meaning for you? When do words become just words?	Clichés have been around a long time and are often repeated because they express a truth or a shared value. However, leaning on clichés is a lazy shortcut. It is far better to express ideas with well-phrased original sentences. Maybe you've heard someone string together a slew of clichés. When the speech is over, you may have no idea what it was about. A slogan can also become a mindless phrase if it is repeated often enough or out of context. In *Animal Farm*, Orwell warns against the danger of slogans that are mindlessly repeated by the masses which sound like the bleating of sheep. Think about what it means when people say, for example, "Support the Troops." What does it mean? How about the phrase "fake news"? Are those self-stick ribbons that people put on their cars just slogans in disguise?
Picturesque language is language that appeals to the senses, otherwise known as description or **imagery**.	Images are powerful in rhetoric. As human beings, we can relate much more to things we can envision or perceive (even vicariously) through our senses. Imagery is highly emotive as well. Think about how visually oriented we are as a modern culture. Some say we live in an image culture. Abstract ideas are sometimes difficult to grasp, but if a writer creates an image that helps us to understand the abstraction, the point is more easily made.

Continued →

Terms and Definitions	Notes
Concrete versus abstract language **Concrete language** uses specific, tangible references. Concrete passages are not difficult to imagine or perceive. **Abstract language** refers to things that are hard to define, or that can be defined in more than one way. Abstract ideas can mean one thing to me and another to you. An example of an abstraction is, "That's interesting," which means many things. What does "interesting" mean?	The basic problem with abstraction is that it is too vague. Ambiguity presents problems for the reader as well as the writer. Terms must be well-defined in order for an argument to be valid. If the reader has to keep asking what this or that means, it's not good. Learn to distinguish between abstract and concrete language in the same way you distinguish facts from opinions.
Equivocation is found when the writer uses words that have more than one meaning in order to be intentionally ambiguous. Equivocation is an avoidance technique. A **double entendre** is a type of equivocation where one meaning is risqué or sexual. **Puns** also rely on double meanings for humor.	If you run into equivocal language, pay attention to both or all potential meanings of the words. Watch for any uses of ambiguous language. The most important question you can ask yourself as you read is, "What is missing or unstated here?"

Test Tip

A good crossword puzzle relies on double or equivocal meanings of words. Practice your word skills by doing the Sunday crossword from your local paper.

IMPLICIT VERSUS EXPLICIT

Implicit means implied. The idea or concept is alluded to or suggested. The "answer" is not directly found in the text but must be inferred or interpreted based on clues. **Explicit** is the opposite and means that an idea or concept is clearly or directly stated in the text. There is no need to infer. The use of the word "explicit" in media to refer to profane or vulgar text or images has created a misunderstanding of the word. "Explicit" does not mean profane or imply any negative association.

LOGICAL FALLACIES

A **fallacy** is a misuse of language or an error in argument that negates the validity of an argument. Please see Chapter 7 for a detailed view of logical fallacies.

PROPAGANDA

Propaganda is language or rhetoric used to persuade a mass audience, generally to convince them of a particular political, religious, or other ideology. Propaganda differs from other mass persuasive messages in that it is associated with a particular agenda and not a particular message. A variety of genres have been used to transmit propaganda including books, films, broadcast messages, and even pamphlets dropped from aircraft to townspeople on the ground.

Think of how social media platforms like Facebook and X have been appropriated as propaganda tools, with bots using artificial intelligence to amplify divisions and spread disinformation. It is crucial for you to recognize valid arguments supported with verifiable evidence.

While totalitarian regimes are most often associated with propaganda, the United States is also well-known for propaganda, such as "Duck and Cover" films for schoolchildren during the Cold War. The term "propaganda" is generally considered to be pejorative. Propaganda techniques are similar to logical fallacies, which pervert or distort the truth.

In Orwell's *1984*, Hate Week and the Two Minutes Hate activities are major components of the Party's propaganda machine, as each works against rational thought and further turns Oceania's citizens into "bleating sheep."

George Orwell's *Animal Farm* is a simple, easy book to read that will help you grasp the concept of propaganda. Each of the propaganda techniques listed below is evident in the novel. In addition, *Animal Farm* is an example of satire (see Chapter 15). Orwell creates an allegory in order to criticize totalitarianism and the abuse of power. Animal and human characters in the novel have direct, real-life correlatives to key individuals from the Russian Revolution.

PROPAGANDA TECHNIQUES

- **Appeal to authority:** Associated with fear, human beings seem reluctant to oppose authority. We're taught that we do not want to get in trouble. Also, we may find it easier to follow than to lead. We tend to blindly follow authority.

- **Appeal to fear:** Fear is one of the most effective methods of controlling others.

- **Bandwagon technique:** Everyone else is doing it; why not you, too? If you think otherwise, you're not patriotic.

- **Glittering generalities:** Using abstract and undefined language to the extent that people want to believe it. Examples: freedom, glory.

- **Obtain disapproval:** Citizens band together to hate or stand against a common enemy.

- **Stereotyping:** It is much easier to disapprove of a group if we believe everyone in the group is the same. Example: All teenagers are lazy and selfish. (Don't you hate that?)

- **Scapegoating:** Find a person or a group to blame it all on.

- **Slogans:** A motto or phrase that is mindlessly repeated and has no particular meaning, but can bring people together in a common bond.

- **Unwarranted emotional appeals:** Even unrestrained joy (the mania of a crowd) can persuade and make people lose their reason.

STYLISTIC DEVICES EFFECTIVE WRITERS USE

- Evocative or emotive language
- Lists of relevant details
- Figurative language, especially to get readers to see things in a fresh way
- Imagery, appeals to senses and draws readers into the text
- Repetition, used for emphasis
- Parallel structure, used for emphasis
- Irony, gets us to see the truth
- Analogy, shows logical relationships

MODES/FORMS OF RHETORIC

- Cause and effect
- Problem and solution
- Narrative
- Description
- Definition
- Humor
- Satire

THE VERBS OF RHETORIC

1. **Analyze:** to break apart; to look at component parts of a text in order to understand an aspect of the whole.

2. **Characterize**: to depict something in a certain way; to give specific characteristics of someone or something.

3. **Cite:** to make reference to.

4. **Claim**: to make an assertion of something you intend to prove. There are also claims of value and claims of policy, all detailed earlier in this chapter.

5. **Clarify**: to draw distinctions, to make more evident, to lessen confusion.

6. **Compare:** to show how two things are alike or have similar qualities.

7. **Contrast:** to show how two things are not alike or have dissimilar qualities.

8. **Describe:** to use vivid language (such as imagery) to characterize or represent.

9. **Develop:** to enlarge or expand upon an idea.

10. **Discuss**: to consider in writing a variety of possible views (ways of interpretation) on a topic.

11. **Dramatize:** to give a story to a situation by adding vivid details, such as imagery, figurative language, etc.

12. **Elaborate:** to give more detail; to make an idea more complex.

13. **Emphasize:** to give added importance or weight to something.

14. **Establish**: to set a foundation for, to base a claim on an observation.

15. **Evaluate:** to assess in value or quality.

16. **Exemplify:** to give one or more examples.

17. **Explain**: to use details to clarify meaning.

18. **Illustrate:** to describe with anecdotes or examples.

19. **Imply**: to state indirectly; to have a logical consequence.

20. **Indicate**: to be a signal of; to state or express.

21. **Itemize**: to list individual items.

22. **Narrate:** to recount events, as in a story.

23. **Observe**: to take notice of, and thereby, it is implied, to draw conclusions.

24. **Offer a hypothesis:** to offer a theory or assumption to investigate or prove.

25. **Paraphrase**: to put into more common, less complex (or less technical) language.

26. **Predict:** to suggest the effects or result of an action or policy (or any idea that may evolve or change).

27. **Propose**: to suggest a plan or a solution to a problem.

28. **Provide a history:** to provide a concise record of past events, policies, beliefs, etc.

29. **Provide an example:** see *exemplify*.

30. **Rebuff**: to reject.

31. **Refute:** to prove something wrong.

32. **State a proposition:** similar to *offer a hypothesis*, a proposition is an idea worth considering.

33. **Suggest:** to offer a perspective, a solution, or a way of thinking about something for consideration.

34. **Support**: to give reasons and examples for a statement of fact or a claim.

35. **Synthesize:** combine various elements to produce a new concept or to make a point.

36. **Trace:** to follow the origins of an idea; similar to *provide a history*.

Logical Fallacies

He who establishes his argument by noise and command
shows that his reason is weak.—Michel de Montaigne

OVERVIEW

A **logical fallacy** is an error in reasoning or logic. When fallacies exist, some aspect of the argument is flawed, or it may be that the entire argument is rendered invalid. The purpose of this chapter is to list and explain the most common logical fallacies.

There are two reasons for you to be aware of these faults in logic. The first is that you are going to be reading a variety of arguments throughout the AP® English Language exam, and being able to detect lapses in reasoning will help you view these arguments realistically. You are also going to be arguing your own point of view in one of the essays. It is important that you maintain control of your thesis and support it with solid, reliable reasoning. You will not want to commit any fallacies of your own.

Search the Web for "logical fallacies" and you will find dozens of credible sources that list and define fallacies. The list below is not meant to include all fallacies, only the most common.

COMMON LOGICAL FALLACIES

1. **Hasty Generalization:** A conclusion reached prematurely without sufficient evidence. Prejudices and stereotypes are types of generalizations. Words like "all," "every," "everyone," and "no" are associated with hasty generalizations. Example: All teenagers are lazy and uninterested in anything other than themselves. This

may also be called "jumping to conclusions." Example: Everyone is doing it, so it must be healthy.

2. **Faulty Use of Authority:** The arguer attempts to justify his claim by citing testimony or opinions of experts. Also, the arguer fails to acknowledge disagreements among experts or otherwise misrepresents the trustworthiness of sources. Example: A marine biologist who dispenses advice on investing could be construed as a false authority lacking pertinent credentials and experience in financial affairs.

3. *Post Hoc, Ergo Propter Hoc* **(Doubtful Cause)** (Latin for *after this, therefore because of this*): This fallacy exists when the arguer suggests that because an event follows another event, it is therefore true that the first event caused the second. Example: Everything was fine until we switched to Daylight Saving Time. That's why the economy is in trouble.

4. *Ad Hominem* (Latin for *against the man*): When the writer attacks a person (personal character or reputation) instead of addressing the argument or the issue. This fallacy draws attention away from the real issues. Example: Don't vote for William Smith. He has been married three times.

5. **False Dilemma or Either-Or Fallacy:** This is when the arguer assumes that there are only two ways of looking at an issue. Example: America. Love it or leave it.

6. **Slippery Slope:** The arguer predicts that one thing will inevitably lead to another, and that one thing will be undesirable. This is a cause-and-effect error that relies on simplistic, erroneous connections. Example: If students study sex education in high school, they will become sexually promiscuous.

7. **Begging the Question:** The arguer makes an assertion as if she has already proven it. It lacks evidence. Example: Required courses such as freshman English are a waste of time. They should not be required.

8. **Straw Man:** In this diversionary tactic, the arguer attacks a view similar to, but not the same as, his opponent's view.

9. *Non Sequitur*: In Latin, this means *does not follow*. An arguer is guilty of *non sequitur* when he states: "Ms. Johnson is our new English teacher. She's young and should be good."

10. *Ad Populum*: An appeal to the prejudices of the masses that asserts: if many believe it, then it is so. The assumption here is that if everyone is going to agree with me, then I don't really need to support my claim with any evidence. Just because a lot of people believe something doesn't necessarily make it true. Example: Politicians often want whatever the American people want, as if everyone wants/believes the same thing.

11. **Bandwagon Effect or Jumping on the Bandwagon:** This fallacy is similar to *Ad Populum*, but relies on popularity or trendiness. The error in logic is obvious—just because it is popular doesn't necessarily make it correct.

12. **Red Herring:** This fallacy exists when the arguer throws out an unrelated argument to divert the reader's/listener's attention.

13. **Appeal to Tradition:** This fallacy is apparent when the arguer suggests a course of action that is correct "because we've always done it this way." Just because something is traditionally true, that does not make it right or effective. Example: We arrange desks in a classroom in orderly rows. It's the Pencey Prep way.

14. **Faulty Emotional Appeals:** When the arguer seeks sensational or sentimental reactions in the audience; bases an argument on feelings (especially pity or fear), often to draw attention away from the real issues or to conceal another purpose. Example: If you don't study at least an hour every night, you won't get into college and you won't have a successful life.

15. **Guilt by Association:** Relies on prejudice instead of thought. When a person is negatively judged by the actions of those with whom he associates. Example: Senator Adams cannot be trusted. He played golf last year with Senator Jones, who has been indicted for campaign-finance fraud.

Test Tip

After you learn these fallacies, look for them in television commercials or in political ads. This will reinforce the fact that these fallacies exist and will help you remember the different types. It also will help you consider the "arguments" of commercials with a more critical eye.

Style–The Writer's Choices:
Diction, Tone, Structure, Imagery, and Figurative Language

Good writing is like a windowpane.—George Orwell

OVERVIEW

Writers have many tools to use when writing an essay, a speech, a letter, or any genre, and exactly how they use words is determined by many things: their purpose, the intended audience, and even the historical, social, and political context in which they write. There is much more to a writer's work than simply putting words together in a grammatically correct way.

One can find simple, persuasive texts in many places. On the side of a box of a popular breakfast cereal, we find a brief appeal to our desire to improve our environment. The writer has used statistics to support the company's claim that it is striving for sustainability. But, there is no imagery, no figurative language, and the words used are simple—we don't need a dictionary to help us understand what we're reading.

The short pieces you will be reading on the AP® English Language exam will, of course, demand more of your reading and thinking skills than those required when reading a box of cereal, so it is important that you know the ways writers use words to achieve their goals.

This chapter is an overview of the basic tools writers use to manipulate and manage words, so that the resulting text is effective, arresting, and above all, persuasive.

OVERALL STYLE

One way to think of **style** is as the voice of the writer. Many decisions a writer makes—such as types and lengths of sentences (see Chapter 9 for an explanation of syntax), types of words used (see diction), and the extent to which he or she uses imagery and figurative language— contribute to what we recognize as his or her style.

For example, Hemingway's style is characterized, in part, by short, simple sentence structure, while William Faulkner is known for excessively long sentences.

However, we also use the word "style" to mean something similar to tone.

Consider the difference in style of the two examples below:

a) She was like, pizza is so, like, fattening. (Casual, conversational)

b) She understood that pizza was excessively high in fat and calories. (Formal)

You will be expected to understand that style impacts other elements in a passage, such as the attitude of the speaker, and the treatment of a topic.

SOME TYPICAL STYLE DESCRIPTORS:

- **authoritative**: the voice is commanding and knowing
- **didactic**: the voice is preachy, insistent
- **emotive**: the voice evokes emotion
- **objective**: the voice is uncommitted, without judgment
- **ornate**: the voice is pretentious, flowery, or ostentatious
- **plain**: the voice is simple, straightforward, to the point
- **scholarly**: the voice is learned and authoritative, erudite
- **scientific**: the voice is precise and relies on the language of science (Latinate words)

See a more comprehensive list of style descriptors at the end of this chapter.

DICTION

Diction is often defined as the "author's choice of words."

There are two ways to think of diction:

1. Specific effect of word choice: connotation and denotation

2. Overall style

DENOTATION

Denotation refers to the literal or precise meaning of a word. An author's use of the right word for the passage can be key to their clarity of expression. Knowing a wide variety of words and their meanings is critical to being able to understand complex prose passages.

One of the main reasons students misread a passage is that they do not understand the vocabulary in the text. Unfortunately, you won't be able to consult a dictionary when you are taking the exam. Please review the list of potentially difficult vocabulary words in Chapter 12. You can also create your own list from any of the complex texts you are studying. Your goal should be to reinforce your vocabulary skills.

It is also important to be open-minded regarding word meanings. Be careful to not automatically attribute a common meaning to a word, especially when you are reading older texts, as meanings of words change over time. For example, the word "terrific" means "wonderful" or "great" in a contemporary context, but in the context in which it appears on one released exam, it means "terrifying." Another example is the word "awful," which means in its context "to be in awe of," not "horrible," as a contemporary reader might reasonably assume. Considering the context in which words appear is critical to determining meaning.

Test Tip

To avoid misreading the material, especially when confronted with archaic language, determine word meanings from the broader context of the text. Archaic, obscure, or overly specific language will generally be defined in footnotes on the exam.

CONNOTATION

In analyzing word choice, you should also consider the connotation of specific word choice and the effect of those associations in the passage. **Connotation** is the emotional sense of a word or the cultural meaning associated with a word. Connotations are generally positive or negative.

Jonathan Swift, in one section of *A Modest Proposal*, wants to suggest to his readers a connection between poor women and animals used for breeding, and so he refers to a newborn baby as "a child just dropped from its dam." Connotation and denotation are both important to Swift's purpose here. According to *Webster's* dictionary, a "dam" is a female parent of an animal. It's not "dame," which is a British term for a woman of rank, station, or authority, and therefore power. A "dam" is just the opposite. In this context, the connotation suggests lowliness, perhaps even filth, as in barnyard filth. A woman called a "dam" is not really considered human. All the connections to human motherhood are diminished in this one word. The connotation of the word "dropped" is important also. Human mothers do not drop their children in the birthing process. They are aided by doctors (or midwives) who help them, as much as possible, ease their child into the world. "Dropped" connotes mindlessness, as an animal that simply lets its body do its work. The overall effect of this language is to reduce the already wretched Irish poor to the same state as animals and therefore devalue them. If Swift can get his intended audience to accept this premise, the real proposal he has in store for them will seem to be a logical conclusion. There is so much meaning in just a few words.

Test Tip

When you read, if you begin to notice several words that fit together in connotative meaning, make a list of them in the margin (or circle them in the text). You are noticing a series of words that create a dominant impression. While this impression may not drive an essay's thesis, the list is probably a key to understanding it and is worth noting.

TONE

Tone is a critical element of diction, particularly in establishing (or identifying) connotations. Writers choose words based on the emotional or social associations they conjure in readers. What's more, tone is also a key aspect of style. If you have a broad understanding of tone, in particular, and how it plays into a writer's purpose, it will help you answer a wide range of questions on the exam.

Tone is the attitude of the speaker toward another character, a place, an idea, or a thing. In thinking of tone in this regard, it is important to pay attention to not only what a character or speaker does, but also to what he or she says. Sometimes we know more than the character does (dramatic irony) and this impacts our understanding of tone.

We also say that a passage or paragraph has a specific tone, which refers to its emotional quality. This quality comes from details like imagery, diction (a speaker's or narrator's speech, for example), even syntax, in which short, simple sentences seem more urgent and less reflective than more ornate sentence types.

Tone is created in a variety of ways. Diction and imagery are major influences on tone. This is because images evoke emotions and certain words have emotional connotations. When you recognize tone, you most likely "feel" it first. But you also have to have an intellectual understanding of what you feel.

The key to an analysis of tone is, first of all, to recognize it. You must acquaint yourself with typical tone descriptors (see the list at the end of this chapter), so that you aren't fumbling for a word to express what you think you see. The wider the variety of tone descriptors you are able to use, the better you'll be at providing a precise analysis. In other words, if you say a passage is "sad" instead of "melancholy" you may be limiting the precision of your analysis.

Test Tip

While there is most likely a prominent or dominant tone in a passage, you should be aware of tone shifts. If the tone changes suddenly, it can signal an epiphany or some change in a speaker's or narrator's thinking. Tone shifts are critical markers in a passage. See the end of this chapter for a comprehensive list of words that can be used to describe tone.

STRUCTURE

Structure can be a confusing concept. An argument itself can be organized by a required structure, such as the five parts of a classical argument (see Chapter 6). A haiku is an example of a structured poem. A structure is an effective order of component parts. Perhaps you've written a five-paragraph essay in the past. This is only one possible way to structure an argument. Structure should never supersede purpose. For example, not every argument fits into five paragraphs.

However, it's also important to think of structure more broadly.

Organizational framework

- Classical argument, etc.

- Basic paragraph: topic sentence, supporting details, transitional sentence

- Any overall method of organizing information in a piece of writing

Rhetorical purpose

- Compare/contrast, problem/solution, etc.

Sentence level structure

- Syntactical patterns (see Chapter 9)

- Parallelism

- Repetition

IMAGERY

Although imagery is one of the most important elements of poetry, it also serves prose writers. **Imagery** is language that engages the senses and evokes emotion. We relate to imagery on a gut level, responding with our emotions. The more detailed the imagery, the more we can put ourselves into the writing.

TYPES OF IMAGERY

- **Visual:** what we can see

- **Auditory:** what we can hear

- **Tactile:** what we can touch

- **Olfactory:** what we can smell

- **Gustatory:** what we can taste

- **Kinesthetic:** sense of movement

- **Organic:** internal sense of being (well or ill)

These sensory perceptions created through language are vicarious (through the experience of the character or the narration). We might also consider these perceptions to be virtual. We don't actually experience them, but the emotions they evoke in us are real. The more vivid the imagery, the more real the emotion.

To become good at recognizing good imagery, make sure you are always looking for it. Stop when you recognize a particularly imagistic passage. Study it. What kind of imagery is it? How do you feel as you experience the passage? And, most importantly, what is the effect of this image?

EFFECTS OF IMAGERY:

- Helps establish tone

- Creates realistic settings

- Creates empathy in readers for characters

- Helps readers imagine themselves as part of a narrative

Test Tip

Engage your imagination in everything you read to practice this important cognitive reading skill. Visualize situations, settings, people involved, and actions. Not only will this practice deepen your understanding of the work, but it will help you remember what you read.

FIGURATIVE LANGUAGE

When we read any text, we must read carefully and critically, and assume that not everything we read is meant to be taken literally. Writers use **figurative language**, language that is not literal, for various purposes. Many times, figurative language helps us understand complex ideas more clearly, especially if the writer connects to common things or ideas.

METAPHOR

A **metaphor** implies or states a comparison between two unlike things or individuals that helps us see them in a new or more meaningful way. **Similes** are also metaphors, but use the words "like," "as," or "than" in making the comparison. "Life is like a river" is a simile.

Specific Types of Metaphor

- **Direct Metaphor**: the comparison is made directly using the word "is"; for example: Life is a river.

- **Indirect Metaphor**: "The river of life" also compares life to a river, but does so indirectly.

- **Extended Metaphor**: the comparison extends throughout the text (or part of a text) and is fully developed. The ultimate extended metaphor is allegory, which layers two narratives, a literal version with a figurative version. Allegory is more typically found in fiction, drama, and poetry, but is also a technique of satire.

- **Metonymy**: a metaphor in which one word or phrase is substituted for another with which it is closely associated (such as "hand" for "worker" or "crown" for "royalty").

- **Metaphysical Conceit**: an elaborate, intellectually ingenious metaphor (often extended) that shows the writer's realm of knowledge.

- **Analogy**: a comparison based on similarities; showing how two things are alike. An analogy differs from a basic metaphor in that a metaphor is typically completed in one statement or sentence, whereas an analogy can be a paragraph, such as an example to support a claim, or an entire essay as a pattern of exposition.

Comparison is one of our basic patterns of reasoning. We perceive the world and compare new things and experiences with what we already know to see how they are alike or different, and in this process, we make judgments and understand ideas.

OTHER TYPES OF FIGURATIVE LANGUAGE

- **Personification**: giving something non-human, human characteristics

- **Oxymoron**: juxtaposing two things apparently contradictory that still reinforce one idea. For example, jumbo shrimp, deafening silence

- **Hyperbole (overstatement)**: using exaggeration to extend reality. Hyperbole gets us to look more closely at what is actually true by giving us a sharp contrast.

- **Understatement**: this works in the opposite way from hyperbole. We use understatement when we say less than is appropriate for the situation or for our meaning.

STYLE AND TONE DESCRIPTORS

Many of the descriptors in the following lists come from questions about tone, style, attitude, and mood seen on released AP® English Language exams. You will notice overlap, which is typical. Some tone/attitude words can be used to describe style equally as well. The purpose of this list is to expand your ability to describe style and tone.

Tone & Attitude

acerbic	fervent	remorseful
ambivalent	genial	respectful
appreciative	harsh	reverent
callous	indecisive	sanguine
capricious	indifferent	sarcastic
churlish	informal	scornful
civil	irate	self-aware
conciliatory	ironic	self-deprecating
condescending	jealous	self-effacing
contemplative	judicious	serious
critical	mocking	solemn
cynical	nostalgic	strident
defensive	optimistic	superficial
detached	petulant	suspicious
disapproving	prudent	sympathetic
disillusioned	reassuring	zealous
dismissive	reckless	
enthusiastic	reconciled	

Style

abstract	discursive	petulant
accusatory	disdainful	pompous
acerbic	disjointed	pretentious
allusive	earnest	quaint
ambivalent	eloquent	quizzical
apathetic	glib	reflective
bitter	gloomy	reverent
callous	haughty	ridiculing
candid	idiosyncratic	sarcastic
choleric	indignant	sardonic
churlish	informal	scornful
colloquial	jovial	self-deprecating
complex	judgmental	sincere
conciliatory	malicious	sinister
condescending	mocking	smug
contemplative	morose	solemn
contemptuous	objective	speculative
critical	obsequious	symbolic
cynical	optimistic	terse
derisive	ostentatious	urbane
descriptive	patronizing	vulgar
despairing	pedantic	
detached	pessimistic	

Style–Syntax:
Sentence Construction and Word Order

*I like the construction of sentences and the juxtaposition
of words—not just how they sound or what they mean,
but even what they look like.*—Don DeLillo

OVERVIEW

Syntax is the structure of a sentence or the order of words in a
sentence that results in various sentence types used for a variety of
rhetorical effects. We can also think of syntax as the rhythm of prose.
Sentence variety creates interesting, fluent, readable prose. Aspects of
syntax, such as repetition and placement of ideas, are used for emphasis.

A study of syntax is important for several reasons:

- Sentences impact the narrative pace of a passage, making it read
  fast or slow, which therefore impacts the idea/theme.

- Certain types of sentences or arrangements of clauses and phrases
  are better at emphasizing ideas or making key notions prominent
  through repetition, parallel structure, or juxtaposition.

- According to the College Board, "Writers may strategically use
  words, phrases, and clauses as modifiers to qualify or limit the
  scope of an argument." Learn to read not just the words, but also
  the effect of how the words are used.

- Learning to go beyond basic sentence construction and deftly
  craft purposeful and sophisticated syntax will not only aid
  your expression, but it will also help you earn that coveted
  "sophistication" point in the free-response rubric.

WORD ORDER

In English, we have a common or typical word order in a sentence:

Subject ▶ Verb ▶ Object

Sometimes writers use **inverted syntax**, which is simply an atypical or unusual word order. There are several reasons why a writer would use inverted syntax:

- The reverse order makes us pay close attention.

- It creates emphasis.

- It slows down our reading of the text.

Typical/Normal Syntax	Inverted/Unusual Syntax
Stephen ate a blueberry muffin for breakfast.	A blueberry muffin Stephen ate for breakfast. *or* For breakfast ate Stephen a blueberry muffin.

When Robert Frost wrote, "Whose woods these are I think I know," he was no doubt using inverted syntax to satisfy his rhyme scheme, and writing "I think I know whose woods these are" was just not going to work for him. As a result, he created an unusual but highly memorable line.

It's not just poets who use inverted syntax. You will notice examples in prose as well. Again, the main reason is to draw attention to some aspect of the text worthy of an extended or second thought.

Test Tip

When you notice inverted syntax in a passage on the exam, mark it and make an annotation. Even if there is no question about it, you may have discovered an important marker worth further exploration.

SENTENCE TYPES AND ATTRIBUTES

Sentence Type	Attributes
Periodic	The most important idea (or the main or independent clause) comes at the end of the sentence. **Example:** Doctors were convinced they had destroyed the pernicious infection, but just when they thought he'd recover fully, Mario became savagely febrile and died.
Loose	The most important idea is revealed early and the sentence unfolds loosely after that. **Example:** After her chemotherapy failed, Margaret lay moribund in the hospice, glad for the kindness of nurses, thankful for each new morning that she was able to enjoy.
Parallel	A parallel sentence (sometimes called a balanced sentence) contains parts of equal grammatical structure or rhetorical value in a variety of combinations. Two examples of parallel structures: 1. The dog ate voraciously, joyously, and noisily. (The verb "ate" is modified by three multisyllabic adverbs, which seems somewhat lofty in style for such a mundane act as a dog eating.) 2. Joyce was worn down by the constant invasion of her co-workers, by their insistent stares, by their noisy whispers, by their unveiled disdain. She knew she had to find another job. (The parallel phrases are set off by commas; this also is an example of anaphora.)

Continued ➡

Sentence Type	Attributes
Repetition	Types of repetition in sentences: **Anaphora:** The repetition of the same word or words at the beginning of a series of phrases, clauses, or sentences. *Example:* The new paradigm was threatening, the new paradigm was bold, and the new paradigm made students angry as they struggled with the new dress code that would force them all to wear plaid jackets. **Epistrophe:** Ending a series of lines, phrases, clauses, or sentences with the same word or words. *Example:* Clara's eyes sparkled inscrutably in her wizened old face as her twenty-something boss told her that he no longer needed her, that he no longer had use for her, that he no longer would employ her. **Asyndeton:** Conjunctions are omitted between words, phrases, or clauses. *Example:* The only way the commoners could mitigate the Queen's rage was to lie humbly prostrate before her, to be temporarily subservient, to feign obedience for the moment. **Chiasmus:** Two corresponding pairs ordered in an ABBA pattern. *Example:* The Queen reveled in the villagers' adulation, but the villagers' adulation was false as they feared her peremptory decree that everyone should turn their surfeit of grain over to the court. **Polysyndeton:** The obvious repetition of conjunctions (*and, but, or*) between words, phrases, or clauses. *Example:* The mountain climber felt immense trepidation as he faced his arduous climb up K2, but he knew the rewards would be great and the thrill exhilarating and the press conference flattering, and he gained momentum from that renewed vigor.

Sentence Type	Attributes
Grammatical Sentence Types	**Simple:** One subject, one verb, modifiers, complements. Simple sentences are generally short, direct, and, in combination with more complex sentences, can be used for emphasis. *Example:* Puppies need a lot of care. **Compound:** Two independent clauses joined by a coordinating conjunction. Remember this mnemonic device: FANBOYS: for, and, nor, but, or, yet, so. *Example:* The king's edict that adulterers would be punished by death caused a raucous din in the local taverns, for even the common folk knew that he had many indiscretions of his own for which to atone. **Complex:** Contains an independent clause and at least one dependent/subordinate clause. *Example:* Since the nun's ascetic life provided her few material comforts, the wool shawl the novitiate knitted for her was a cherished treasure. **Compound-complex:** Contains two independent clauses and a dependent (subordinate) clause. *Example:* Even though Rafael's muse had sparked his fertile imagination, he nonetheless lost his drive to paint, so he eased his plight by driving a taxi.
Grammatical Sentence Purposes	1. Declarative sentence: Makes a statement. 2. Imperative sentence: Gives a command. 3. Interrogative sentence: Asks a question. 4. Exclamatory sentence: Makes an emphatic or emotion-filled statement.

Test Tip

Copy several sentence pattern examples and rewrite them using as many vocabulary words as you can from Chapter 12. You'll reinforce your vocabulary and practice your sentence types at the same time.

MORE ASPECTS OF SYNTAX

1. **Climax**: The main idea or most important point in a sentence. The position of the climax may be varied for effect.

2. **Cadence**: The rhythm or "music" of a sentence that comes through parallel elements and repetition.

3. **Narrative Pace**: The pace or speed of a passage comes through the following elements:

   - Length of words

   - Omission of words or punctuation

   - Ellipsis (series of dots) indicates a portion is omitted

   - Length of sentences

   - Number of dependent/subordinate clauses

   - Repetition of sounds

Generally, the shorter the words (fewer syllables) and the shorter and simpler the sentences, the faster the pace. Conversely, the longer the words (more syllables) and the longer, more complex the sentences, the slower the pace.

REMEMBER THE THREE P's OF SYNTAX

1. **Prominence:** Prominence refers to the importance given to an idea in a sentence. Prominence is achieved both by placement and repetition. Sometimes an idea is isolated in a short sentence where it is given sole prominence. If a word is ever set off alone as a fragment, it is being given prominence that you'd best not ignore. Instead, ask the question, "Why is this word isolated?"

2. **Position:** Position means where the key idea is located. It will most often come at the beginning of the sentence (loose sentence) or at the end of the sentence (periodic sentence). But sometimes, writers use nonstandard syntax, or inverted word order, to draw attention to certain words or ideas.

3. **Pace:** Pace is when the speed of the text generally complements the author's purpose. While the following two examples are literature-based, they demonstrate the concept perfectly, and you may be familiar with each example. Quentin's section in Faulkner's *The Sound and The Fury* is presented primarily in stream of consciousness, with fast-paced narration that emphasizes the character's fragile state of mind. Another great example of how pace complements the writer's purpose is Maya Angelou's poem *Woman Work*. The first stanza in which she describes all the tasks to be done is meant to be read so fast that the reader actually feels tired after reading it. The rest of the poem is composed of four-line stanzas that read much, much slower. The images in these stanzas evoke peace, coolness, and rest.

Test Tip

Your syntax is important in the essay section of the exam. See Chapter 10 for more on using sentence variety in your writing.

Grammar Basics

*I never made a mistake in grammar but one in my life and
as soon as I done it I seen it.*—Carl Sandburg

The AP® English Language exam is not exactly a grammar test.
You are not going to be asked to identify parts of speech or parts of
sentences. However, one key to comprehending challenging texts—
especially those with complex syntax—is understanding the relationship
of a word to a word, of a word to a sentence, or of phrases or clauses to
sentences and more. In the free-response portion of the exam, it is just as
important that you demonstrate your ability to control the elements of
grammar, mechanics, usage, and syntax in your own writing. The more
sophisticated your control, the better.

Therefore, the purpose of this chapter is to refresh your knowledge
of grammar basics that you will be expected to have mastered prior to
exam day.

PRONOUNS AND ANTECEDENTS

Antecedent means "that which comes before."

Generally speaking, you can think of an antecedent as any clause,
phrase, or noun to which a pronoun or other part of speech refers.
The AP® English Language exam is going to expect you to make such
referential connections.

Specifically, pronouns have antecedents. The antecedent of a pronoun
is the noun to which the pronoun refers. In the sentence, "Jim suddenly
realized **his** work on the project wasn't finished, which would make **him**

late for the meeting to discuss **it**," the pronouns "his" and "him" refer to Jim, while the pronoun "it" refers to the project. One easy way to identify antecedents is to use the object of the pronoun in a question.

> **Example**   The object of the pronoun "his" is "work." You next ask, "Whose work?" The clear answer would be Jim's.

This strategy seems ridiculous when we're looking at this silly little sentence, but what if the syntax of the sentence were much more complicated? Then what? You'll need to look and think carefully and not simply assume that the actual antecedent is the noun closest to the pronoun. You may be wrong!

The following excerpt from Michel de Montaigne's essay "Of Books" is a bit more complex than my previous example. Read it, and then answer the question that follows.

> I have often observed that those of our times, who take upon them to write comedies (in imitation of the Italians, who are happy enough in that way of writing), take three or four plots of those of Plautus or Terence to make one of their own, and, crowd five or six of Boccaccio's novels into one single comedy. That which makes **them** so load themselves with matter is the diffidence they have of being able to support themselves with their own strength. They must find out something to lean to; and not having of their own stuff wherewith to entertain us, they bring in the story to supply the defect of language.

Question: What is the antecedent of the pronoun in bold? Find the answer at the end of this chapter.

Pronouns and their antecedents need to agree in three ways: person, number, and gender.

- Person: first, second, or third person
- Number: singular or plural
- Gender: masculine, feminine, or neuter

THE GENDER ISSUE

At one time, if one did not know the sex of the subject or if one was writing about people in general, one would always use masculine pronouns and male references. "We hold these truths to be self-evident, that all men are created equal," for example. Today, the once ubiquitous "he" is rightly considered a mark of sexism, as it excludes all but cisgender males.

One attempt to solve this problem in writing was to blend male and female pronouns throughout the work, but that strategy was not fully inclusive either, and it led to awkward prose. English teachers winced at the logical but grammatically incorrect use of plural "they/them" instead.

However, these days, more and more people have accepted a new solution: using "they/them" as singular pronouns. In his July 10, 2019, op-ed in *The New York Times*, Farhad Manjoo wrote, "According to linguists who study gender and pronouns, 'they' and 'them' are increasingly and widely seen as legitimate ways to refer to an individual, both generically and specifically, whether you know their gender or not. . . ." Manjoo's point is evidence that the English language is a dynamic language that continues to grow in how we use it.

Therefore, a young writer who wishes to avoid sexism and show *their* audience *they* are considering all perspectives will take care with the pronouns *they* use. (See what I did there?)

As a practical note, if you sense your reader will not yet be receptive to this new solution, it may be best to avoid the issue by following the standard pronoun antecedent rule, which states that pronouns and antecedents must agree in number (singular or plural) and person (first, second, or third person). Nevertheless, it is critical you work to avoid sexist language, no matter what.

PHRASES AND CLAUSES

Phrases and clauses are important parts of sentences that serve a variety of functions. There is much more to the study of phrases and clauses than what is presented here. This section of the book will help you know and understand the basics.

1. PHRASES

A phrase is never a sentence. A **phrase** is a group of related words that does not contain BOTH a subject and a verb. There are several common types of phrases:

A. Appositive Phrase

An **appositive phrase** gives more information about the word (noun, subject) it follows and is set off by commas.

> **Example**   The band director, *a veteran of 31 years*, led his students to first place in the national competition.

B. Infinitive Phrase

An **infinitive phrase** consists of an infinitive—the root of the verb preceded by "to"—and the modifiers or complements associated with it. Infinitive phrases can function as adjectives, adverbs, or nouns.

> **Examples**   *To see the sun set* off the shores of Key West can be a spiritual experience. (This infinitive phrase serves as a noun or subject of the sentence.)
>
> Anita went to Harvard *to study criminal law*. (This infinitive phrase tells us why she went to Harvard, so it serves as an adverb.)

C. Prepositional Phrase

A **prepositional phrase** is a group of words that begins with a preposition that links to an object.

You can easily consult the internet or a grammar handbook for a complete list of prepositions, but you are no doubt quite used to seeing them in what you read and perhaps even using them in your own writing.

Common Prepositions

at	over	before
on	under	up
in	into	down
above	among	beneath
beyond	after	

Examples of prepositional phrases:

Preposition	Object (of the preposition)
under	the *bed*
into	the *wild* (title of Jon Krakauer's book)
before	breakfast
after	an *understanding*

A stylistic aspect of some writers is to add information or emphasis with a string or series of prepositional phrases. Here is an example from Jonathan Swift's *A Modest Proposal*. As an exercise, underline all the prepositional phrases you see. What do you think the effect of this style is?

> I think it is agreed by all parties that this prodigious number of children in the arms, or on the backs, or at the heels of their mothers, and frequently of their fathers, is in the present deplorable state of the kingdom a very great additional grievance. . . .

AN ANALYSIS OF WHY PREPOSITIONAL PHRASES MATTER

You may never have to identify the subject of a sentence on the AP® English Language exam, but you can be certain that you will never find the subject of a sentence in a prepositional phrase. In fact, prepositional phrases are somewhat inert components of sentences. You could cross them all out and still end up with a grammatically viable independent clause (sentence). Knowing this may help you isolate core ideas. If you need to simplify the sentence, try crossing out all the prepositional phrases to leave the skeleton of the sentence visible. This strategy can help make a complicated sentence much easier to understand or analyze.

Here is the same sentence from Swift with all the prepositional phrases, conjunctions, and modifiers crossed out. What is left is the skeleton of the sentence or the core idea.

I think it is agreed by all parties that this prodigious **number** ~~of children in the arms, or on the backs, or at the heels of their mothers, and frequently of their fathers,~~ **is** ~~in the present deplorable state of the kingdom~~ a very great additional **grievance.** . . .

The most essential meaning can be boiled down to *number* (subject) *is* (verb) *grievance* (object). But, of course, Swift would not have been very convincing if he had written it that way. He'd have come off sounding like the proverbial cave man. The point is that we can cross out prepositional phrases to more easily find these basic sentence elements.

Why is "children" not the subject? "Children" is in the prepositional phrase, "of children." The actual subject is "number." But of course, "of children" is necessary to the meaning of the sentence. Without it, we would ask, number of what?

Stylistically, Swift creates imagery in the string of prepositional phrases that shows children "clinging" to their parents, in an almost burdensome way. Their prodigious number feels, to a careful reader, weightier.

2. CLAUSES

A **clause** is a group of related words that contains a subject and a verb. An independent clause can stand alone (see more on sentences). A dependent or subordinate clause is incomplete if used alone, and must be joined with an independent clause to form a complete sentence. Dependent or subordinate clauses that are presented alone are called **fragments**.

Dependent (or subordinate) clauses sometimes begin with a subordinating conjunction.

Common Subordinating Conjunctions		
since	after	while
when	if	when
because		

Here are examples of dependent or subordinate clauses (so called because they are dependent on something else to make them complete sentences or they stand subordinate to the main sentence).

- *Since Sue first began to play the piano,* she understood it took practice to play well.

- John left the house early *when he knew the traffic would be bad.*

Both of these examples are embedded in sentences. When the dependent clause comes first, we set it off with a comma. When it comes second, we do not.

Because . . .

Do you remember a teacher saying we never start a sentence with "because"? He or she probably did not trust that you understood the difference between a dependent clause and an independent clause. It is actually not uncommon to see a sentence that begins with "because." "Because" is an important transitional marker in a sentence that shows cause and effect. Just don't forget that the dependent clause depends on something else to make it independent.

Example   Because the child could not identify all the letters in the alphabet, she was not allowed to move on to first grade.

However . . .

The transition "however" is not a subordinating conjunction. The use of the word "however" in the following example does not make it a dependent clause.

Example   However, Jane was still opposed to having her taxes done by her brother.

The previous example is an independent clause. It stands by itself as a sentence. Students who believe that words like "however" and "therefore" create dependent clauses will incorrectly link them to independent clauses with a comma and will create comma splice errors. (See the section on sentence faults for more about this.) "However" and other words are conjunctive adverbs (see the list that follows). They are followed by commas.

Common Conjunctive Adverbs		
accordingly	however	nonetheless
also	incidentally	now
anyway	indeed	otherwise
besides	instead	similarly
certainly	likewise	still
consequently	meanwhile	then
finally	moreover	thereafter
further	namely	therefore
furthermore	nevertheless	thus
hence	next	undoubtedly

WHAT CONSTITUTES A SENTENCE?

A **sentence** must contain a subject, a verb (often referred to as a predicate), and express a complete thought or idea. "I am" is a sentence because it has a subject (I) and a verb (am) and expresses a complete thought (the subject understands him or herself to exist). We are almost always going to need more than two words in a sentence, however.

The subject of a sentence is typically a noun, but it can also be a pronoun, or even a phrase that serves as a noun. If you need to identify the subject of the sentence, the fastest way is to first find the verb and then ask the questions, who? or what?

What is the subject of this sentence?

After the swim meet, a bunch of players went to Cal's house for pizza.

Think it through.

Well, the verb is "went," so I can ask "who went?" The answer is "a bunch of players." But, wait! I read that the subject can never be in a prepositional phrase, so if I cross out "of players," I am left with "bunch." I guess "bunch" must be the subject.

This example is simple, but knowing the subject of a sentence will help you comprehend its message.

BASIC SENTENCE STRUCTURES

There are four basic sentence structures. (Refer to Chapter 9 for more complex sentence types.)

1. **Simple:** Consists of a single independent clause.
   Example: Dad mowed the yard every Saturday.

2. **Compound:** Consists of two or more simple sentences joined by a comma and coordinating conjunction or by a semicolon.
   Example: Dad mowed the yard every Saturday, but on Sunday he refused to do any work.

3. **Complex:** Contains one or more dependent or subordinate clauses as well as one independent clause.
   Examples: (a) Since Margaret found the shortcut to work, she is never late.
   (b) When Bill cranks up the air conditioner, his wife complains since she is always too cold.

4. **Compound Complex:** Combines a compound sentence with a complex sentence.
   Example: Allison and Bill shared the day shift, but creating the schedule took compromise since Bill always wanted Friday afternoon off.

Test Tip

Work to eliminate sentence faults from your writing, especially if it's a known weakness. Part of your essay score is based on your ability to control the conventions of language.

BASIC SENTENCE FUNCTIONS

1. **Declarative:** Makes a statement (most of our sentences are declarative).
   Example: Tulip bulbs can be planted in the fall for a spring bloom.

2. **Interrogatory:** Asks a question.
   Example: What's wrong with you?

3. **Exclamatory:** Declares with urgency.
   Example: A tornado is coming!

4. **Imperative:** Commands.
   Example: Don't touch that!

COMMON SENTENCE FAULTS AND HOW TO CORRECT THEM

Professional writers sometimes intentionally use sentence fragments for emphasis or variety. However, in general, sentence fragments are not found in formal writing. In your case, a fragment could be an effective syntax tool, but using one is a risky strategy, because an AP® reader judging your work would have to instantly recognize the use as purposeful and not an error. What if he or she misunderstands your intentions? It's best to avoid fragments entirely.

All other sentence faults are absolutely unacceptable in the writing you do on the AP® English Language and Composition exam.

FRAGMENT

A **sentence fragment** is generally a dependent or subordinate clause left to stand on its own, which we know it can't. Phrases are also not independent. To fix fragments, they need to be attached to independent clauses.

Fragment	Sentence
Since time was running out.	Genevieve realized she needed to finish painting her bedroom since time was running out.
Longing for the next vacation.	Longing for the next vacation, Mario kept studying travel magazines.

FUSED OR RUN-ON SENTENCE

When two independent clauses are joined together, we call it a **fused** or **run-on sentence**.

COMMA SPLICE

A **comma splice** is two independent clauses joined by a comma.

Four Ways to Fix These Major Sentence Faults

	Fused or Run-on	Comma Splice
Wrong ▶	Arianna loved to get up early the air was so light and things were peaceful at 5:30 a.m.	Some people think it is difficult to grow roses, it just takes good soil, plenty of sunshine, and some basic care. Sometimes people call long sentences "run-ons" when they may not be that at all. The confusion stems from the perception that the sentence is going on, or running on, a long time. However, such usage is not technically correct.
▼ Four ways to correct the error		
1. Add a period at the end of the sentence.	Arianna loved to get up early. The air was so light and things were peaceful at 5:30 a.m.	Some people think it is difficult to grow roses. It just takes good soil, plenty of sunshine, and some basic care.
2. Create a compound sentence by adding a comma and a coordinating conjunction. (See list below.)	Arianna loved to get up early, for the air was so light and things were peaceful at 5:30 a.m.	Some people think it is difficult to grow roses, but it just takes good soil, plenty of sunshine, and some basic care.

Continued ➡

3. Add a subordinating conjunction to turn an independent clause into a dependent clause.	Arianna loved to get up early because the air was so light and things were peaceful at 5:30 a.m.	While some people think it is difficult to grow roses, it just takes good soil, plenty of sunshine, and some basic care.
4. Add a semicolon, but only if the two halves have a strong logical connection: parallel in meaning or cause and effect.	Arianna loved to get up early; the air was so light and things were peaceful at 5:30 a.m.	Some people think it is difficult to grow roses; it just takes good soil, plenty of sunshine, and some basic care.

LIST OF COORDINATING CONJUNCTIONS

As I've said, the acronym FANBOYS will help you remember the seven coordinating conjunctions: **for, and, nor, but, or, yet, so.**

When you create a compound sentence, a comma must precede the coordinating conjunction.

To avoid making punctuation errors in your essays, rely on what you know. If you aren't an expert in using semicolons, don't use them. As for commas, when in doubt, leave them out. Students tend to put commas where they do not belong. Instead of worrying about punctuation, write clear sentences that say what you mean, but keep them lean. Learn the basic sentence structures and vary your use of them. If you stay with the familiar in your prose, you should be competent in your use of punctuation.

PUNCTUATION SIMPLIFIED

This short section is meant to help you avoid common punctuation errors by reminding you of a few basic rules. If punctuation is a real problem for you in your writing, consult a good grammar handbook and study the rules.

A. COMMAS

1. Use commas to separate items in a series of repeated parallel elements.
   Examples:
   Bring me the scissors, the paper, and the glue.

   "We shall fight on the beaches, we shall fight on the landing grounds, we shall fight in the fields and in the streets, we shall fight in the hills; we shall never surrender." —Winston Churchill.

2. Use commas to set off appositive phrases or non-essential phrases or clauses.
   Example:
   John, my uncle's second cousin, sells fresh produce every Saturday at the farmer's market in Westfield.

3. Use a comma after an introductory dependent clause, phrase, or word.
   Examples:
   After the rain stops, we should go for a walk.

   While the children play, let's make lemonade.

   Well, we should visit Aunt Mary soon.

4. Use a comma to separate two or more adjectives if they are not connected with a conjunction.
   Examples:
   The lush, verdant garden was inviting to visitors.

   The garden was lush and verdant and inviting to visitors.

5. **A comma must never separate a subject from its verb.**

B. QUOTATION MARKS

1. Set off quoted text with quotation marks and discrete words used to prove your point about diction.
   Example:
   The author's use of the words "riled," "annoyance," "steamed," and "vehemently" clearly point to the fact that the speaker is angry.

2. Use quotation marks to set off a direct quotation.
Example:
"I am tired of pizza," Mark said. "I want to cook something healthy instead."

3. Indirect quotations do not need quotation marks.
Example:
Mark said that he was tired of pizza and wanted to cook something healthy for a change.

4. Use single quotation marks for a quotation inside a quotation.
Example:
Senator Smith remarked, "The economic recovery is in sight, and as for this latest recession, all I can say is 'all's well that ends well.'"

5. In or out? Do the following punctuation marks go inside or outside quotation marks?

1. Commas? Inside

2. Periods? Inside

3. Semicolon? Outside

4. Question Mark? Inside if it belongs to the quotation. Outside if it doesn't belong to the quoted matter.

C. COLONS AND SEMICOLONS

1. Use a colon to introduce a long quotation. In addition, a long quotation in an essay is generally indented.

2. A colon can precede a long explanation.

3. Use a colon to introduce a list.
Example:
For a great day at the beach, pack the following items: sunscreen, a blanket, a jug of water, and your sunglasses.

4. Use a semicolon to link two independent clauses of parallel or other logical connection, such as cause and effect.

D. APOSTROPHES

1. Use apostrophes to show omission.
   Examples: We're, they're, and o'er (over).

2. Use apostrophes to show possession:
   Examples: Mel's van, everyone's favorite.

3. Never use apostrophes to indicate plurals.
   Wrong ▶ There were too many banana's.

You can't really edit the world, but I was recently driving on a country road and saw a nice (professionally made) sign promoting the sale of "raspberry's." By this point in the book I'm sure you know that the sign should have promoted the sale of "raspberries."

E. MORE PUNCTUATION

1. Em dashes—generally the equivalent of two hyphens—are used to set off interrupters or appositive phrases in the same way commas can. Do not confuse an em dash with a hyphen.

2. Exclamation points!!!!!!! Avoid them. The danger is that you will overuse or misuse them. If an exclamation point exists in the text you're quoting, that's different. But steer clear of them in your own prose.

Test Tip

It's = it is. Always! In this case, the apostrophe does not show possession. To show something belongs to *it*, omit the apostrophe. Example: That dog is chasing *its* own tail.

COMMON USAGE ERRORS AND CONFUSED WORDS

I've seen some really smart students make these errors, so let's look at some common errors and help you avoid them in your writing. These are the kinds of errors that drive English teachers (and no doubt AP® readers) crazy!

accept, except	I accept this award. No one except Ryan may speak right now.
affect, effect	The effect (noun) of the sun's rays can be harmful. Turning in that paper late will affect (verb) your grade. [effect: a result; affect: a change]
a lot, allot	"A lot" is two words meaning "many;" "allot" means "to disperse." "Alot" is a misspelling. (Avoid using "a lot" because it sounds too casual.)
bring, take	Bring me my slippers then take the trash to the curb, please. Bring = come towards you; take = go away from you.
could have, not could of	should have, *not* should of; would have, *not* would of
fewer, less	There are fewer students in Forensics this year, so our meetings will take less time. Use "fewer" when referring to plural things; use "less" when referring to singular things.
good, well	You will do well today since you ate a good breakfast. "Good" is an adjective; "well" is almost always an adverb.
it's, its	Its fur is brown and it's in need of washing. "Its'" is a possessive pronoun. "It's" is a contraction for "it is."
knew, new	I knew you would ruin your new shoes. "New" is state of age; "knew" is past tense of "to know."
know, no	No, I don't know the capital of Rhode Island. "No" is a negative response. "To know" is to be aware of something.
lead, led (verb)	Lead on, Kyle, or do you prefer being led? "Lead" is present tense; "led" is past tense.
loose, lose	If you keep your hold on that leash so loose, you will lose the leash and the dog will run away. "Loose" is not tight. To "lose" is to have something disappear.

past, passed	In the past, people with manners would have asked for the potatoes to be passed instead of reaching over someone to get them. "Past" is a time before now. "Passed" is past tense of "to pass."
quiet, quite, quit	Be quiet or you will have to quit practicing with the band in our garage. Our neighbors are quite beside themselves because of the noise. "Quiet" is softer volume. "Quit" is to end something. "Quite" is a modifier.
than, then	If I knew then what I know now, I would have chosen this rather than that. "Than" is used to make a comparison. "Then" is a time transition or adverb.
their, there, they're	If they're going to play over there with their toys, then they are going to need to be careful. "They're" is a contraction for "they are." "There" shows where. "Their" is a possessive pronoun.
threw, through	She threw the ball through the air. "Threw" is past tense of "to throw." "Through" is a preposition showing where.
to, too, two	I, too, have had two choices to make. "Too" means also, "two" is "one more than one," and "to" is a preposition.
waist, waste	Her waist was so small that we made a size 4 dress and the extra material went to waste. "Waist" is the middle of the body. "Waste" is to not use, to throw unnecessarily away.
weather, whether	The weather was so bad, we didn't know whether or not to go to the lake. "Weather" is rain, snow, and all that meteorological stuff, and "whether" is a transition used to show a choice.
which, witch	Which wicked witch in *The Wizard of Oz* did Dorothy's house fall on? "Which" is a relative pronoun used to refer to something. "Witch" is a sorceress.
who's, whose	Whose article won an award? Who's going to go pick it up? "Whose" is a pronoun. "Who's" is a contraction for "who is."

Continued ➝

| woman, women | A woman I know was voted Woman of the Year for her work in helping battered women. "Woman" with an "a" is singular, one woman; "women" with an "e" is plural, two or more women. |
| your, you're | I'm happy to announce that your team won, and now you're going to go to the next round in the Brain Brawl. "Your" is a possessive pronoun, and "you're" is a contraction for "you are." |

Answer to the antecedent question (page 106): "those of our times." Another way the AP® English Language exam might ask you to look at the Montaigne passage is to question to whom "those of our times" might refer. With nothing else to base your answer on than the text given in this book, what would you say? If you said "writers," you'd be correct.

PART III

ANALYTICAL READING
AND THINKING

Engaged and
Active Reading

Tis the good reader that makes the good book.
—Ralph Waldo Emerson

OVERVIEW

In the multiple-choice section of the AP® English Language and
Composition exam, you will have 60 minutes to read five texts
(approximately 500–600 words each) and answer 45 questions related
to those texts. There is also quite a bit to read in the essay section. The
synthesis question will provide six to eight resources that include a variety
of genres: articles, excerpts from books, graphs, charts, or pictures. For
another question, you will have a short persuasive document to read,
analyze, and write about. If you don't understand what you've read,
you will not be able to choose a correct response to a question or write
intelligent essays.

Whatever the case, you will not have time for leisurely reading. You
may only have time to read each text once, so you need to read carefully
and with purpose.

ANALYZING YOUR READING HABITS

You know your reading habits need some improvement if any of the
following is true for you:

- You find yourself thinking of something else about every other
  sentence;

- You have to reread a paragraph about five times to know what
  it means;

- You have to look up nearly every other word;

- You are bored by the passage and just skim through it, but then you have no idea what it is about;

- You sometimes characterize the text as "stupid," "dumb," "pointless," etc.

Some of the problems listed above have to do with **your attitude** about the reading. It is fair to say that not all the texts on the AP® English Language exam will be to your liking, but it will be important for you to control your negative emotional response. Negative emotions will kill your motivation and will cloud your ability to think clearly. The fix? Approach each passage as something you can *mostly* understand. You aren't expected to be an expert on any of the passages.

A FEW STRATEGIES TO IMPROVE YOUR BASIC READING HABITS

If you find yourself rereading often, you may actually be reading too slowly, letting extraneous thoughts creep into your head. This is a matter of **concentration** and it is something you can control. Way before exam day, practice reading complex texts at a speed faster than your normal rate. Don't read so fast so that you are skimming. Instead, read the passage quickly without reading every single word.

More strategies for improving your reading:

- Make a conscious effort to understand what you're doing as you read. As soon as you start to wander off mentally, toss out a mental lasso and pull yourself back. Work on keeping your focus.

- Visualize as you read. Picture the setting, the "characters," and the action of the passage as much as possible. Visualization will help you comprehend and remember what you read.

- If you start to get tired, drink water (not energy drinks) and remember to breathe. Do some neck exercises to get blood to your brain. You won't be able to get up and walk around during the exam, so try to get accustomed to reading and thinking for periods of an hour or more at a time.

- Practice reading while sitting at a desk or table, as this is most likely where you'll be for nearly four hours during the exam.

- Because the exam is given digitally, being a digital native used to working on-screen gives you an advantage. If, however, you prefer dealing with paper-based text, you will need to get used to reading—and comprehending—complex literary works on a computer screen. To reduce potential eye strain, the Mayo Clinic suggests using the 20-20-20 rule. They say, "Every 20 minutes, look at something 20 feet away for at least 20 seconds."

- Minimize distractions. DO NOT read with your ears plugged with ear buds listening to your music or Spotify. You may believe you can concentrate, but you are forcing your brain to think of two things at once, a practice that is stressful and counterproductive for exam prep. You will not be allowed to have any electronic devices with you for the exam, so get used to reading in relative silence.

- Practice controlling your emotions by choosing some tough texts to read. Read them, annotate them, and feel good about your progress. Start with Voltaire, Jonathan Swift, Ben Franklin, or Mark Twain. After these, Hunter S. Thompson might seem easy. A lot of older texts are online. You can download them to an e-reader, or read them online. It is best to have hard copies of texts, however, if you really want to practice annotating. You could search Project Gutenberg (*http://www.gutenberg.org*), for example, to find many of the authors listed in Chapter 4.

- Give yourself permission to skip words. You don't have to read every single word to know what's going on. This is not to say that you should skim—not at all, but if you think you have to look up every word, you may miss the "big picture." *Everything in its context* is a good mantra to keep.

- Before you read a passage for a set of questions in the multiple-choice section of the exam, try quickly skimming the questions first. Doing so can give your reading a sharper focus. For example, if there is a question on rhetorical strategy and another on irony, you will be alert to those aspects of the text as you read. Be careful not to spend too much time pre-reading the questions. Also, when you come back to the questions, be sure you read each one again (and not rely on your memory) so you don't misinterpret what is being asked.

- Learn how to annotate texts and then practice annotating. This may be the most important thing you can do to improve your reading skills for the AP® English Language exam. Read more on this later in this chapter.

Test Tip

Empower yourself! A positive attitude will go a long way. Tell yourself "I CAN DO THIS!!" Think of each text on the exam as a noble, worthy opponent, but one that will not defeat you. Respect these rhetorical opponents, recognize their strengths and special elements, but feel confident that you can read, understand, and respond to them. Never think you are too weak for any reading challenge.

ANNOTATING OR MARKING A TEXT

WHY DO IT?

When you read a difficult text, you're not reading for pleasure. You want to understand it deeply and, at least for the AP® English Language exam, quickly. Difficult texts are not easy to grasp with the test clock ticking, so marking the text as you read can help you pick out the key ideas and easily reconnect with your thinking upon a second look.

For example, if you immediately recognize the dominant tone, mark that down, and if the tone shifts in the last paragraph, note that as well. If a question follows the passage asking you to determine the tone, you'll probably be able to answer it without rereading the text.

HOW TO DO IT ON TODAY'S DIGITAL EXAM

Annotating a text is a proven way to learn close reading and deepen your understanding. Even though the English Language exam is administered digitally, it is still essential to read and study paper-based texts. This approach will give you valuable practice to hone a skill critical to your success on the exam. Annotation strategies will easily translate from the print medium to the digital medium. The key is to put in the practice to be able to read and mentally annotate digital texts. What follows is a guide for annotating a paper document.

Annotating—marking a text—means that as you read you are highlighting key words, marking key phrases or ideas, and especially making margin notes of key ideas by paraphrasing them to show your deep understanding. This process facilitates active and engaged reading. If you are making notes while you read, if you are actively looking for what to mark, you will be less likely to drift off and begin thinking about something else. The digital AP® exam lets you highlight and annotate exam stimuli and questions, use scratch paper to plan and outline your response, cross out answer choices, and mark questions for later review. You'll also be able to use control +/- or command +/- to zoom in and out.

WHEN TO START?

Start now, so you can train yourself. At first, practicing this skill may slow down your reading, but with time you'll be able to read more quickly and more deeply at the same time. Always read with a pen or pencil in hand, even if you're reading something like a magazine, just for practice.

SUGGESTED SYMBOLS OR MARKERS

Whether you use the suggested symbols below or create your own, it is important to keep your system simple (use only a few symbols) and stay consistent.

⬯	Circle unfamiliar words. You won't be allowed to use a dictionary on the AP® English Language exam, but just circling unfamiliar words reminds you to try to understand them by using context clues. When you do have a dictionary available, it might be a good idea to look up a word if you cannot fully grasp its meaning from the context. Also, you can add these unfamiliar words to your list of words to know. See Chapter 12.
___	Underline words in close proximity that share connotative or denotative associations; pair any underlined section with a textual note in the margin. Also underline to make note of a key idea.
!	An exclamation point in the margin near a group of lines indicates a key idea; pair with brackets around specific text. A star also works for this purpose.
?	A question mark in the margin means "I don't understand." Noting questions prompts you to answer them later.

Continued →

notes	Write brief notes in the margins to make your thinking visually accessible and easy to connect with upon a second look. Your notes can be about anything, but should be summaries of conclusions you've drawn about the text so far. Paraphrase key ideas in quick margin notes.
[ ]	Use brackets around phrases or chunks of text (or enclose in a rectangle) to mark significant literary or rhetorical devices, such as appeals, imagery, figurative language, etc. Label the device in the margin. Make corresponding notes about what these might mean. Example: Don't just mark that the writer uses an ethical appeal, but make a note about shared values that make the appeal effective.

WHEN TO MARK A TEXT?

Mark now, as you are learning this skill—on nearly everything you read just to practice, but eventually only on texts you wish to study. It is really not something you'd use for pleasure reading, unless your pleasure is to read and understand difficult books. Then, yes, you would read with a pen in hand. Be sure you are looking for, marking, and commenting on key ideas, as well as rhetorical strategies and techniques.

Making annotation a habit will prepare you to mark your AP® English Language and Composition exam—not only the passages in the multiple-choice section, but also the passages in the free-response section.

Mark in college—of course! You will have developed a reading skill that will help you read and study all kinds of texts in college.

WHAT TO LOOK FOR? THE "ETCEAS" STRATEGY

Use the acronym ETCEAS to find the basic elements of any nonfiction text. Find a full description of this strategy in Chapter 4.

E Exigence

T Thesis

C Claims

E Evidence

A Appeals

S Style

A NOTE ABOUT THE SUBJECT

The texts chosen for the exam convey interesting and important ideas. Try to avoid a simplistic statement regarding the subject. For example, a journal from an organic gardener is probably not simply about gardening. It may be about the ways plants can teach us about our environment. Look for ideas that are

- important (are of consequence)

- universal (important to most or all people)

- enduring (vital historically, vital now)

SAMPLE ANNOTATED TEXT

On the next page is an excerpt from Margaret Fuller's *Woman in the Nineteenth Century, and Kindred Papers Relating to the Sphere, Condition, and Duties of Woman.* I include this sample to show annotating skills in action. As you study this text, you may find ideas or elements that you would have marked or for which you would have made notes. If so, this shows you are thinking critically. Good for you!

Exercise: Write an essay for this text using the insights in the annotations. Use one of the following prompts to guide you:

1. The "good era" for women that Fuller imagines already exists in Miranda, a woman whose self-dependence is a model for other women. Analyze Miranda's own attitude toward her sense of self, especially as a model for others.

2. What, does Fuller argue, is the role of a parent in a daughter's sense of self?

3. Imagine the section that follows this one. What will Fuller focus on next and how will she support that argument?

Fuller's main claim is a claim of value: She believes women are to be equally free with men, to live, think, and grow according to their talents.

from *Woman in the Nineteenth Century, and Kindred Papers Relating to the Sphere, Condition, and Duties of Woman*

by Margaret Fuller (1855)

If men were so progressive/ enlightened to consider women as equals, we'd not need to discuss...

Man/ Woman— refers to the sex in general

Were thought and feeling once so far elevated that Man should esteem himself the brother and friend, but nowise the lord and tutor, of Woman,—were he really bound with her in equal worship,—arrangements as to function and employment would be of no consequence. What Woman needs is not as a woman to act or rule, but as a nature to grow, as an intellect to discern, as a soul to live freely and unimpeded, to unfold such powers as were given her when we left our "common home." If fewer talents were given her, yet if allowed the free and full employment of these, so that she may render back to the giver his own with usury, she will not complain; nay, I dare to say she will bless and rejoice in her earthly birth-place, her earthly lot. Let us consider what obstructions impede this good era, and what signs give reason to hope that it draws near.

mother's womb: each person comes to his/her life in the same way.

God/Interest

Author states her purpose: to consider what stands in the way of the ideal situation for women and to look at signs that the "good era" is close.

She's not angry that she's a woman

I was talking on this subject with Miranda, a woman, who, if any in the world could, might speak without heat and bitterness of the position of her sex. Her father was a man who cherished no sentimental reverence for Woman, but a firm belief in the equality of the sexes. She was his eldest child, and came to him at an age when he needed a companion. From the time she could speak and go alone, he addressed her not as a plaything, but as a living mind. Among the few verses he ever wrote was a copy addressed to this child, when the first locks were cut from her head; and the reverence expressed on this occasion for that cherished head, he never belied. It was to him the temple of immortal

Miranda's story is Fuller's example that another reality for women can exist.

intellect. <u>He respected his child</u>, however, too much to be an indulgent parent. <u>He called on her for clear judgment, for courage, for honor and fidelity; in short, for such virtues as he knew.</u> In so far as he possessed the keys to the wonders of this universe, he allowed free use of them to her, and, by the incentive of a high expectation, he forbade, so far as possible, that <u>she should let the privilege lie idle.</u> appeals to our self-actualization needs

Miranda's father serves as an example of an ideal father. He believes
- *equality of sexes*
- *respects children's minds*
- *expects a female child to do all in life that any male child would be expected to do*

This section characterizes Miranda's relationships with both men and women.

Thus this child was early led to feel herself a child of the spirit. She took her place easily, not only in the world of organized being, but in the world of mind. A dignified sense of <u>self-dependence</u> was given as all her portion, and she found it a sure anchor. Herself securely anchored, her relations with others were established with equal security. <u>She was fortunate in a total absence of those charms which might have drawn to her bewildering flatteries,</u> and in a strong electric nature, <u>which repelled those</u> who did not belong to her, and <u>attracted those</u> who did. With men and women her relations were noble,—affectionate without passion, intellectual without coldness. The world was free to her, and she lived freely in it. Outward adversity came, and inward conflict; but that faith and self-respect had early been awakened which must always lead, at last, to an outward serenity and an inward peace.

Miranda emerges from childhood fully self-reliant.

She's not beautiful, at least not in the ordinary way, which Fuller says is a benefit.

Her strong personality brought her together with others who were like her.

Despite having a progressive father + self-dependence, M.'s life is like everyone's: Includes conflict to adversity (Normal troubles)

hindrance, obstacle

Of Miranda I had ~~always~~ thought as an example, that the restraints upon the sex were |insuperable| only to those who think them so, or who noisily strive to break them. <u>She had taken a course of her own, and no man stood in her way.</u> Many of her acts had been unusual, but excited no uproar. Few helped, but none checked her; and the many men who knew her mind and her life, showed to her confidence as to a brother, gentleness as to a sister. And not only refined,

Being a woman is a problem only if you think it is.

Reinforces the idea that M. is self-reliant— she lives how she wants.

but very coarse men approved and aided one in whom they saw resolution and clearness of design. Her <u>mind was often the leading one,</u> always effective.

> She was a clear voice + others listened to her. She's a role model for other women.

When I talked with her upon these matters, and had said very much what I have written, she smilingly replied; "And yet we must admit that <u>I have been fortunate, and this should not be.</u> My good father's early trust gave the first bias, and the rest followed, of course. It is true that I have had less outward aid, in after years, than most women; but that is of little consequence. Religion was early awakened in my soul,—a sense that what the soul is capable to ask it must attain, and that, though I might be aided and instructed by others, I must depend on myself as the only constant friend. This self-dependence, <u>which was honored in me</u>, is <u>deprecated</u> as a fault in most women. <u>They are taught</u> to learn their rule from without, not to unfold it from within.

> My situation should not be unusual.

Too many women accept their subservient role; weakness is a learned role/behavior.

"This is the fault of Man, who is still vain, and wishes to be more important to Woman than, by right, he should be."

M. is example that it (weakness) is <u>not a</u> female trait.

"Men have not shown this disposition toward you," I said.

"No; because the position I early was enabled to take was one of self-reliance. And were <u>all women as sure of</u> their wants as I was, <u>the result would be the same.</u> But they are so overloaded with precepts by guardians, who think that nothing is so much to be dreaded for a woman as originality of thought or character, that their minds are impeded by doubts till they lose their chance of fair, free proportions. The difficulty is to get them to the point from which they shall naturally develop self-respect, and learn self-help.

if <u>all</u> women recognized their need to live freely to express themselves, they'd be like me, says M.

ethical appeal

The goal must be to get women to recognize they are more powerful than they realize.

In a way, women allow men to rule them.

Men continue to "rule" women because they're vain and believe they're more important.

Enhancing Vocabulary

One forgets words as one forgets names. One's vocabulary needs constant fertilizing or it will die.—Evelyn Waugh

OVERVIEW

I like what British writer Evelyn Waugh said about fertilizing our vocabulary, as if it's something that grows like a flower garden. Plants are tenacious and will strive to live despite our neglect of them, but if we water and fertilize our garden, we will have abundant blossoms to reward us. Our word vocabulary is like our garden. We must create the rich soil (lots of words) that will give us, in an instant, the exact word for our purpose. Think of this chapter's "Words to Know" list and the one you create yourself as fertilizer for your vocabulary. A prominent goal for you as you prepare for the exam is to strive to express yourself clearly and precisely. The ability to choose the best or most apt word for the task is not to be undervalued.

There are also two practical reasons for this chapter. One is that you are expected to read and comprehend complex texts on the AP® exam. If you have a limited vocabulary, you will struggle with finding meaning. While archaic or overly specific terms will generally be defined in footnotes, you are expected to know a lot of words. AP® readers also expect a certain level of vocabulary in your essays. If you use sixth grade words, it *does* make a difference in how your writing is perceived. I would never suggest that you use "big" words just for the sake of using them, especially if you are not quite comfortable with their meanings. However, since you are expected to use college-level vocabulary, you should be comfortable with more sophisticated word choices.

Test Tip

For fun, get a *Mad Libs* tablet and use some of the more difficult words below to create crazy little stories. They'll be silly, fun, and may make it easier for you to remember the words.

WORDS TO KNOW

The following words were taken from released AP® exams. They were chosen for a variety of reasons: level of difficulty, archaic quality, obscure usage, or specific cultural connotation. This list is merely meant to fertilize your vocabulary garden.

1. acuity (noun): sharpness, keenness

2. adept (adjective): having or showing knowledge and skill and aptitude

3. admonish (verb); admonition (noun): warn, scold, caution

4. ambiguous (adjective): unclear meaning, two possible interpretations

5. apocalyptic (adjective): involving or portending widespread devastation or ultimate doom

6. apocryphal (adjective): of questionable authenticity

7. appellation (noun): a name, title, or designation

8. archetype (noun); archetypal (adjective): an original model, pattern, or type (after an original model)

9. artifice (noun): pretense or ploy; clever or artful strategy

10. ascertain (verb): to determine; to find out

11. assiduous (adjective): diligent, persistent

12. baize (noun): a type of coarse woolen cloth, often green, usually used for covering card tables

13. base (adjective): inferior; dishonorable

14. bastion (noun): a well-fortified position

15. berate (verb): to rebuke, reprimand, or scold

16. bourgeoisie (noun): the middle class; in Marxist theory, the social group opposed to the proletariat (working class)

17. calumny (noun): slander; a false statement maliciously made to injure another's reputation

18. cant (noun): tedious talk; monotonous talk filled with platitudes

19. censure (verb): to reprimand; to excommunicate (expel, as from the priesthood)

20. charismatic (adjective): charming, compelling, appealing personality

21. chink (noun): crack or weakness in structure or armor

22. coarse (adjective): lacking refinement or rough grained in texture

23. confute (verb): to prove to be wrong or in error

24. connoisseur (noun): a person with expert knowledge or training, especially in the fine arts

25. corporeal (adjective): having physical substance, material form

26. decorous (adjective): well behaved, particularly according to social norms

27. decry (verb): express strong disapproval of

28. defer (verb); deference (noun): submit or yield to another's wish or opinion

29. deliquesce (verb): to disappear as if by melting

30. dilatory (adjective): inclined to waste time and lag behind

31. disparage (verb): to criticize someone or something in a way that shows you do not respect or value them

32. dogmatic (adjective): strict; inflexible expectations to adhere to a dogma (systemic belief, typically religious)

33. draught (noun): a current of unpleasantly cold air blowing through a room (archaic for draft)

34. dray (noun): a large low carriage with four wheels pulled by horses

35. dyspeptic (adjective); dyspepsia (noun): always angry or easily annoyed or having indigestion

36. elicit (verb): to call forth, draw out, or provoke; to bring or draw out

37. emit (verb): to send out a beam, noise, smell, or gas

38. enfranchised (adjective): empowered; the opposite is "disenfranchised"

39. engender (verb): to create

40. espionage (noun): spying; the discovering of secrets, especially political or military information, of another country or the proprietary information of a business

41. explicit (adjective): clear, precise; overtly stated

42. facile (adjective): easy, effortless

43. faux (adjective): false, fake

44. feign (verb): to pretend, to dissemble, to misrepresent

45. fester: to become infected, to suppurate; an infection (can be a noun or a verb)

46. festoon(ed) (verb): draped, decorated as for a parade or state event

47. fledgling (adjective): new and inexperienced

48. fobs (verb): employ trickery; pass off a fake as genuine

49. gainsay (verb): challenge, dispute

50. genuflect (verb), genuflections (noun): to bow as before a priest (obeisances, reverent gestures)

51. grandeur (noun): magnificent, splendid, vast beauty

52. grudging (adjective); grudgingly (adverb): done in an unwilling way; unwillingly

53. hack (noun): a reporter, artist, or writer whose work is not very good

54. husband(ed) (verb): to use something carefully so that you do not use all of it

55. illicit (adjective): contrary to accepted morality (especially sexual morality) or convention

56. illusory (adjective): not real, based on illusion

57. imbibe (verb): to drink, especially alcohol

58. impracticable (adjective): not possible, unusable

59. inexorable (adjective): without end, interminable

60. ingenuity (noun): cleverness; resourcefulness

61. introspection (noun): examination of and attention to your own ideas, thoughts, and feelings

62. kowtow (verb): to show too much respect to someone in authority, always obeying them and changing what you do in order to please them; what a toady does; sucking up

63. languid, languished, languor (noun): without energy; pleasant mental or physical tiredness or lack of activity

64. latent (adjective): potentially existing but not presently evident or realized

65. magnanimity (noun): great generosity of spirit or money

66. malevolent (adjective); malevolence (noun): ill will, maliciousness

67. mutton (noun): meat from a sheep

68. orthodoxy (noun): a belief or orientation agreeing with conventional standards

69. paramount (adjective): supreme or dominant

70. parochial (adjective): provincial; country-like, or of a parish (church community or region)

71. pathos (noun): poignancy; quality of emotion in a work of art or literature

72. pecuniary (adjective): relating to money; monetary

73. permeate (verb): pervade, penetrate, get into everything

74. pernicious (adjective): deadly, harmful, pestilent

75. pious (adjective); piety (noun): godly, reverent, holy (state of being pious)

76. plait (verb); plaits (noun): to braid; braids

77. porter (noun): a railroad employee who assists passengers

78. pragmatic (adjective): realistic, practical, expecting logical results

79. prattle (verb): idle talk, to go on and on meaninglessly

80. precipitate (verb); precipitous (adjective): to cause to happen, especially suddenly or prematurely; done hastily, without thought

81. precocious (adjective): characterized by or characteristic of exceptionally early development or maturity, especially mental development

82. prerogative (noun): privilege, right

83. profligate (adjective): wasteful, extravagant, prodigal

84. prostrate (adjective or verb): to lay face down on the ground in humility, submission, or adoration

85. prudent (adjective): careful and sensible; marked by sound judgment

86. qualm(s) (noun): an uncomfortable feeling of doubt about whether you are doing the right thing

87. randy (adjective): sexually aroused

88. recitation (noun): an event when one recites a literary work (usually) orally for an audience

89. reiterate (verb); reiteration (noun): to say or explain again

90. reputed (adjective): alleged, presumed

91. resonant (adjective); resonance (noun): strong and deep in tone or strongly reminiscent; evocative

92. rheumatism (noun): any painful disorder of the joints or muscles or connective tissues

93. sated (adjective); satiety (noun): satisfied; full

94. scant, scanty (adjective): barely sufficient

95. schizoid (adjective): of, relating to, or having a personality disorder marked by extreme shyness, flat affect, discomfort with others, and an inability to form close relationships; a person who is reclusive

96. seethe (verb): churn with anger or rage

97. self-abasement (noun): to put oneself down, to denigrate oneself

98. skirmish (noun): clash, battle, scuffle

99. sodden (adjective): drenched, soaked, sopping; expressionless, stupid, or dull, especially from drink

100. synergy (noun): interaction; parts working together

101. tawdry (adjective): cheap, gaudy, trashy, tacky

102. throes (noun): condition of agonizing struggle or trouble

103. timorous (adjective): fearful; shy; timid

104. torpor (noun): listlessness; languor, without energy, apathetic

105. torrent (noun): an overwhelming number or amount or a violently fast stream of water

106. transcendent (adjective); transcendence (noun): beyond ordinary; sublime

107. transient, transience (noun): fleeting; not lasting

108. tremulous (adjective): quivering as from weakness or fear

109. turbid (adjective): churned up; cloudy, muddy, murky

110. unabashed (adjective): not embarrassed

111. unimpeachable (adjective): impossible to discredit, without fault

112. variegated (adjective): having streaks, marks, or patches of a different color or colors; varicolored

113. veracity (noun): truthfulness

114. veritable (adjective): being truly or aptly called; real or genuine

115. vigilant (adjective); vigilance (noun): on guard, cautiously aware, continuous attention

116. vigilante (noun): one who takes or advocates the taking of law enforcement into one's own hands

117. vociferation (noun); vociferous (adjective): cry out loudly and vehemently, especially in protest

118. voluble (adjective); volubility (noun): talking easily, readily, and at length; fluent

119. weft (noun): the horizontal threads interlaced through the warp in a woven fabric

120. wholly (adjective): fully, completely

 Make learning new words a game. When you learn a new word, commit to using it at least ten times a day in a variety of contexts. Bonus: You might have fun annoying those around you!

YOUR OWN LIST

Use this space to record new words and their definitions. Come back to this section often to reinforce your memory.

Word	Definition
1.	
2.	
3.	
4.	
5.	
6.	
7.	
8.	
9.	
10.	
11.	
12.	
13.	
14.	
15.	

GREEK AND LATIN ROOTS

The ability to determine the meaning of an unfamiliar word in context is an invaluable comprehension skill. If you have a working knowledge of some basic Greek and Latin prefixes and roots, you can often quickly decipher word meanings, particularly when words are scientific in nature. Perhaps you've learned many of these roots in a science or world language class. If so, concentrate on those in this list that are new to you. This list is by no means complete, but it does contain a good sampling of roots that will aid your decoding skills.

For fun, take note of the English examples below that contain more than one of the roots. *Autograph*, for example, means "self-write."

Root/Prefix	Meaning	English Examples
ab-, a-, abs-	away, from	abstain, absent
ante-	before	anteroom, antecedent, antebellum
anthrop-	human	anthropomorphic, misanthrope
anti-	against	antidote, antipathy
auto-	self	autobiography, autoimmune, autocratic
bell-	war	bellicose, belligerent
bene-	good	benevolent, beneficiary, beneficial
bi-	two	biennial, bisect, bicycle
bio-	life	biology, biosphere, biogenesis
cede-	go, yield, surrender	concede, recede
circum-	around	circumference, circumlocution
con-	with	conspire, connect
contra-	against	contraband, contrary, contrast
de-	down, from	devolve, decline, devoid
dic-, dict-	say, speak	diction, dictate
dis-, di-	apart, away	dissolve, dissuade, diverge, divest

Continued ➜

Root/Prefix	Meaning	English Examples
ex-, e-	out of, from	eject, emerge, extricate, example
fid-, fide-, feder-	faith, trust	confide, bona fide, fidelity
graph-, gram-	write, draw	graphic, telegram, autograph
hyper-	beyond, over	hyperbole, hyperactive
hypo-	under, less	hypodermic, hypocrite
inter-	among, between	interstate, intercede, introspection
intra-	within	intramural, intravenous
log-, logo-, -ology	reason, learning	logistics, catalog
loqu-, locut-	talk, speak	eloquent, colloquial, loquacious
mis-	ill, mistaken, wrong	misunderstood, misogyny
mal-	bad, evil	malnourished, malinger
morph-	shape, form	amorphic, metamorphosis
para-, par-	beside	paralegal, parameter
phil-	love	philosophy, philanthropic
post-	after, following	postpone, postgraduate
pre-	before	precursor, preface, premonition
pro-	forward, outward	project, protract
soph-	wisdom	sophomore, sophist
super-	above	superior, superimpose
tele-, tel-	far	television, telekinesis, telemarketer
trans-	across	transpose, transcontinental, transgender
vert-	turn	revert, convert, introvert
vid-, vis-	to see	visual, video, envision
viv-, vita-, vivi-	alive, life	vivacious, vitality, vivid
vol-	will, wish	malevolent, voluntary

Point of View, Perspective, and Position

*And this, our life, exempt from public haunt, finds tongues
in trees, books in the running brooks, sermons in stones,
and good in everything.*—William Shakespeare

OVERVIEW

It is important to really understand the distinction between a few terms that may seem basically interchangeable: point of view, perspective, and position. The goal of this chapter is to help you see the nuances of these concepts.

POINT OF VIEW, PERSPECTIVE, AND POSITION

A. POINT OF VIEW

Think of point of view as a literary or rhetorical construct. We define the types of point of view based on various factors that limit what a narrator or speaker can control as well as the grammatical markers (pronouns).

However, sometimes the terms "point of view" and "perspective" are used interchangeably, so take care not to be too pedantic about their meanings.

B. PERSPECTIVE

Perspective refers to how one views an issue in terms of personal experience and individual environmental influences. In a way, it is how we see the world as only we can see it. Think of perspective as a social lens.

The factors that influence perspective are the same as those that create our biases: age, sex, gender, ethnicity, religious affiliation, culture, and accumulated personal experiences.

The degree to which one limits their access to knowledge also influences perspective. If we get all our news from either a left-leaning or a right-leaning source, we are less likely to possess a broader, perhaps more truthful, perspective. Narrow perspectives are sometimes called information "silos." To break out of a silo, we need to cultivate empathy.

Empathy is the ability to see things from another's perspective. Being able to acknowledge another's perspective, without necessarily adopting it, is a necessary critical reading skill. Read more about empathy below.

C. POSITION

Think of position as a writer's rhetorical stance on an issue. A position can be thought of as the belief that leads to one's thesis in an argument.

YOUR OWN PERSPECTIVE

An inherent disadvantage to youth is that it comes with a limited worldview. Most high school students have limited life experience. We cannot blame them for this, but as experience affects one's ability to conceive of complex world issues, it is a matter worth addressing here. Plus, each of us, despite our age, can work to broaden our experience so we can have a fuller worldview.

In addition to your age, your perspective is influenced by:

- Your sex and gender;
- Your culture (ethnicity, religion, etc.);
- Your environment (urban, rural, specific region of the country);
- Your family values;
- Your economic status;
- Your life experiences such as travel, personal interactions with people who are different, even having been "in love."

These influences cause us to have particular biases. Everyone has biases. It is important for us to recognize that fact and understand that our point of view and our biases affect how we read. To be good critical readers, we must control and limit the effect of our biases by improving our ability to be empathetic readers.

CONSCIOUSLY AND PURPOSEFULLY ADD TO WHAT YOU KNOW ABOUT LIFE

One of the best ways to understand the world and its problems is to read. But sometimes we need to have experiences that help us understand what we read. To do this, consider expanding your knowledge of the world in the following ways:

- Engage in conversations with people from different cultures.

- Talk to older adults about their life experiences and try to see the world from their perspective.

- Read opinions that seem directly counter to your own and carefully consider how these arguments are constructed. Mentally defend, challenge, or qualify such arguments.

- Add variety to your media preferences:
  - Read a variety of books and articles, both old and new;
  - Listen to different types of music;
  - View foreign films, with subtitles;
  - Read national and international newspapers;
  - Watch historical documentaries;
  - Download lectures and philosophy podcasts. (iTunes U is a fantastic resource for free materials at a college level.)

BECOMING AN EMPATHETIC READER

Empathy is the ability to put yourself in someone else's place, to see things as he or she sees them. As readers, we must be empathetic if we are to truly understand the books we read. To do this means to actually put yourself into the perspective of the speaker, the narrator, or the character.

When you read, visualize yourself in the text. Make a mind movie in which you walk through the setting, follow the characters, listen to them speak, and observe their actions. Allow yourself to see and hear what the speaker sees and hears. Even more importantly, allow yourself to feel what the speaker feels. This is empathy.

To be fair, it is much easier to empathize with the action of fictional characters in narratives. They are like us in a direct way. But the AP® English Language and Composition exam does not ask you to analyze fictional characters. Instead you will be reading nonfiction prose, such as essays, diaries, memoirs, or even letters. Such works typically feature one speaker defending a position on an issue. And if you can't relate to or empathize with the speaker, you may have a difficult time acknowledging his or her position. Even a purely expository essay will have some recognizable elements that help us visualize the text: setting (context of time and space), character (the speaker and any others necessary to the text), conflict (a problem to solve, an issue that begs exploration), even imagery (look for what you can perceive with your senses to help you fully experience the text).

In addition, many questions on the exam ask you to determine the attitude or perspective of a speaker. If you can improve your empathetic reading skills, this task will be much easier for you.

The more you practice empathetic reading, the more you will develop a kind of "double vision," where you'll view the text from within and also from without as a critical reader who sees the parts as they relate to the whole.

In your double vision, you'll learn to appreciate how the writing conveys enduring and universal ideas through the perspective of a character, narrator, or speaker.

THE IMPORTANCE OF IRONY

AP® readers say that students have difficulty recognizing irony in passages on the exam. And questions about irony are prevalent in the multiple-choice section. Recognizing irony is an aspect of seeing clearly. If something is not what it seems, perhaps there is something ironic there. But it will never be enough to simply identify irony—you will need to determine the effect or function the ironic element has in the text as a whole. See Chapter 15 for a detailed analysis of irony and satire.

- **Dramatic irony** is a powerful tool authors employ to reveal thematic insight. Whenever you know something a character or speaker does not know, you should make note of the discrepancy in the margin of the text. As you follow your character around in your mind movie, pay attention to moments when you feel smarter or more aware than the character. What does that show you?

- A narrator's speech is not always meant to be taken literally. Watch for **verbal irony** when what the speaker says differs from what he or she really means. The voice may even be sarcastic. Look for the underlying truth and how that truth functions in the text.

- Watch for evidence of **situational irony**. This can be a discrepancy in the setting or situation that is not what you expect. For example, you would not expect a very wealthy widow to be eating cat food. What might that detail mean?

- **Socratic irony** is a method in which an arguer feigns ignorance by taking a position he or she does not actually hold in order to push an argument to its limits.

TONE AND POINT OF VIEW

Tone is an important tool in understanding a speaker's attitude. The author will create a specific tone that reinforces how the narrator or speaker feels about someone or something creating emotional impact. When you are asked to determine the speaker's reaction to another person, an idea, or an event, look for the underlying emotions in the passage. Chapter 8 has a list of tone words to help you express what you see.

Shifts in tone are important to notice as they often signal an important change in position. If the text is at first congenial but then evolves into bitterness and indignation like Swift's *A Modest Proposal,* you've got something worth examining closely.

REVIEWING MAIN POINTS OF VIEW

- **First Person:** The narrator tells his/her own story using first-person pronouns. This point of view is limited by what the narrator can know, see, or understand. First-person narrators cannot always be trusted to assess the situation honestly. They may be blind to their own faults, etc. Those who write autobiographies or memoirs do not always capture reality exactly, but no one expects them to do this. Look for places where first-person narrators are being self-deprecating. This may be honesty or irony.

In providing evidence for your claims for Questions 1 and 3 in the free-response section, AP® readers now want to see that you are fully engaged in the topic by providing personal evidence, such as supportive data or facts, from your own observations or experiences. Evidence of this kind will require you to use first person. However, remember to default to authoritative third person (see explanation below) for the bulk of your essay, transitioning to first person only when you need it. This blending of two points of view is a skill you can practice. Look for examples of how student writers have blended points of view in the sample essays at AP® Central.

- **Second Person:** The narrator uses second-person pronouns to make immediate connections with readers.

- **Third-Person Limited:** A third-person narrator tells another's story using third-person pronouns. A third-person limited narrator is similar to a first-person narrator in that the narrator can only see and know what his character can see and know.

- **Third-Person Omniscient:** This third-person narrator is godlike, seeing and knowing all without constraints of time or space, seeing even beyond earthly existence. Third-person narrators often digress into contemplative or philosophical forays. Third-person omniscient narrators will often voice the viewpoint of the author. This would be a rare point of view in nonfiction.

- **Objective:** An objective narrator tells a story in a similar way to that of a video recorder, simply revealing the sights and sounds it perceives (though not, of course, as strictly as that). You will recognize an objective narrator by the lack of emotion or personal interest in the subject.

When using first person in a rhetorical argument, always avoid phrases like "I think," "in my opinion," or "in my view." They reduce the impact of your evidence by unnecessarily qualifying it and suggest the point you are making is "only" your perspective.

SHIFTS IN PERSPECTIVE (POINT OF VIEW)

A shift in point of view is something to examine closely. It is often a critical marker in understanding meaning or theme. Use the following list of questions as your guide:

1. Identify the shift. Where does it occur? From whose point of view to whose?

2. Why does the shift occur? What can the author accomplish with this new narrative point of view?

3. What changes are evident in narrative style, narrative voice, even syntax and diction?

4. What can you see that you did not see before? Something new, different, something opposite?

5. What limitations exist?

6. What does this new "viewer" know that the previous one did not? Or vice versa?

7. What is the overall effect of this shift?

As you consider your observations, certain points will probably jump out as truly significant or insightful. Use one of these points to create a defensible claim for an essay.

POINT OF VIEW IN YOUR OWN ESSAYS

LITERARY-PRESENT TENSE

Characters or persons in a literary text live in the present time. To write about them, we use what is called the literary-present tense, in which we use present-tense verbs. We would write, for example, "Atticus *is* a great father to Scout and Jem," or "Huck fakes his own death to escape his abusive father." While these examples are from fictional literature, literary-present tense is relevant when we write about nonfiction texts as well. You might write, "Swift argues that. . . ." or "Franklin writes . . ."

TENSE

Because it's best that you use literary-present tense verbs in your essay and when you cite source material, conflicts of tense can arise if the passage you cite is in past tense. However, when you use a direct or indirect citation, it is not always necessary to change the tense to conform. Purdue's Online Writing Lab (Purdue OWL) advises you to "establish a primary tense for the main discourse, and use occasional shifts to other tenses to indicate changes in time frame."

You have probably been taught to mark any changes you make to a direct citation by presenting the change in [brackets]. In your essays on the exam, you probably won't need to do this. Instead, follow the Purdue OWL's guidance. See the following for an example of how blending tenses can be effective:

Woolf says that by the nineteenth century "it was the habit for men of letters to describe their minds in confessions and autobiographies." She is suggesting that these men were expressing the effect of their environment on their work as writers.

AUTHORITATIVE-THIRD PERSON

The essays you will write for the AP® English Language exam are best written in third person, which gives you an authoritative voice. You will be taking a stance and supporting it. Whenever you write your own point of view, the tendency is to want to qualify your opinions by adding phrases such as "I think," "I feel," and "In my opinion." It is actually better to avoid such qualifiers.

Instead, write strong, confident claims that sound as if they are fact. It will be your task to provide evidence for your claims so your reader accepts your opinions, but don't intentionally limit your claims with qualifying phrases. Think of how you would respond to the example below. Which one of the pair seems stronger and more like a fact?

Qualified Claim	Authoritative Claim
In my opinion, Jefferson should have heeded Adams' advice and left the anti-slavery language in the Declaration of Independence. I feel it would have catapulted our country's sense of human rights ahead by hundreds of years.	Jefferson should have heeded Adams' advice and left the anti-slavery language in the Declaration of Independence. It would have catapulted our country's sense of human rights ahead by hundreds of years.

UNIVERSAL FIRST PERSON

In general you will be using authoritative third person for all of your essays. And, as I said earlier, when you present evidence from your own experience, you will transition to first person. A second type of first person is called universal-first person. We use universal-first person when we include ourselves in the masses that understand universal truths or themes. We'll use "we" instead of "I" to show our alliance in a common understanding or purpose. It may be appropriate to use the universal-first person, especially in your conclusion, if you are extending your understanding of the theme as something we all know or should know.

USING FIRST PERSON: A SAMPLE PROMPT AND WRITING EXERCISE

When the prompt on the exam asks you to support your argument with evidence from your reading, observation, and experience, you will present this evidence using first-person voice. Even if the prompt specifically doesn't cue you to use your own experience and observations, some of your best evidence may come from your life, so don't be afraid to use it. Effective use of such evidence will amp up your ethos better than anything else.

However, you don't want to overdo it. An AP® essay is not equivalent to a personal narrative. And, by default, you should use authoritative third person, transitioning to first person when you need to, then back again.

The prompt below, for free-response Question 3, is from a recently released AP® English Language and Composition Exam.

> In her book *Gift from the Sea*, author and aviator Anne Morrow Lindbergh (1906–2001) writes, "We tend not to choose the unknown which might be a shock or a disappointment or simply a little difficult to cope with. And yet it is the unknown with all its disappointments and surprises that is the most enriching."
>
> Consider the value Lindbergh places on choosing the unknown. Then write an essay in which you develop your own position on the value of exploring the unknown. Use appropriate, specific evidence to illustrate and develop your position.

This prompt seems to beg for an introspective essay. While it is possible to know about how notable figures benefited from taking steps into the unknown by having read their memoirs or biographies, you may lack that information. One source is wide open to you—your own experience, and this prompt opens the door for you to relay your own experience.

GENERATE EVIDENCE

As an exercise, make a list of times when you forged ahead, maybe even fearfully, into the unknown and were rewarded for your courage. Clarify the "how" and "why" aspects of each experience. Next, think about how other people you know personally (or through your reading) did the same thing. List those as well, with all relevant details.

WRITE IT

Now go beyond a mental exercise. Actually develop an essay following the directions above. Take care to default to authoritative third person voice, but weave in your evidence using first person where it fits.

Encourage your study group to do the same, then share your essays and critique each other's work.

I can't help but think your resulting essays might serve a double purpose. College entrance essay prompts often ask similar questions.

The World of Ideas:
Philosophies, Concepts, and Literary Themes

You can never learn less, you can only learn more.
—R. Buckminster Fuller

OVERVIEW

Human beings are by nature curious. We want to know how our world works. For thousands of years, people have pondered the universe, both the world outside us and the inner world of the mind and soul. Typically, those who ask the big questions and expound upon them are called philosophers. The root definition of the word "philosopher" is lover of wisdom. In the same way, the writers you'll encounter on this exam are concerned with the big ideas of life.

Additionally, it is important to understand that sometimes arguments are constructed through a particular perspective as a thought exercise. For example, one might develop claims to support both a feminist and a Marxist perspective of human rights in order to more fully understand the two positions. A Venn diagram can be helpful in such comparisons.

So treat this chapter as a very brief summary of the history of ideas as well as a reminder of common literary themes. And if your time is limited, spend most of it on the literary themes.

THINKING: A FEW KEY TERMS

- **Aesthetics**: philosophy that deals with the nature and expression of beauty.

- *A posteriori*: *a posteriori* knowledge or justification is dependent upon experience or empirical evidence.

- *A priori*: *a priori* knowledge or justification does not depend on experience.

- **Axiomatic:** self-evident or unquestionable.

- **Empiricism:** knowledge comes from the **senses**, as we look, listen, smell, touch, and taste the various objects in our environment.

- **Epistemology:** the study of knowledge.

- **Ethics:** the study or philosophy of what is right or good.

- **Metaphysics:** the study of the nature of reality, including the relationship between mind and matter, substance and attribute, fact and value.

- **Ontological:** referring to the study of the nature of being, existence, reality.

- **Rationalism:** constructing knowledge of the external world, the self, the soul, God, ethics, and science out of the simplest, indubitable ideas possessed innately by the **mind**.

- **Skepticism:** we do not, or cannot, know anything, or at least we do not know as much as we think we do.

50 KEY "ISMS"

There are hundreds of terms that end in "ism" that represent political, literary, social, and religious views. This list is only meant to remind you of some of the more common "isms." To give you a simpler reference, these terms are given in alphabetical order—not chronological, and not according to any category.

1. **absurdism:** doctrine that we live in an irrational universe.

2. **agnosticism:** doctrine that we can know nothing beyond material phenomena.

3. **anarchism:** doctrine that all governments should be abolished.

4. **anthropomorphism:** attribution of human qualities to non-human things.

5. **antinomianism:** doctrine of the rejection of moral law.

6. **asceticism**: doctrine that physical (bodily) self-denial permits spiritual enlightenment.

7. **atheism**: belief that there is no god.

8. **atomism**: belief that the universe consists of small indivisible particles.

9. **bipartisanism**: the state of being composed of members of two parties or of two parties cooperating, as in government.

10. **capitalism**: doctrine that private ownership and free markets should govern economies.

11. **centrism**: adherence to a middle-of-the-road position, neither left nor right, as in politics.

12. **collectivism**: doctrine of communal control of the means of production.

13. **Communism**: a theory or system in which all property is owned by all of the people equally, with its administration vested by them in the state or in the community.

14. **conservatism**: belief in maintaining political and social traditions.

15. **deism**: belief in a god but rejection of religion.

16. **determinism**: doctrine that events are predetermined by preceding events or laws.

17. **dualism**: doctrine that the universe is controlled by one good and one evil force.

18. **egalitarianism**: belief that humans ought to be equal in rights and privileges.

19. **egoism**: doctrine that the pursuit of self-interest is the highest good.

20. **empiricism**: doctrine that the experience of the senses is the only source of knowledge.

21. **existentialism**: doctrine of individual human responsibility in an unfathomable universe.

22. **Fascism**: a political philosophy that exalts nation and often race above the individual and that stands for a centralized autocratic government headed by a dictatorial leader, severe economic and social regimentation, and forcible suppression of opposition.

23. **fatalism**: doctrine that events are fixed and humans are powerless.

24. **feminism**: belief in the liberation of women in society to a social stature equal to that of men.

25. **gnosticism**: belief that freedom derives solely from knowledge.

26. **hedonism**: belief that pleasure is the highest good.

27. **humanism**: belief that human interests and mind are paramount.

28. **imperialism**: policy of forcefully extending a nation's authority by territorial gain or by the establishment of economic and political dominance over other nations.

29. **individualism**: belief that individual interests and rights are paramount.

30. **libertarianism**: doctrine that personal liberty is the highest value.

31. **Marxism**: the economic and political theories of Karl Marx and Friedrich Engels that hold that human actions and institutions are economically determined, and that class struggle is needed to create historical change, and that capitalism will ultimately be superseded by communism.

32. **materialism**: belief that matter is the only extant substance.

33. **monotheism**: belief in only one god.

34. **nihilism**: denial of all reality; extreme skepticism.

35. **objectivism**: a philosophical system founded by Ayn Rand, being one of several doctrines holding that all reality is objective and external to the mind and that knowledge is reliably based on observed objects and events.

36. **pantheism**: belief that the universe is God, that God is revealed in nature.

37. **polytheism**: belief in multiple deities.

38. **positivism**: philosophical view that whatever exists can be verified through experiments, observation, and mathematical/logical proof.

39. **pragmatism**: doctrine emphasizing practical value of philosophy.

40. **progressivism**: the principles and practices of those advocating progress, change, or reform, especially in political matters. When capitalized, the political and economic doctrines of the Progressive Party or Progressive Movement.

41. **radicalism**: the holding or following of principles advocating drastic political, economic, or social reforms.

42. **rationalism**: belief that reason is the fundamental source of knowledge.

43. **secularism**: the concept that government or other entities should exist separately from religion and/or religious beliefs.

44. **self-determinism**: doctrine that the actions of a self are self-originated.

45. **skepticism**: doctrine that true knowledge is always uncertain.

46. **socialism**: doctrine of centralized state control of wealth and property.

47. **solipsism**: theory that self-existence is the only certainty.

48. **stoicism**: belief in indifference to pleasure or pain.

49. **transcendentalism**: theory that emphasizes that which transcends perception.

50. **utilitarianism**: belief that utility of actions determines moral value and that the goal of human conduct is happiness.

POLITICAL CONTINUUM

What follows is a very basic map of the political continuum based on the wings in the British Parliament building. The purpose for including this graphic is to help you have a basic understanding of the often-used, but often-misunderstood, terms "left wing" and "right wing."

Left Wing

Liberal

Solving problems using
new methods, active
role of government

Progressive

Right Wing

Conservative

Solving problems using
old methods, limited
role of government

Laissez-Faire

Within the oval below we find concepts associated
with democracy and outside the oval we find concepts associated
with absolute rule (monarchies and dictatorships).[‡]

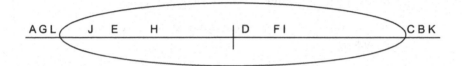

Examples

A. Karl Marx	B. Adolf Hitler	C. Mussolini	D. George W. Bush
E. Teddy Roosevelt	F. Calvin Coolidge	G. Stalin	H. John F. Kennedy
I. Ronald Reagan	J. Franklin D. Roosevelt	K. Osama bin Laden	L. Fidel Castro

COMMON LITERARY THEMES

Why study themes? At the heart of any piece of writing, whether a
memoir or an essay on economics, is some underlying truth about human
existence. In literature, we refer to these truths as "themes." Expanding your
awareness of key themes might trigger a deeper grasp of a complex passage.
Do take note: no author is going to tell readers directly that the point of the
essay is to reaffirm that, for example, "power is a corrupting force." However,
as an astute reader, you will be expected to draw that conclusion as you read.

THEMATIC STATEMENTS:

- All life is connected.

- Each life, no matter how small, matters.

[‡]This graphic was created by Sheboygan Falls High School social studies teacher
Lee McGlade. Similar graphics can be found online from various accredited sources.

- Life is too brief.

- Youth (innocence) and beauty don't last.

- We don't appreciate what we have until it's gone.

- Pride can blind us to the truth.

- Small acts of kindness and/or generosity can have a tremendous effect.

- Courage can reward those who push themselves.

- Sometimes we learn too late what we need to know.

- Social status, beauty, wealth, etc., do not matter.

- We learn through trial, hardship, or pain those lessons most valuable.

- The individual is sometimes in conflict with society.

- Individuals are often alienated and alone.

- Self-determination is a fierce inner force, but is often thwarted or delayed by outside forces.

- Fantasy is sometimes more real than everyday reality.

- Mortality (death) is inevitable.

- Human beings are sometimes too weak (or too blind) to do what is right.

- We often want what others have or we often want what we cannot have.

- Fear, jealousy, and greed are destructive emotions.

- We sometimes hurt those we love.

- People (of all cultures and of all times) are more alike than they are different.

- Nature does not care about people.

- Each of us is alone (often feeling small or frightened) in the world.

- Evil exists in the hearts of men (women).

- Power can be a corrupting force.

THEMATIC QUESTIONS:

- What is truth?
- What is beauty?
- What is real?
- What is justice?
- What is honor?
- What is love?
- What does it mean to live a good life?
- What does it mean to be a hero?
- What does it mean to have courage?

Chapter 16 includes a list of common topics and themes you may find on the AP® English Language exam.

Make a card listing your top ten literary themes and carry it with you. Pull it out to look at it often. Make these themes serve as the lens through which you view the world. You will start to hear these themes in songs, see them in movies, and recognize them on TV shows. More importantly, you will be better able to recognize them in the literature you read. The result of rehearsing themes is that when you read those complex passages on the exam, you will be better able to recognize them quickly.

Irony and Satire:
Reading Between the Lines

Satire is focused bitterness.—Leo Rosten

OVERVIEW

The concepts of irony and satire—even though they are all around us—remain a struggle for many students. I think the reason for this is that irony and satire do not communicate messages directly, but do so indirectly. Their meaning is not obvious, but subtle. As there are typically questions about irony or about satirical passages on the exam, it is important to devote some extra time here to study them. This chapter will provide you with a good foundation to maximize your ability to both recognize and understand the function of these concepts.

IRONY

While irony is a tool (the main tool) of satirists, it is, on its own, an important element in all literature. Yearly, there are questions on the exam about irony. Basically, *irony* is the term we use to signal an uncomfortable space between appearances and reality. Irony gets us to pay attention, since it is a kind of cognitive dissonance that our brain wants swept up and made orderly. We want things to make sense or fit a constructed order.

In general, irony lives in any technique meant to create contrast, such as hyperbole, understatement, oxymoron, and more. Be sure you are a master of the following types of irony and can easily spot them in the texts you read.

At the end of this chapter, you will find an annotated satirical essay by Mark Twain. Use it as one more example of how close, critical reading is important and as an illustration of some of the concepts in this chapter.

FOUR TYPES OF IRONY

1. **Verbal Irony**: what the speaker says is different from what he or she means. Sarcasm is a type of verbal irony, but it is harsh, even bitter, and typically expresses a veiled anger or resentment.

2. **Dramatic Irony**: the reader or listener knows something that the character or speaker does not know.

3. **Situational Irony**: a discrepancy between what is real and what is perceived. Situational irony refers to an occasion in which the outcome is significantly different from what is expected or considered appropriate.

4. **Socratic Irony**: Socrates taught his students by pretending to be ignorant about the subjects they were discussing in order to get them to think on their own. Related to this playing "devil's advocate" is the situation in which an arguer ironically takes a position he or she does not actually hold in order to push an argument to its limits.

Test Tip

If understanding irony is difficult for you, start an irony journal. When ironic situations or comments "pop up" in your everyday life, make a list of them. Actively collecting examples of irony will force you to pay attention to it and will thus sharpen your irony radar!

SATIRE

Satire is language or writing (even if the mode is visual) with a specific purpose. The purpose of **satire** is to point out the inadequacies, vices, and corruptions in people, institutions, and cultures with the intent of bringing about change. Satire is often wryly funny, sometimes even knee-slapping funny, but sometimes the satirist hits a raw nerve, and we may be too uncomfortable to laugh at what is clearly no laughing matter. The satirist is a person in tune with what ought to be, and he or she may see what others cannot see or are too timid to express: the truth. The ultimate goal of a satirist is to bring about positive change for the betterment of all.

As ordinary citizens, we expect that people in power, especially if we bestow that power upon them, will not abuse it and will not exploit, undermine, or cheat us in the execution of their duties. We also know that human beings are innately flawed, which provides a rich field for satirists, whose job it is to point out people and institutions that break our explicit or implicit social contract.

THE SOCIAL CONTRACT

To be good at analyzing satire, it is important that we understand that human beings have, in general, a social contract with each other. Satirists point out a break or departure from this social contract. To understand this social contract, think in terms of humanity's norms. A **norm** is a universally agreed upon standard of behavior. In this social contract, we also include rules (laws). The commandment "Thou shalt not kill" is a good example of a long-standing rule that most people in all cultures agree is an important rule by which to live. Three aspects of norms and rules determine the extent to which we universally value them in our social contract. The chart below illustrates these aspects of "universality."

Qualities of Universality ▶	Long-standing	Most reasonable people agree that it is just/fair	Accepted in many cultures
"Thou shalt not kill."	✓	✓	✓
Stealing is wrong	✓	✓	✓
Lying is wrong	✓	✓	✓
You should not wear white shoes after Labor Day‡.			
Women must not express their opinions in public.			

‡Ask your grandmother about this one. ☺

Test Tip

Create your own list of universal truths that you believe are central to our universal social contract.

Why not simply be a muckraker or a whistle-blower? It is sometimes politically or personally dangerous to stand up to powerful figures, be they institutions or individuals. Surely you've heard stories of whistle-blowers losing their jobs, *or worse*. Since satire is inherently ambiguous, there is safety in the gray areas. All satirical techniques allow the satirist to say two or more things at the same time. Satirists mainly insinuate instead of attack directly. This aspect of satire provides relative safety for the satirist, but can also present difficulty for AP® English students. We must read carefully and learn to read what's implied or insinuated. This can sometimes be very difficult to do, which is why you need to practice the skills shown in this chapter.

For example, while the targets for *The Daily Show*'s writers are corrupt politicians, *we* are their audience. Their goal is for *us* to snap out of our lethargy and become aware and eventually act. They want us to stand up for what we know is right. Similarly, Jonathan Swift could not have solved the problems of the Irish poor by himself, but he expected the landowners and the politicians to begin acting in honorable ways. *A Modest Proposal* is outrageous, but its intent is to shame those who abandoned the poor.

Most satirists are also, to some extent, entertainers. Even Geoffrey Chaucer's portrayal of the cheating Miller in *The Reeve's Tale* is initially laugh-out-loud funny. When we examine the story more closely, we see all kinds of human foibles there and good lessons for us all.

It is also a fact of human nature that we don't respond to the dictates of a know-it-all. We shun the arrogance of those who tell us what to do. But when a satirist first astonishes us or makes us laugh and gives us an oblique picture of ourselves in a mirror, we somehow are more willing to accept our faults.

STYLES AND TYPES OF SATIRE

Two Styles

1. **Direct** satire (also called Formal): directly stated by the satirist
2. **Indirect** satire: communicated through characters in a narrative

Two Types

1. **Juvenalian Satire**: Named after Juvenal, a Roman poet active in the late first and early second century; author of the *Satires*. This type of satire is bitter, angry, contemptuous, and full of moral indignation. If you do not laugh but instead react with outrageous surprise, you are probably reading Juvenalian satire.
2. **Horatian Satire**: Named after Horace, Roman poet who lived 65–8 BCE. It is characterized by gentle, urbane comedy that corrects through sympathetic laughter.

TYPICAL SATIRICAL TARGETS

Powerful People	Institutions	Events/ Conditions	Human Nature
Politicians	Congress	Oil Spills	Cowardice
Religious Leaders	Churches	Wars	Greed and Corruption
Teachers	Broadcast Networks	Social Trends/ Fads	Hypocrisy
Police Officers	Corporations	Neglect of Duty	Incontinence (inability to control desires)
Parents	Sports Teams		Arrogance
Celebrities			Ignorance

SATIRICAL TECHNIQUES AND DEVICES

Lists of satirical techniques will vary from source to source. The list below is meant to give you a broad view. As with any list of literary terms, there is some overlap. Various sources use different terms for similar concepts. The Quick Guide (following the list) is a more summarized approach. If you are short on time, rely on the Quick Guide, but also familiarize yourself with this list as well.

1. **Allegory/Parable:** An **allegory** is a narrative with a literal and a symbolic meaning. By using allegory, writers can disguise their satirical targets as a character. A **parable** is a story that teaches a lesson. Parables are sometimes cautionary tales such as narratives that warn what might happen if behavior does not change.

2. **Ambiguity:** Inherent in most of these techniques, ambiguity is simply when the meaning of something is unclear and it may mean more than one thing.

3. **Exaggeration:** To enlarge, increase, or represent something beyond normal bounds so that it becomes ridiculous and its faults can be seen. *Caricature* is the exaggeration of a physical feature or trait. Cartoons, especially political cartoons, provide extensive examples

of caricature. *Burlesque* is the ridiculous exaggeration of language. An example is when a character who should use formal, intelligent language speaks like a fool or a character who is portrayed as uneducated uses highly sophisticated, intelligent language. To enlarge, increase, or represent something beyond normal bounds so that it becomes ridiculous and its faults can be seen.

4. **Diminution:** Taking a real-life situation and reducing it to make it ridiculous and showcase its faults. Also, **Reduction**.

5. **Distortion:** Taking something out of its ordinary surroundings sometimes reveals its idiocy or inadequacies.

6. **Farce:** Similar to burlesque, a farce is a narrative in which the ridiculous characters in the situation are exaggerated and the outcomes of the plot are absurd. It is essentially a comedy.

7. **Incongruity:** To present things that are out of place or absurd in relation to their surroundings. Particular techniques include oxymoron, metaphor, and irony. Much of irony—and thus satire—can be summed up by incongruity between what is said and what is meant.

8. **Innuendo:** An implied remark that disparages another's reputation.

9. **Invective:** A direct insult. A longer version of invective is a **diatribe** (we'd call it a rant).

10. **Knaves and Fools:** These clowns of satire are exaggerations of our follies. Taken to the extreme, their ridiculous behavior still rings true, and we see in them something of ourselves. Knaves and fools are key elements of farce.

11. **Malapropism:** Absurd or humorous misuse of a word, especially by confusion with one of similar sound. Example: "Republicans understand the importance of bondage between a mother and child." (Dan Quayle)

12. **Oxymoron:** Words or phrases used together that present a paradox. Examples are "wax fruit" and "electric candles."

13. **Parody:** To imitate the techniques and/or style of some person, place, or thing, mimicking the techniques and/or style in order to ridicule the original. For parody to be successful, the reader must know the original text that is being ridiculed.

14. **Reduction:** To belittle the satirical target, reducing power or stature. Caricature is one way to reduce status, since it makes the target look ridiculous or silly.

15. **Reversal:** To present the opposite of the normal order. Reversal can focus on the order of events, such as serving dessert before the main dish or having breakfast for dinner. Additionally, reversal can focus on hierarchical order—for instance, when a young child makes all the decisions for a family or when an administrative assistant dictates what the company president decides and does. To present the opposite of the normal order (e.g., the order of events, hierarchical order).

16. **Understatement:** The opposite of exaggeration, understatement does basically the same thing, but instead draws attention to the truth.

SATIRE: QUICK GUIDE

I created this quick guide for students to take with them since it is more portable than a book. During our satire unit, I encourage students to see through the lenses of a satirist, which means everything they encounter should be viewed as fodder for its potential to be satirized. Learning the tools a satirist uses means more than just memorizing a few terms. It means that you must recognize irony and exaggeration when you see it and decide if the writer has a barb in mind.

SATIRE: Quick Guide

What is it? A satirist points out, usually through humor, what is wrong in people and institutions. In any analysis of satire, we look for three things: Target, Purpose, Techniques. You want to know what is being mocked or ridiculed in order to know what the satirist wants us to know and do.

1. What is the satirical target?

   - A person? A company/corporation? An idea? A social trend/ convention?

2. What is the satirical purpose?

   - Force a recognition of common sense. "Let's get real, people."

   - Urge a change in policy. "This is not how it should be done."

   - Create an understanding that something is wrong/illegal/ immoral or should be.

Continued →

3. How is the satire achieved? What techniques are used? There are more than these nine, but these are often cited as the main ones.

- **Exaggeration**
  Hyperbole/overstatement, or plain exaggeration is used to take something to the extreme. The contrast gets us to see the reality.

- **Understatement**
  The opposite of exaggeration, understatement does basically the same thing. By contrast, it draws attention to the truth.

- **Distortion**
  Taking something out of its ordinary surroundings sometimes reveals its idiocy or inadequacies. Distortion unmasks an idea.

- **Irony**
  Plain old irony points out discrepancies that perhaps should be obvious, but might take the satirist to show us.

- **Oxymoron**
  A good example is "deafening silence." An extremely loud noise would be deafening and silence is the absence of any noise. When the words don't fit, the meaning becomes obvious.

- **Innuendo**
  Innuendo is an indirect attack or insinuation. It's useful when the target is dangerous or powerful. Intention can always be denied.

- **Reversal**
  To present the opposite of the normal order, which is a type of distortion, but reversal gets us to look at what should be by way of the contrast.

- **Reduction**
  Look for caricatures or other ways to knock the corrupt and powerful off their self-made pedestals. Does a sneaky politician look clownish in a cartoon? That's reduction.

- **Ambiguity**
  While many aspects of satire are ambiguous, some statements are directly so. Look for fuzzy statements that can mean more than one thing.

4. Put in your own words what it is that the satirist wants us to **know** or **do**.

Note: In addition to common satirical techniques, any piece of satire may also employ typical rhetorical strategies. Be sure to know all of those as well as the list of appeals. See Chapter 6.

GENERAL GUIDE FOR ANALYZING SATIRE

I created the following guide for my students to help them analyze several texts that we study together in our satire unit. My students sometimes work independently, but also with partners, especially if a text is complex. If you have a study team, you might want to consider sharing this guide with them. In your group, read and study some of the texts listed in the chart at the end of this chapter.

General Guide for Analyzing Satire

Title of work: _____   Author: _____

1. What is the main satiric target (social institution, social convention/norm, etc.)?

2. Who are the specific representatives of the target (individuals or groups)?

3. Which aspects of our social "agreement" are flawed?

4. What change does the author want to see?

5. Find and label in your text examples of specific satirical techniques. (See the list above.) Then, choose two and, in the space below, explain their effectiveness.

6. How are wit and humor employed? Give specific examples.

7. Is this work a sample of Juvenalian or Horatian satire, and how do you know?

8. How well does the author achieve his/her purpose? Do you think the message is clear or too ambiguous? Explain.

(Copy and use to analyze a variety of satirical texts.)

RESOURCE GUIDE

Some academics say satire is dead, but it may just be that good satire is harder to find. The list that follows should give you a good start in finding new and old satire to study. If you find the genre difficult, please do spend some time with this. It will pay off in the end. This list of works is not meant to suggest the full range of literary or cultural satire, but rather to remind you of what is out there that is generally easy to access.

Do not limit yourself to what is listed here. Instead, be open to satirical possibilities anywhere. If you're laughing and the writer or commentator is making fun of someone who did something not quite right, that's satire. Analyze it. Think it through. You'll become an expert in no time.

Cautionary note: It is easy to get caught up in the humor when you watch some of these shows or read some of the articles, but keep your analytical head about you. Always work on identifying the satirical target and what techniques are used to blast away at the stupidity, hypocrisy, or corruption.

Test Tip

Photocopy several copies of the General Guide for Analyzing Satire (see previous page), and study some examples from the current media. Do the same with a text from a classic satirist such as Jonathan Swift or Mark Twain.

Current Examples		Classic Satirists
Television/ Movies	**Books/Newspaper/Internet**	
The Daily Show	*The Onion* (an article from *The Onion* was featured in the free-response section of the 2005 exam). *The Onion* was originally a print paper. They have published several books as well.	Geoffrey Chaucer: *Canterbury Tales*
Family Guy, Seth MacFarlane	Andy Borowitz, *The Borowitz Report, The New Yorker*.	Jonathan Swift: *A Modest Proposal, Gulliver's Travels*
Saturday Night Live	*The Heckler* (satirical look at Chicago sports)	Voltaire: *Candide*
The Simpsons, Matt Groening	Garry Trudeau's comic strip, *Doonesbury* (first published in daily papers in 1970). Look at the editorial cartoons in your own newspaper as well (or those published and shared online).	Benjamin Franklin: *Rules by Which a Great Empire May Be Reduced to a Small One* (public domain)
South Park, Matt Stone and Trey Parker	Dave Barry: variety of titles	Mark Twain: *The Adventures of Huckleberry Finn, Advice to Youth* (earlier AP® prompt)
This is Spinal Tap, Best in Show, Waiting for Guffman, Christopher Guest	Joseph Heller: *Catch-22*	

SAMPLE WORK WITH ANNOTATIONS

The following is a speech by Mark Twain called *Advice to Youth* (1882).

Primary Satirical Target: Hypocritical adults (parents) who tell children one thing but live the opposite.

Being told I would be expected to talk here, I inquired what sort of talk I ought to make. They said it should be something suitable to youth—something <u>didactic, instructive,</u> or something in the nature of good advice. Very well. I have a few things in my mind which I have often longed to say for the instruction of the young; for it is in <u>one's tender early years</u> that such things <u>will best take root</u> and be most enduring and most valuable. First, then, I will say to you my young friends—and I say it <u>beseechingly, urgingly—</u>

Tone – initially sincere

Genre: speech

The young are impressionable

My message is very important! (It actually is – the real message.)

Series of maxims/moral truths

1) Always obey your parents, when they are present. This is the best policy in the long run, because if you don't, they will make you. Most parents think they know better than you do, and you can generally make more by humoring that superstition than you can by acting on your own better judgment.

First indication that he may not always be serious, or mean what he says.

2) Be respectful to your superiors, if you have any, also to strangers, and sometimes to others. If a person offends you, and you are in doubt as to whether it was intentional or not, do not resort to extreme measures; simply watch your chance <u>and hit him with</u> a brick. <u>That will be sufficient.</u> If you shall find that he had not intended any offense, come out frankly and confess yourself in the wrong when you struck him; acknowledge it like a man and say you didn't mean to. Yes, always avoid violence; in this age of charity and kindliness, the time has gone by for such things. Leave dynamite to the low and unrefined.

Reversal: Such behavior is not at all socially acceptable. Exaggerated example of how people sometimes act poorly and then say "Sorry, didn't mean it."

3) Go to bed early, get up early—this is wise. Some authorities say get up with the sun; some say get up with one thing, others with another. But a lark is really the best thing to get up with. It gives you a splendid reputation with everybody to know that you get up with the lark; and if you get the right kind of lark, and work at him right, you can easily train him to get up at half past nine, every time—it's no trick at all.

Ambiguity→"Lark"
Lark is an early bird but also a whim. Getting up early is a relative virtue, but maybe getting up each day w/a sense of newness + adventure is good.

tongue-in-cheek

Now as to the matter of lying. You want to be very careful about lying; otherwise you are nearly sure to get caught. Once caught, you can never again be in the eyes to the good and the pure, what you were before. Many a young person has injured himself permanently through a single clumsy and ill finished lie, the result of carelessness born of incomplete training. Some authorities hold that the young ought not to lie at all. That of course, is putting it rather stronger than necessary; still while I cannot go quite so far as that, I do maintain, and I believe I am right, that the young ought to be temperate in the use of this great art until practice and experience shall give them that confidence, elegance, and precision which alone can make the accomplishment graceful and profitable. Patience, diligence, painstaking attention to detail—these are requirements; these in time, will make the student perfect; upon these only, may he rely as the sure foundation for future eminence. Think what tedious years of study, thought, practice, experience, went to the equipment of that peerless old master who was able to impose upon the whole world the lofty and sounding maxim that "Truth is mighty and will prevail"—the most majestic compound fracture of fact which any of woman born has yet achieved. For the history of our race, and each individual's experience, are sewn

⚔︎1
⚔︎ Yes – careful, but not in a traditional way.

If you're going to lie well, it takes practice.

The typical view of all adults/parents.

⚔︎2
⚔︎2 These are actually good traits.

This maxim is in itself a lie. Good ex. of hypocrisy.

nice phrase, a complicated lie

Society doesn't really value the truth.

thick with evidences that a truth is not hard to kill, and that a lie well told is immortal.

Lying is so common that some lies become immortal.

There is in Boston a monument of the man who discovered anesthesia; many people are aware, in these latter days, that man didn't discover it at all, but stole the discovery from another man. Is this truth mighty, and will it prevail? Ah no, my hearers, the monument is made of hardy material, but the lie it tells will outlast it a million years. An awkward, feeble, leaky lie is a thing which you ought to make it your unceasing study to avoid; such a lie as that has no more real permanence than an average truth. Why, you might as well tell the truth at once and be done with it. A feeble, stupid, preposterous lie will not live two years—except it be a slander upon somebody. It is indestructible, then of course, but that is no merit of yours. A final word: begin your practice of this gracious and beautiful art early—begin now. If I had begun earlier, I could have learned how.

Example of an immortal lie.

This seems like a cynical truth.

Irony – Emphasizes his earnestness. He's not able to lie. But of course, he writes fiction.

Never handle firearms carelessly. The sorrow and suffering that have been caused through the innocent but heedless handling of firearms by the young! Only four days ago, right in the next farm house to the one where I am spending the summer, a grandmother, old and gray and sweet, one of the loveliest spirits in the land, was sitting at her work, when her young grandson crept in and got down an old, battered, rusty gun which had not been touched for many years and was supposed not to be loaded, and pointed it at her, laughing and threatening to shoot. In her fright she ran screaming and pleading toward the door on the other side of the room; but as she passed him he placed the gun almost against her very breast and pulled the trigger! He had supposed it was not loaded.

And he was right—it wasn't. So there wasn't any harm done. It is the only case of that kind I ever heard of. Therefore, just the same, don't you meddle with old unloaded firearms; they are the most deadly and unerring things that have ever been created by man. You don't have to take any pains at all with them; you don't have to have a rest, you don't have to have any sights on the gun, you don't have to take aim, even. No, you just pick out a relative and bang away, and you are sure to get him. A youth who can't hit a cathedral at thirty yards with a Gatling gun in three quarters of an hour, can take up an old empty musket and bag his grandmother every time, at a hundred. Think what Waterloo would have been if one of the armies had been boys armed with old muskets supposed not to be loaded, and the other army had been composed of their female relations. The very thought of it makes one shudder.

irony — real guns/ weapons are ... "the most deadly ever created by man."

Distortion — A wild youth with a gun is ridiculous — but compared to reality — harmless. Guns in real life are not unloaded + they kill for real.

Reversal – But war isn't silly stuff.

 4

There are many sorts of books; but good ones are the sort for the young to read: Remember that. They are a great, an inestimable, and unspeakable means of improvement. Therefore be careful in your selection, my young friends; be very careful; confine yourselves exclusively to Robertson's Sermons, Baxter's Saint's Rest, The Innocents Abroad, and works of that kind.

Didactic texts that are most likely worthless. He's mocking himself by including his own book. Learn from life, not books!

Biblical allusion

But I have said enough/ I hope you will treasure up the instructions which I have given you, and <u>make them a guide to your feet and a light</u> to your understanding. <u>Build your character thoughtfully and painstakingly upon these precepts,</u> and by and by, when you have got it built, you will be surprised and gratified to see <u>how nicely and sharply it resembles everybody else's.</u> Cynical tone.

Appeal to identity + esteem needs; we want to find our own way + not follow.

Twain's main point: If you want to be like all the other adults in the world, learn to lie + use violence to solve your conflicts.

PART IV

RESEARCH AND COMPOSITION

Free-Response Questions

*I do insist on making what I hope is sense so there's always
a coherent narrative or argument that the
reader can follow.* — Howard Nemerov

OVERVIEW

While each of the three free-response questions presents a distinct
task, they all require you to do your best rhetorical reading and writing.
All three questions require you to develop and defend an argument.

The College Board is committed to what they call "stable prompt
wording," in which they promise to maintain a standard approach for
each question from year to year. Knowing that the core task for each
question will remain constant not only helps your teacher develop
appropriate lessons, but it also helps you know exactly what you can do
to prepare.

The language for these stable prompts comes directly from the latest
AP® English Language and Composition Course and Exam Description.

You will find a detailed analysis of each free-response question along
with sample essays later in this book, in Chapters 19–21.

QUESTION 1   SYNTHESIS

You will be presented with an issue to consider. There will usually be
six sources, at least one of which is a visual text. Your task is to develop
your own position on the issue that is presented and defend your thesis
with evidence from at least three of the provided sources. See the detailed
explanation of this question in Chapter 19.

STABLE PROMPT WORDING

Carefully read the following six sources, including the introductory information for each source. Write an essay that synthesizes material from at least three of the sources and develops your position on [specific subject from the introduction].

QUESTION 2   RHETORICAL ANALYSIS

For Question 2 you will be presented with a prose passage (approximately 600–800 words) to read and analyze. In general, you will be asked to analyze the writer's rhetorical choices and the function or effect of those choices in accomplishing his or her purpose. You will not generally be given a list of rhetorical appeals, devices, or strategies because you are expected to have a functional knowledge of these elements of argument. (See Chapter 6.)

Question 2 is most likely to be presented as follows.

STABLE PROMPT WORDING

[Background on the rhetorical situation]. Read the passage carefully. Write an essay that analyzes the rhetorical choices [the writer] makes to [develop/achieve/convey] [his/her] [argument. . . /purpose. . . / message. . .].

QUESTION 3   ARGUMENT

Several situations are possible:

You are given a short quotation (or multiple quotations) or a very brief passage that presents a debatable issue. You are asked to develop your own position on the issue and defend it. Your evidence for this essay comes from your own knowledge, reading, experience, and observations.

You are given a premise and you will choose your own relevant issue to argue. Your support for this essay comes from your own knowledge, reading, experience, and observations.

You may be asked to defend (support), challenge (rebut or refute), or qualify a writer's position. This task may also be worded this way: support, complement, or contradict. *Support* means to agree and explain why. *Complement* means to mostly agree but go further by adding your own argument. *Contradict* means to disagree and explain why.

STABLE PROMPT WORDING

Write an essay that argues your position on [specific subject from the introduction].

READ PROMPTS CAREFULLY

A typical AP® essay prompt does several things:

1. Asks you to carefully read a specific text(s), quotation, or question, including background and introductory information.

2. Gives you a specific task to accomplish

3. Directly tells you to develop a position or argument.

4. May instruct you to defend your claim with specific evidence (though this aspect of any argument should be self-evident).

It is critically important for you to know exactly what a prompt is asking for and respond appropriately. You will earn a very low score if you fail to do what the prompt asks you to do or if you substitute a simpler task for the one presented to you.

ANALYZING AN ESSAY PROMPT: STRATEGY FOR SUCCESS

1. **Analyze your prompt.** Underline key words in the prompt, especially verbs that state your task, but also underline any hints about a topic or perspective.

   ➤ Sample prompt from a previous exam with keywords, verbs, and hints underlined:

   In his 2004 book, <u>Status Anxiety</u>, Alain de Botton argues that the chief aim of humorists is not merely to entertain but "to convey with impunity messages that might be dangerous or impossible to state directly." Because <u>society allows humorists to say things that other people cannot or will not say</u>, de Botton sees humorists as serving a vital function in society.

<u>Think</u> about the implications of de Botton's view of the role of humorists (cartoonists, stand-up comics, satirical writers, hosts of television programs, etc.). Then write an essay that <u>defends, challenges, or qualifies</u> de Botton's claim about the <u>vital role of humorists</u>. <u>Use specific, appropriate evidence</u> to develop your position.

2. **Paraphrase your task**. This step is crucial to your understanding. It will be helpful to you, at least as you prepare for exam day, to write out your paraphrase, but since it only takes a few seconds, why not continue the practice when it really matters? By phrasing, in your own words, what you believe your task to be, you will understand it better and will remember it more as you write, which will help you stay focused. You can also reword the prompt using first person, stating what you need to do. See the example below.

➤ Paraphrase for prompt above:

Alain de Botton says that humorists (comedians, cartoonists, television hosts) do more than entertain us. He thinks we allow them to say things no one else can say, which gives them an important voice in society. I need to think about what this means, and decide if I agree with de Botton or not (or somewhere in between), then develop my claim in my essay.

3. **Use the prompt as your guide**. When you know what you're supposed to do, you can read a passage or source materials more efficiently and more intelligently.

➤ Annotate any supplied texts as you read, with the prompt in mind.

➤ Create a mini-outline that contains your main claim (thesis) and your key points. This is your "answer" to the prompt. It must fit the expectations presented in the prompt. However, never think you are simply "answering" a question. You must take a position and create your own argument.

➤ Write your thesis on your scratch paper. By the time you're ready to write, any subtle changes you wish to make will be easier if your original idea is jotted down for reference.

4. **Review the prompt** as often as necessary to make sure you aren't digressing or losing focus.

Test Tip

If you get in the habit of using the prompt-analysis strategy given above on all your practice essays, it will become an automatic skill for you by exam time and you'll barely be conscious of the process. That's efficiency!

TAKING A POSITION

You are sometimes asked to defend, challenge, or qualify an author's purpose or position in a passage. It is important to know what these terms mean.

Defend (sometimes **support** is used to mean the same thing)	Defending someone else's point of view means that you agree with it. You will create your own argument using evidence from your reading, observations, and experience to support your claim that the author is correct.
Challenge (sometimes **refute** or **rebut** is used to mean the same thing)	Challenging or refuting someone else's point of view means that you disagree with it. You will create your own argument using evidence from your reading, observations, and experience to support your claim that the author is incorrect.
Qualify (sometimes **complement**)	Qualifying someone else's point of view means that you agree with some parts of his or her argument but disagree with other parts. Or, it could mean that while you think the author is generally correct, you want to point out some exceptions or some qualifications that exist. You will create your own argument using evidence from your reading, observations, and experience to support your claim that the author is not exactly correct.

THEMES AND TOPICS

The following is a list of themes and topics from past free-response prompts. As you read through this list, you will notice some obviously similar ideas, which may mean that these topics are favorites of the College Board, that these themes are essential human themes, or even that the most prominent themes may reappear on future exams. The purpose of this list is to show you what issues students have been presented with in the past. You could also use this list to guide your reading. If you are fairly uninformed on a particular topic, you could make it a point to read more about it prior to exam day.

- Value of technology in education
- Slavery
- Function of humor and humorists in society
- Daylight Saving Time
- Midwestern values
- Effects of consumer culture
- Individual and conformity
- Free speech
- Effect of television on society
- Environment
- Effect of adversity on one's character
- Value of penny coin
- Scientific research method
- Corporate advertising/sponsorship in schools
- National school curriculum
- Anti-intellectualism
- Effect of dissent in America
- Effect of advertising on society
- Emigration
- Ethics of rewarding charitable acts in schools

- What museum artifacts represent
- Value of muckrakers/whistle-blowers
- Race
- How fads reflect American values
- Effect of money in society
- Value/effect of personal opinion/commentary in society
- Compulsory voting
- Effect of reading on independent thought
- Consumerism and advertising
- Poverty
- The Mississippi River
- Value of trial-and-error thinking
- Cultural differences
- Common sense and personal values
- Protecting the environment
- Morality
- Cultural norms
- Effect of entertainment on society
- Admiration of birds in flight
- Emigration
- Individual and society
- Plagiarism in schools
- Effects of Civil War from Lincoln's point of view
- Childhood memories
- Abuse of power
- Appreciation for natural world/beauty
- Man versus machine/technology
- Self-awareness

- Limitations of viewing the world through photographic images
- Dress code
- Value of polite speech for society
- Value of public libraries
- Locavore movement
- Role of journalism in national discourse
- Value of college
- Technology versus nature
- Child labor
- Genetically modified food
- Commercial wind farms

See Chapter 4 for lists of authors and texts to consider reading before your exam.

Developing an Argument:
Creating Excellence Through Structure, Style, and Voice

If the writing is honest it cannot be separated from the [one] who wrote it.—Tennessee Williams

OVERVIEW

Please think of yourself not as a student writer, but as a young person with something to say. This perspective is new to the College Board's approach to helping teachers develop their AP® English Language and Composition courses. As your teachers, we are now more aware that we need to appreciate your voice and to envelop you in the world of rhetoric by acknowledging that you have agency. What this means is that we recognize your capacity to think independently and add your voice to the ongoing discussion of important issues. Such a position should be empowering for you. As your teachers, we do care about what you think, and we want to hear from you.

But, we are still your teachers, so we want to guide you to become highly proficient in using rhetorical tools for effective expression. This chapter gives you a summary of those tools and strategies.

Having said that, I do want to point out that you are not going to have to write the most brilliant essays ever written to do well on the AP® English Language and Composition exam, but you *are* going to have to show that you understand the task presented to you, that you can formulate logical, defensible arguments, and that you can write well-organized, insightful essays. Additionally, your essays for the exam are considered drafts and AP® readers are instructed to award points for what students do well. Don't misinterpret "draft." AP® readers will not reward a sloppy, lazy attempt. They do want your best work, but they understand you cannot provide a perfect, final draft in 40 minutes.

See Chapter 16 for a list of the essay types and prompts.

TYPICAL PROBLEMS

If you could ask an AP® reader to list some typical mistakes students make in writing their essays, the AP® reader might mention the following:

- No discernible thesis (therefore, no controlling idea).

- Failure to analyze (the writer summarizes or paraphrases instead).

- Failure to move from "what" to "how" and "why."

- Failure to support generalizations or claims with evidence from the text.

- Poorly developed commentary, perhaps repeating one or two ideas over and over.

- Inability to integrate and embed evidence from the supplied text or sources in sentences.

- Wordy introductions, mostly a restatement of the prompt.

- "Boring" conclusions that simply restate the thesis or prompt.

- Loosely constructed paragraphs that are not unified or coherent.

- Predictable reliance upon a five-paragraph essay, but without real analysis (organization without content is not an essay).

- Imprecise use of language. Never use big words to impress. Instead, use the exact right word for the job. See Chapter 12 for more on vocabulary.

- Failure to synthesize (combine) sources.

GENERAL QUALITIES OF A GOOD ESSAY

- It is far better to write a relatively short essay with a defensible thesis and a few insightful claims supported with textual evidence than to have a longer essay that is about nothing. If you don't understand the prompt or the text, your essay will be about nothing.

- An essay is not a list of separate ideas clumped together.

- An essay is not a summary of the text or sources—it is an **argument** that you control. A generalization without support is not an argument.

- You need a thesis that responds accurately to the task given in the prompt, without repeating the prompt.

- A good essay is well organized, even if it is a draft. It should have discernible parts: introduction, body, and conclusion.

HOW DO YOU GET THERE?

First of all, you have to care about your essays. Show you are engaged and committed to the general debate. One way to do that is to think about how an issue affects you or is at least related to an issue that affects you. What's your stake in the conversation? Establish your agency. **Remember, you are writing about ideas, not answering questions.** Your level of commitment will show in your work.

Secondly, you have to work diligently to attain this level of excellence, which cannot start the week before the exam. There truly can be no cram session for better writing. Writing is a process that takes time, but fortunately, you've been practicing your writing skills since kindergarten.

Lastly, you have to believe you are up to the challenge. If you do not have confidence, all is lost. This book is meant to help you discover just what you need to do your best work on the exam.

VISUAL GUIDE TO EXCELLENCE

Thesis restates the prompt	Thesis reveals writer's position and sets up his or her line of reasoning
Little to no evidence for claims	Apt and sufficient evidence for claims
Evidence not explained	Evidence clearly and concisely explained in controlled and compelling commentary that makes use of rhetorical strategies and appeals
Casual, simplistic word choice	Sophisticated vocabulary
Simple	Complex
Imprecise/Sloppy	Precise/Careful
Simplistic sentences	Varied, complex sentences used for effect
Error-laden	Control of conventions and prose
Off task	Focused on precise understanding of task
Writer lacks commitment	Writer cares about work, goal, audience

See Chapter 22 for a detailed analysis of the new scoring rubrics.

THE WRITING PROCESS

There is no time on exam day for the full-blown writing process: pre-writing, drafting, revision, etc. But that doesn't mean that prior to exam day you should ignore these basic steps of composition. You will be or should be writing many practice essays prior to May. For each one, it is good practice to revise your work. If you are writing essays for a class, your teacher may encourage you to revise. If so, perfect. If not, do it anyway.

Revision is beneficial in a number of ways:

- You are better able to see your strengths and weaknesses.

- Revision makes you a more flexible writer. If you are willing to concede that your word choice could have been better, or that a sentence is wordy, or that your third paragraph is disorganized, then you are much more open to alternative options. Stubborn students who say things such as, "Well, that's how I wrote it," and then refuse to see a different way will also not develop the reflective processes of mind needed on exam day.

- Revision trains your brain. If your teacher scored your last essay in the middle range, how can you make it better? What can you do to earn a higher score? Training your brain to think of these strategies will help you remember them on exam day. Not only that, but you will be writing better essays overall.

Use your peers as revision partners by reading and critiquing one another's work. Be sure you are measuring an essay using a standard rubric, either one given by your teacher or one of the new rubrics for a particular essay found at the College Board's AP® Central website.

STAND IN A DIFFERENT PLACE

Learning to judge the qualities of your own writing fairly and objectively is not easy. One strategy you can employ is to put the work away for a while, at most a day or two, but at least an hour. When you return to it, you will be "standing" in a different place. We always benefit from seeing a thing in a new way. We see things that were not there before. This new view of your own work should reveal weaknesses, such as omitted words, clumsy phrasing, incomplete arguments, and more.

Before you write the first word for any of the three essays on your exam, create a brief plan. Jot down a mini-outline on your scratch paper, noting your thesis and several supporting points. Any quick references to evidence you use and rhetorical strategies you employ will also help keep you from "winging it," which will likely not be an effective approach.

Even though time is limited on exam day, if you find you have ten minutes or so at the end of Part Two, use it to take one more look at the essay about which you felt the least confident. This second look, or second perspective, may show you some minor error(s) that you can easily fix, which will surely have a positive impact on your score.

ELEMENTS OF A GOOD INTRODUCTION

- You must acknowledge the task given in the prompt in your introduction.

- Give the writer's name and the title of the work (watch spelling on both).

- Avoid long exposition or discursive prose meant to engage the reader. Opt for shorter options, such as a compelling fact or rhetorical question or a poignant scenario. You don't have time for much more and it's the body of your argument where the bulk of your points come from.

- Include a thesis that reveals your insightful understanding of the key ideas in the text and clearly presents your position.

- In the scoring rubric, the College Board acknowledges that a thesis may exist elsewhere in an essay, toward the end, for example, after a purposeful line of reasoning. However, the least risky strategy may be to locate your thesis in its standard position—as the last sentence (or two) of your introduction.

MORE ON THESIS STATEMENTS

A **thesis statement** is the sentence where you state your main claim and set up your line of reasoning, though you may not have the time or the foresight to fulfill both aspects of a thesis. In order to earn your thesis point, you must establish your claim (position on an issue). If you don't have something to argue, you don't have a thesis. While reading, you must have come to some conclusion about the text(s) and come to a position that you can defend. Your thesis comes from that. If you have a good thesis statement, it will serve as your guide to creating subordinate claims and choosing the most compelling evidence.

An important rule to remember for your thesis is this:

Respond to the prompt, don't restate it.

SIMPLE THESIS STATEMENT FORMULAS

Claim + Reason = Thesis
Position + Reason = Thesis

HOOKS OR LEADS: DRAWING YOUR READER INTO YOUR WRITING

Journalists grab their readers' attention quickly with engaging leads. They use a variety of strategies that you can adopt in your own writing. The following list of leads is meant to get you to think consciously about how to begin your essays. If you need some variety, some oomph in your introductions, consider playing around with some of these leads.

One way to play is to revise any argumentative essay that you have written. Rewrite the introduction several times using some of these lead strategies. Whatever you decide, you must have a reason for choosing a particular lead style. If your choice seems arbitrary and unrelated to your purpose, it will count against you.

7 TYPES OF LEADS/HOOKS

1. **Factual**: Begin with a startling or arresting statistic or fact.

2. **Quotation**: Start with a controversial or thought-provoking quotation.

3. **Imagistic**: Set the scene or describe the situation.

4. **Narrative**: Begin with a short anecdote or story that relates to the main claim.

5. **Question**: A thought-provoking question gets your reader thinking. Caution: using a question implies that you will use second-person voice, but you should avoid the "did you ever" kinds of questions. Maintain your third-person authoritative voice even in questions. Example: Are seat belts ever harmful to passengers?

6. **Ironic**: Start with an ironic situation or statement.

7. **Dialectic**: Begin with a short dialogue, such as a witty repartee between two hypothetical speakers/characters. The dialogue could also be serious.

EXAMPLE INTRODUCTION

The following generic introduction was written for a prompt on a past AP® English Language exam, which asked students to develop a position on "the ethics of offering incentives for charitable acts." While this introduction is **much longer than desirable**, it shows one way to integrate an engaging lead and still incorporate all necessary aspects of a good introduction.

The two students huddled at lunch, their heads nearly touching as they discussed a brilliant new opportunity to earn an A in English for the semester. "Are you sure it will work?" Joe asked Matt. "Look," Matt said as he punched numbers into the calculator, "at five extra credit points for each pound of food we bring in . . . ." Joe's eyes brightened as he envisioned his weak B changing before his eyes, all with no real effort on his part. "Sweet," he said. In her desire to encourage her students' social consciousness, their English teacher offered extra credit for their donations to the annual fall food drive. The result will no doubt mean more food for the hungry (an incidental but important side effect), but Joe, Matt, and their peers will be no more socially responsible than they were before the food drive. Their focus is not about what they can do to help others; it is about their desire to help themselves. The teacher's actions, while seemingly right, are actually detrimental, as she may unwittingly be promoting a new level of selfishness in her students.

> **Lead:** Combination narrative/dialogue, presents a hypothetical situation that gets the reader thinking and sets up the claim.
>
> **Thesis:** The teacher's actions, while seemingly right, are actually detrimental, as she may unwittingly be promoting a new level of selfishness in her students.
>
> **Summary of Thesis Formula:** Claim (The teacher's actions are detrimental) + Reason (promoting selfishness in her students) = Thesis

See the rest of this essay at the end of this chapter.

Exercise: The sample introduction above is too long. Make copies for your study group and give everyone two minutes (use an egg timer) to cut its length by half without losing effectiveness. Then share your results.

Have each person discuss why they chose to eliminate what they did. Be sure everyone's edited version has a clear thesis statement.

The multiple-choice section of the exam will ask you to make judgments about effective editing. Exercises like this one will help you hone this skill.

DEVELOPING THE BODY OF THE ESSAY

The body of your essay is where you argue your thesis. You will need to make several points or claims that prove your thesis. A good *formula* for developing the ideas in your argument is the CECT formula:

1. State a **Claim** (this may be your topic sentence in a paragraph).

2. Provide **Evidence** from the text in defense of the claim. It is likely you will have more than one piece of evidence. In fact, for the synthesis essay, it is desirable to combine (synthesize) evidence from more than one source for any particular claim.

3. Explain your reasoning through **Commentary** that links the evidence to the claim (and ultimately the thesis) showing how or why.

4. **Transition** fluently from idea to idea, from claim to evidence, from claim to claim within your paragraph.

COMMENTARY: EXPLAINING YOUR REASONING

Sometimes, you will think that your ideas are clearly stated, when they're actually only **implicit** (implied). You need to make your ideas **explicit**, meaning you need to show exactly how and/or why what you say is so. Make connections. Make your ideas transparent. One of the biggest problems in student essays is that they contain too many implied ideas.

If you (or your reader) can still ask the following questions about your essay, you have not fully explained what you mean:

- Why?
- What is important or significant about this idea?
- What does this have to do with the claim?

The main purpose of commentary is to connect evidence to thesis and claims and to transition to the next point in your argument.

ORGANIZATION AND LENGTH

There is no set number of paragraphs expected for your AP® essays. You should let the essay develop organically from your position and the points you want to make. AVOID using the five-paragraph formula. It is too constrictive, and it forces you to think about the formula instead of your ideas. You may have three body paragraphs, or you may have four, five, or even six. Your paragraphs do not have to be the same length, either. If you make your point in three sentences and need to move on to the next paragraph, then do it. The next point you make may need seven sentences. Let your argument determine how you write.

Regardless of the number of paragraphs in your essay, remember that a paragraph is a coherent collection of sentences that support one main idea. The sentences belong together. A topic sentence sets the purpose for the paragraph. Some paragraphs may be extensions of topics set up in the preceding paragraph. If this is the case, make the transition clear to your reader with transitional phrases such as, "Another example of __," or "One more way to think about __ is ___."

WRITING A CONCLUSION THAT INSPIRES: HOW TO END YOUR ESSAY WELL

Avoid generic summary conclusions that simply restate the thesis. They're uninspiring, and they rob you of the opportunity to go beyond your analysis of a text to relate your personal insight. While your conclusion should not be personal, your particular insight **does** come from you and sometimes the conclusion is where your voice is most strong. Still, remember to stay focused on the text and leave readers with a memorable thought or image, especially one that compels them to fully accept your argument.

CONCLUSION TIPS

- Never introduce a new claim in the conclusion. Claims must be supported with evidence. Your conclusion is not the place to continue your argument. It is the place to wrap up your argument.

- You generally should not cite the text in the conclusion.

- A good conclusion should remind readers of the most important concepts of your essay.

- A good conclusion makes the essay feel finished.
- Avoid overused phrases like "in conclusion," "to sum up," or the like. Instead, make a smooth transition to the end of an essay.

CONCLUSION STRATEGIES

- Restate the central idea or argument. Phrase the idea differently than you did in your introduction.
- Make suggestions: possible solutions to a problem, a new way of thinking about something, a plan of action, etc.
- Reiterate the topic's significance: explain how an issue or idea affects people or will affect people.
- Use a rhetorical device:
    — relevant quotation;

    — anecdote;

    — metaphor;

    — ironic statement;

    — reference to historical event.

    — begin with "because" to create a sort of cause/effect conclusion, offering the weight of the effect or "so what" for your argument.

"BUT WHAT IF I RUN OUT OF TIME?"

It is possible that you will not have time to write a conclusion. Of course it is best if you can end with something, even a sentence or two, but in the event that the proctor is standing over you with his hand out, your essay will have to stand without its ending. Do not fret too much. The introduction and the body are the most crucial parts and should show your insightful analysis. It is possible to score well without a true conclusion.

COMMON TRANSITIONS

Transition is the "T" in CECT. Learn and use transitional words and phrases in your writing. If you do, you will be less likely to write confusing or foggy prose.

Transitions not only lead your reader through your thinking, they help you organize your argument. Find transitions for comparing and contrasting later in this chapter.

Purpose			
Show Location	above away against along amid among around from back behind	below beneath between off of down in front of inside near beyond	by beside outside over across under onto on top of into throughout
Show Time	about third prior to next week next second tomorrow yesterday then	first today tomorrow as soon as during meanwhile afterward immediately before	until later after at till soon in the meantime
Emphasize a Point	again in fact indeed	with this in mind for this reason to emphasize	truly to repeat
To Conclude or Summarize	as a result thus in summary consequently	due to all in all accordingly to sum up	in short therefore finally in conclusion
To Add Information	again besides for example together with and next	additionally another furthermore finally in addition further	along with as well for instance also likewise moreover

ABOUT ERRORS

The essays you write for the AP® exam are meant to show off your lucid thinking and your ability to write well. However, even the most brilliant writers do not write perfect drafts the first time. Moreover, 40 minutes is not nearly enough time for you to go through the stages of the writing process. Be realistic: You are expected to produce a solid essay, not a perfectly polished one. Exam readers will forgive minor errors. Just be sure to proofread your work as best you can. Since you'll be typing, not writing by hand, you can easily clean up spelling errors.

Sometimes you may find you want to rewrite an entire sentence. If you have finished all three essays and are going back to reread the one you think is weakest, you may want to do some minor revisions. If you finish early, using that extra time to improve one of your essays will pay off!

Test Tip

The best way to train yourself to be able to write a complete AP® essay in 40 minutes is to practice again and again. It is not an effortless goal, but your diligence will reward you.

INTEGRATING OR EMBEDDING TEXTUAL EVIDENCE

Weaving textual evidence into an essay is a skill that you can practice and learn to do well. You should study good models. Reading a newspaper can help you. Journalists are experts at integrating quotations into their text. They must attribute quotations to their sources also. Chapter 18 provides a fuller explanation of this skill, particularly as employed for Question 1.

1. Learn these rules for integrating your textual support:

   - Use partial quotations; it will be rare that you need an entire sentence from a text. Use only the part that helps you prove your point.

   - You need to supply context for the full or partial quotation. This means to set it up somehow, or transition into the quotation with your claim.

   - As a general rule, don't begin the sentence with the quoted text.

   - Use quotation marks around anything you take from the text, even isolated words.

   - If your essay is mostly quotations from the text, you are probably summarizing, which is one of the worst things you can do. Don't overquote!

   - When you weave in the cited text, you must end up with a grammatically correct sentence. If you have to change tense or wording of a direct question, use [brackets] around the parts you change.

   - A quotation or cited text is not self-evident; you must still explain it. Why did you include the quotation? What does it show or prove? Master your commentary skills.

2. Practice your skills by using these model phrases:

   - The writer or speaker argues, claims that, suggests, etc. _____.

   - His description of _____ shows how _____.

   - _____ reads quickly, even frantically. This narrative pace suggests that something _____.

   - When *author* writes that _____ she shows how _____.

   - The imagery in paragraph four contrasts with the imagery in paragraph one. _____ suggests _____, while _____ is clearly meant to _____.

   - *Speaker's name* relates the process by which she learned about _____ from her observations of _____. She writes _____.

Notice the use of strong verbs, particularly in the first model phrase. Review the verbs of rhetoric in Chapter 6 to familiarize yourself with more verbs to use in your own arguments.

When you read student essay samples from the AP® Central website, look specifically at how the writers of top-scoring essays incorporate evidence from the text to prove their claims.

USE PRECISE LANGUAGE: CONFIDENTLY SAY WHAT YOU MEAN

- **Use Higher-Level Vocabulary**

  I have admonished you to not toss in showy "big" words that you don't know. However, you should show that you have a sophisticated vocabulary. Begin to use the words you are learning (see Chapter 12). If you never use a "big" word, your prose may sound simplistic. AP® readers are looking for your ability to use a college-level vocabulary.

- **Use Strong Verbs**

  Avoid using being verbs or linking verbs, as they do not express action. Instead choose strong, vivid action verbs. Your writing will be more powerful and clear. Your writing also will be more visual. When we write with linking and being verbs, we rely too much upon adjectives. Adjectives can be vague or ambiguous. See the samples below.

Being/Linking Verbs

is	been	should have been
am	being	would have been
was	have been	feels
were	had been	seems
are	shall be	
be	will be	

How do you know if it's an action verb? If you can do it (act it out), it is an action verb. I can act out "dance," but I cannot act out "was."

Test Tip Check your own writing for strong verb use. Choose any essay and highlight all the linking/being verbs you have used. Then, revise the essay and replace those highlighted verbs with action verbs. Notice the difference in the quality of your essay.

EXAMPLES:

Weak	Strong
Sylvia was clumsy.	Sylvia tripped over the smallest pebble.
The images are interesting.	The images in the first paragraph evoke pity for the narrator.
The simile is effective.	The simile conjures images of wickedness.

WORDS AND PHRASES TO AVOID

Some words are inherently ambiguous. Others are simply meaningless. Others are clichés or overused expressions that are out of place in a scholarly essay. It is best always to avoid words and phrases that promote imprecision.

- "Very," "really," "completely," etc. Qualifiers added to adjectives are generally not needed. As far as that goes, adjectives are often not needed. Adjectives tend to carry opinions along with them, opinions you may not intend to express.

- "Interesting." We all know that saying "that's interesting" can mean so many different things that it can actually mean nothing. Avoid all ambiguous language. See Chapter 7 for details about effective use of language.

- "This," "that," and "it" can be ambiguity traps. It's best not to use them. For example: "That is why he never told even his closest friends about it." What is *that*? Furthermore, what is *it*?

- "Like," as in "the character was so like suffocated by his mother's dreams for him." Watch out for slang or colloquial language when writing. You are writing, not speaking.

- "Talks about" as in "This passage talks about." Passages do not talk. Instead say, "The author writes, shows, reveals," etc.

- "Wonderful," "skillfully," "fantastic," when meant to compliment the writer. Do not "suck up" to the writer. This gains you no points. Praising the prose is not analyzing the prose.

NEVER, NEVER . . .

- Begin a sentence with a pronoun.

- Begin a paragraph with a pronoun.

- Use ambiguous pronouns: "this," "that," "those," "it," etc.

- Write in the same manner as you speak. That is, do not use a conversational style that screams out, "I am not serious."

- Use words you do not understand. If you misuse a word, you will lose credibility.

- Use more words than necessary to make your point.

AVOID CLICHÉS, TRITE EXPRESSIONS, AND REDUNDANT PHRASES

If you have heard a phrase many times before, it may be a cliché. Clichés are empty expressions that may have been clever at one time, but now simply distract from your writing. If you rely on clichés, you are avoiding your job as a writer, which is to use precise language to say what you mean.

A Few Common Clichés:

- A close call

- A fish out of water

- At wit's end

- Bird's-eye view
- Coming down the pike
- Fall on deaf ears
- Never a dull moment
- Nerve-wracking
- Nipped in the bud
- Out of the box
- What goes around comes around.

Redundant Phrases

Redundant Phrase	Replace with
at this point in time	at this point; at this time
cancel out	cancel
complete opposite	opposite
each and every	every
evolve over time	evolve
join together	join
look back in retrospect	in retrospect
nostalgia for the past	nostalgia
overexaggerate	exaggerate
past experience	experience
past history	history
plan ahead	plan
the reason why	the reason
this day and age	in our time; presently
ultimate goal	goal

ACTIVE AND PASSIVE VOICE

Being aware of the difference between active and passive voice is important. If you've ever run a grammar check in Microsoft Word on a document you've written, you may have been told that you have too many passive sentences. Typically, it is better to write in active voice rather than passive. Passive voice can seem weak, indecisive, or tentative. Active voice is much more authoritative sounding.

An active verb is one in which the subject is the doer. With a passive verb, the subject is not the doer, but is the object, receiver, or effect of the action. When you add forms of "be" to a verb, you change the verb to passive, such as "is," "are," "was," "were," etc.

EXAMPLES

Passive	Active
The cookies were baked by Susan.	Susan baked the cookies.
The movie was chosen by Arthur.	Arthur chose the movie.
Invitations to her party were sent by Beth.	Beth sent invitations to her party.

VALUE OF PASSIVE VOICE

If the subject is less important than the object, passive construction may be an advantage.

Active	Passive
The farmer gathered these eggs yesterday.	These eggs were gathered yesterday.
The boss hired a new computer tech today.	A new computer tech was hired today.

YOUR OWN SYNTAX

You must be able to write effective and fluent sentences for effective prose. You can use syntactical patterns, which is what the writers whose work is featured on the exam use. Study the patterns (Chapter 9) and learn the value of each. Practice writing various types over time. For example, during one week, just write simple sentences. During the next week, write compound sentences, and so on. End up being able to use anaphora or polysyndeton without even thinking about how to do it, just knowing why you want to.

The best way to get better at sentence crafting is by recognizing effective sentences in the texts you read by emulating the patterns and effects you see.

To practice writing better sentences, use the following activity:

COPY-CHANGE ACTIVITY

Find and copy a highly effective paragraph from a text and study it. Learn the sentence patterns. Label the sentence types you see. Then, rewrite the paragraph with a new topic. Change the nouns and verbs to fit the new topic, but don't change their placement. Replicate phrases, clauses, and punctuation exactly. Learn by imitating.

EXPOSITORY PATTERNS

Practice developing your paragraphs using a variety of rhetorical or expository patterns. Use what seems appropriate for the text. In other words, you can't force something that doesn't work. Here are a few basic ways that you can argue your point. See more expository patterns in Chapter 6.

- **Exemplification**: Use examples from the text to prove your point. Of course, you will want to choose the best examples for your purpose.

- **Definition:** a piece of writing that explains what a term or a concept means can be helpful, particularly when exploring gaps or gulfs between cultures, paradigms, or historical periods.

- **Process Analysis**: If you recognize a process (how something works or operates) in a text, you can identify it and analyze its elements.

- **Cause-and-Effect Analysis:** Show why something happens, the series of events leading to or causing a concluding event.

- **Compare and Contrast**: Comparing two texts to show similarities and differences.

COMPARE/CONTRAST

On past exams, Question 2 asked students to write an essay analyzing the elements of two comparable texts. Therefore, the following guide is meant to help you understand the basics of compare/contrast essays. *Compare* means to show similarities. *Contrast* means pointing out differences.

The texts you will be presented with have some obvious similarities; otherwise, they would not be paired. What will differ will be the ways the authors treat the subjects. For example, the speaker's attitude toward the subject may be completely different. It will be important for you to understand both overt and subtle similarities and differences. As you read, annotate each text and make marginal notes listing what you find.

COMPARE/CONTRAST TRANSITIONAL WORDS AND PHRASES

To compare:

In the same way	Also
Likewise	Like
Similarly	

To contrast:

Conversely	On the contrary
However	On the other hand
Rather	

INTRODUCTION

Mention both texts and be sure your thesis suggests the main ways the two texts are similar. Do not say, "Jones's journal is similar to Smith's in some ways, but there are also some main differences." Instead say, "Even though both writers characterize women as intelligent and nurturing, Jones's view deprecates women when he says 'they are emotionally weak and incapable of managing tough business situations.' "

ORGANIZING THE BODY OF THE ESSAY

Main Methods

1. Whole to whole (subject to subject):

   - Discuss the important aspects of one text, then the other. You may lose track of your main points if you're not careful.

2. Show all similarities, then all differences:

   - Can seem less integrated, less fluent.

3. Subject by subject:

   - For example: tone in each speech or text.

SAMPLE ESSAY

Now let's examine a completed essay that was introduced earlier in this chapter when students were asked (for Question 3) to develop a position on "the ethics of offering incentives for charitable acts."

Note that this essay was not scored by an AP® reader and that it is longer than would be typical in order to show all components.

The two students huddled at lunch, their heads nearly touching as they discussed a brilliant new opportunity to earn an A in English for the semester. "Are you sure it will work?" Joe asked Matt. "Look," Matt said as he punched numbers into the calculator. "At five extra credit points for each pound of food we bring in. . . " Joe's eyes brightened as he envisioned his weak B changing before his eyes, all with no real effort on his part. "Sweet," he said. In her desire to encourage her students' social consciousness, their English teacher offered extra credit for their donations to the annual fall food drive. The result will no doubt mean more food for the hungry (an incidental but important side effect), but Joe, Matt, and their peers will be no more socially responsible than they were before the food drive. Their focus is not on what they can do to help others; it is on their desire to help themselves. The teacher's actions, while seemingly right, are actually detrimental, as she may unwittingly be promoting a new level of selfishness in her students.[1]

The need to provide for others less fortunate than we are is ingrained in our common sense of self.[2] We are taught as young children in churches, in schools, and at home that there are others who don't have what we do. The story of the Good Samaritan teaches that we must always help others when we see they are in need. Some states even have Good Samaritan laws that protect passersby who intervene from liability in case something goes wrong. Scouting America, postal workers, and other community organizations regularly sponsor food drives for the hungry. Even in our own homes, moms admonish us to finish all the food on our plate, because we don't throw food away when others in the world are starving.[3] In general, we deem charitable acts to be good, even noble.

And yet,[4] while no reward for giving should be necessary, we live in a culture that actively promotes reward for giving.[5] It seems we[6] are a society that needs to be prodded to do what is right. When public radio and television stations conduct their pledge drives, they offer gifts in return: coffee mugs, tote bags, or t-shirts.[7] Take your

---

[1] An analysis of this introduction can be found earlier in this chapter in the section on introductions.
[2] Topic sentence/claim
[3] Series of examples in support.
[4] Transition signaling a contrasting idea.
[5] Claim
[6] Universal first person—the writer includes herself as a member of this society.
[7] Begins a series of examples from real life to support the claim.

coffee mug to work and you can subtly let everyone know that you support public broadcasting. Some charities entice giving up front by sending address labels or personalized stationery, like note pads or greeting cards, hoping to "guilt" people into giving. They're saying, "Hey, we gave you this nice gift, so don't you want to thank us with your donation?" Even those pseudo-documentary infomercials for "adopting" a needy child in a third-world country promise a reward for one's generosity. If you sponsor a child, you will receive letters from him or her that let you know how things are going. Perhaps the letter serves more to keep the organization honest than as a reward,[8] but if you slap that letter on the refrigerator with the free magnet you got from the March of Dimes,[9] then you remind yourself daily what a good person you are, and that is also, of course, a reward.

Even bigger gifts to communities, like endowments that provide money for a new hospital wing, a state-of-the-art technology center for the local community college, or a new auditorium for the high school are rewarded by naming the facility after the benefactor.[10] Gala parties are thrown to honor and publicly thank the donor, whose real reward is a kind of eternity that only money can buy. By contrast, those rare anonymous gifts make the news simply because they're so unusual.

The culture of reward for giving is unfortunately prevalent in schools.[11] In my school, student council sponsors a food drive every year around Thanksgiving time.[12] They entice students by awarding a pizza party to the first-hour class with the most donations. Matt and Joe are my hypothetical classmates. My English teacher wanted us to win. She told us how important it was for us to replenish the food pantry, especially with the economy in such bad shape. Too many people were out of work and it was hard for

---

[8] Acknowledges an alternative point of view.

[9] Notice the writer's cynical tone here. The tone reinforces the idea that it is wrong to need a reward for doing what is right.

[10] This short paragraph gives more examples, but they are grouped separately because they share a common quality: all are examples of large philanthropic gifts.

[11] Claim

[12] Example from personal experience.

parents, especially single parents, to feed their kids. She should have stopped with her appeal to our sense of what is right. Where she went wrong was in following society's model by offering a tangible reward for doing what we should do anyway.[13] Maybe she even wanted the esteem of her peers. After all, if we won, it would show that she could persuade us and get us to work together.

It may seem benign to give a student extra credit for bringing in ten cans of corn, but it's not.[14] The end goal may have been reached. The food pantry is full again. Fewer people will go hungry, but the negative results must not be ignored. Students who manipulate the system for a grade are cheats. An A not earned through intellect and effort is worthless. A transcript with that A on it is a lie. A system that allows, or even worse, promotes extra credit for charity is hypocritical. In such a system, grades mean nothing.[15] In this situation, students give not because they should, but because they will benefit. They act selfishly instead of selflessly, and no one can blame them. The system encourages selfishness.

To truly be good people, we should give from the heart because it is the right thing to do. We should not need others to praise us. We should not need public accolades, whether they are our name on a building or a simple sticker saying "I gave blood." At most, our reward must come from within, from the satisfaction we get from doing what is right. We may nurture our esteem without proclaiming it to anyone, and that is how it should be.[16]

Parents can teach this concept to their children and teachers must reinforce it as well. Adults must begin to work against the reward model prevalent in the media and begin to reinforce a different narrative, appealing to nobility and morality and not

---

[13] Transition sentence that sets up the claim in the next paragraph.
[14] Claim
[15] Series of statements that show the effect of rewarding charity.
[16] This transitional paragraph sets up the premise for the solution. This paragraph explains the concept the writer wishes us to believe and act upon.

to our own desires or needs.[17] For example,[18] my friend's parents decided to stop the crazy cycle of gift giving one Christmas. The idea was that the family would buy no presents for each other. And what's more, each one was to give something, either time, or a gift, to someone else who needed it more. In the end, the family did both. They worked together on Christmas Day to serve a turkey dinner to the homeless. And when they did their Christmas shopping, it was to buy toys and warm clothes for someone they would never meet. My friend wasn't too excited about it at first. In fact, all she did when she first found out about the plan was complain about how unfair it was. I was on her side, too, initially. But[19] then I listened to all of her "I wants," and she started to sound so selfish and petty. When we got together after Christmas, however, she sounded much different. She told me how the people she met at the homeless shelter affected her and how she felt like she could not do enough to help them. Her stories were moving, and I was even a little jealous of her experience.[20] She never once mentioned that she didn't get a single present from her parents for Christmas. That didn't matter anymore.

My friend didn't go around school bragging about how great she was now, for helping the homeless. I don't think she told anyone but me. But how are we to learn what noble charity means if we are not exposed to stories like hers? I do not believe that people are innately selfless. We need to be taught.[21] What if[22] the consumer machine included stories like this? I know our economy would crumble if people just stopped buying and consuming, but if we could also follow a less selfish model just because it is right,[23] we could have it all and still give to those who don't. In such a world, we

---

[17] Call to action. The writer states specifically what must be done.

[18] The writer includes an anecdote that illustrates how the desired change might occur.

[19] Don't overlook simple transitions. "But" introduces a contrasting idea.

[20] The effect of the story is to draw the reader into a scenario, but the writer shows how he is also affected. This empathy helps establish the writer's credibility.

[21] Final claim, but this is not a new idea presented in the conclusion. Instead, the writer restates an earlier claim in order to reinforce it here.

[22] Using "what if" statements allows the writer to suggest what could be if the desired change occurred. As readers, we are asked to imagine an ideal situation.

[23] Ethical appeal

would not need to entice charitable giving with silly or even harmful rewards,[24] and we would be better people as a result.

Test Tip

Footnote and analyze your own essay. Find an engaging prompt (in school or online) and write the essay. Then assign a code for things like thesis, topic sentence, evidence, explanation, etc. Insert a superscript number in your essay to those corresponding elements. In your analysis, also look for examples of appeals as well as times you used a sentence pattern or repetition device for effect. Circle all your "being" verbs. Can you change them to more active verbs? Learning to judge the quality of your own work is one of the most important ways you can prepare yourself for the exam.

MORE COMMENTS ON THE SAMPLE ESSAY

POINT OF VIEW

Notice how the writer uses first, third, and even second person interchangeably as the document dictates. The writer maintains authority, but effectively engages the reader by putting him or her in the situation. The first-person point of view in this essay is also effective. The risk in sharing examples from personal experience is that they are unique and limited to the individual, but this writer's examples seem likely to be shared by most high school students.

LANGUAGE

Underline words in this essay that seem beyond what a typical high school student would use in everyday speech. What effect does scholarly diction have on the reader? Which words in particular help the writer create a more effective argument?

EXPOSITORY PATTERN

This is a problem-solution essay that argues for society in general, but parents and teachers specifically, to teach children that it is good to be

---

[24] Reiterating the main thesis: rewards for giving are not ethical.

charitable and that charitable acts do not require external rewards. The first part of the essay illuminates the problem and gives many examples to support the writer's main premise. The second part of the essay uses an anecdote, the story about the writer's friend, in support of a solution.

APPEALS

The writer uses ethical and emotional appeals as well as appeals to readers' esteem needs.

Test Tip

Go one step further. Instead of merely studying the sample essay above, write your own essay in response. Defend, refute, or challenge this writer's point of view. If you have a study group, suggest that each of you do the same. Then share your essays and talk about what you have learned.

Citing and Documenting Sources Effectively

Weave, don't plop.—Dawn Hogue

OVERVIEW

There are three distinct essays on the AP® English Language and Composition exam and each requires a different approach regarding your source material. The synthesis essay looks much like a typical research paper and will require you to document your use of supplied sources. The rhetorical analysis essay requires you to cite the provided text in your argument. Finally, evidence for your argument essay comes primarily from your reading, general knowledge, experience, and observations, all of which are sources stored in your memory. You may mention titles, authors, and ideas in books, but it will, of course, be impossible to quote a text directly for Question 3. You may also make reference to the supplied quotation or short excerpt used in the prompt for Question 3. This chapter aims to give you a summary of the basic skills and techniques you will need to manage your evidence in your essays on the exam.

Not only will you be expected to cite and document sources correctly, you may also be asked several questions about effective documentation in the multiple-choice section of the exam. These questions are not meant to prove your knowledge of MLA or APA styles (see below), but rather are meant to test your general understanding of how and why writers reference, cite, and document sources.

ABOUT STYLE GUIDES

A style guide is basically a set of rules about how to use and cite sources in research and academic writing. Style guides are also known as stylebooks. They help writers and publishers maintain consistency and clarity. The examples in this chapter use MLA style (Modern Language Association), which is generally preferred in English and humanities courses. APA (American Psychological Association) has its own style rules. APA is the dominant style used in the social sciences. There are also Turabian and Chicago styles. The latter, formally known as the *Chicago Manual of Style* and published by the University of Chicago, is widely used by book publishers, including REA, the publisher of this *Crash Course* study guide. Journalists mainly use *The Associated Press Stylebook*.

When you are in college, you will be directed by your professor to use one style or another. No one memorizes the rules for any given style. You will probably own one or more style guides in your life and rely upon them when needed. The AP® English Language and Composition exam is not a test of your "style savvy." It is a test of your writing and thinking ability. However, there is a presumption that your teacher has given you some general instruction in using one or more style guides. If you have no concept of what a style guide is or what it means, this chapter gives you a brief primer in MLA. There are numerous websites available to give you a more in-depth look if you need it. An excellent resource for MLA and APA is Purdue University's OWL (Online Writing Lab).

DOCUMENTING SOURCES

When we embed quotations, summaries, or paraphrases from various sources to use as evidence in our own work, we must document the source, which simply means to show from where the information originates. Plagiarism is a failure to document source material.

PARENTHETICAL REFERENCES

In each of the examples below, notice the punctuation and follow the model. The source used for illustration here is fictional. It is important to note that you will rarely need to make a page number reference on the exam. However, the general research papers you do in your high school or college courses will require page numbers.

1. The directions for the synthesis question tell you that you can simply refer to each source by its designation: Source A, for example. Default to this simple model for question 1.

   > The availability of newspapers online helps "democratize society because anyone with internet can access not only the local paper, but also national and international papers" (Source A).

   If you mention Source A in your sentence, you won't need to add it in parentheses. Example: According to Source A, the availability of. . . .

2. Another method is to include the author's last name and page number, if available, in parentheses at the end of the sentence or section that uses the citation. This information is also provided in the synthesis question.

   > The availability of newspapers online helps "democratize society because anyone with internet can access not only the local paper, but also national and international papers" (Sanders, 219).

3. Use the author's name in the sentence and give only the page number.

   > Sanders says that the availability of newspapers online helps "democratize society because anyone with internet can access not only the local paper, but also national and international papers" (219).

4. Another option is to give the author and the title in your sentence.

   > In "The Demise of Dailies: An Honest Look," Sanders says that the availability of newspapers online helps "democratize society because anyone with internet can access not only the local paper, but also national and international papers" (219).

5. For your exam essays, you'll be citing short texts without page numbers. To help you document your evidence, line numbers will be provided. You do not have to cite line numbers. It might be cumbersome or unnecessarily time consuming to do so, but

if you think citing a line number makes your reasoning clearer, you can do so. Here's an example.

> Sanders argues that online newspapers help "democratize society because anyone with internet" has access to news from a variety of sources (Line 24).

Once you've shown that you are referencing line numbers in parentheses by using the word "line" or "lines," you can omit those words and simple include the numbers themselves.

6. Very likely, excerpts from longer passages will be noted by lines, which you can reference by replacing the page number with the line number.

Take a look at the sample essay for the Synthesis Question in Chapter 19 to see how the writer cites and documents sources.

While you would be expected in ordinary circumstances to use MLA, APA, Chicago, or another style according to your instructor's needs, time given for the exam simply prohibits truly accurate adherence to any style. AP® readers are far more interested in your ideas and how well you express and support them than in your uncanny knowledge of any particular style. While the guidelines above can be helpful, if it's easier to simply cite the source by its letter, do so. You will not be penalized.

DIRECT AND INDIRECT REFERENCES

It is preferable to use both direct and indirect references or citations. The hope is that you will not rely too much on direct quotations. A direct reference is simply a direct quotation, text taken word for word from a source and shown to be such by use of quotation marks. An indirect reference is a paraphrase, where you cite the writer's idea, but in your own phrasing, which is sometimes shorter than the original. Being able to use both types of references shows your skill as a writer and improves fluency.

CLARIFYING TERMINOLOGY

When I refer to "quotation," I mean any text taken from a source to use as evidence in an argument, whether a single word, a short phrase, or a complete sentence. To indicate a direct quotation (replicated exactly as shown in the original text), quotation marks must be used.

Some students have expressed confusion about using quotations, as they have inferred this means they must search the source for something already in quotation marks. But this is not what we mean when we say "quote the text."

QUOTING SOURCES

The following is a quick guide to the different ways you can quote a source. The sources used for illustration here are fictional.

1. Weave the quoted passage into your own sentence. The following example is a **partial quotation**.

   Sanders says that the availability of newspapers online helps "democratize society because anyone with internet can access not only the local paper, but also national and international papers" (219).

2. **Introduce the quotation** with a sentence and a colon.

   Anyone wanting to explore various points of view can easily do so by reading a variety of newspapers online: "Easy access to national and international newspapers online gives ordinary citizens, especially those in rural or remote areas a portal to world views" (Sanders, 220).

3. Use a **long quotation** by introducing it with your own sentence. A long quotation is one that is four or more lines long. There are specific style rules (MLA) for long quotations. Since it is indented ten spaces or one inch from the left margin, there is no need to use quotation marks. In this case, the final period goes before the parenthetical reference.

   In "Celebrating the Death of Newspapers," Roger Sanders argues that the loss of tangible newsprint papers is not the lamentable situation that some claim it is:

   There are, of course, some legitimate reasons to be sorrowful at this time of transition. No more will the gritty presses roll in pre-dawn hours inking papers to be sold on the street just a short time later. The industry and ingenuity that made newspapers a critical part of America in the last 400 years, however, is not dead. Instead it is something new, something for the future, and we must see the possibilities that lie within these changes that will make us even stronger as a nation. (195)

You would not use such a long quotation in an essay you write for your exam. An in-class essay might be different, however.

MAKE IT GRAMMATICALLY CORRECT

If you are using a direct quotation that does not fit grammatically into your prose, you may need to change a word or two. For example, you might have a situation in which using a quotation as it is results in a subject/agreement error. In such a case, make the change but recognize it by putting the changed word in [brackets].

Whenever you weave in a quotation, paraphrase, or summary, the end result must be a complete, correct sentence. Review Chapter 10 on grammar basics. The longer and more complicated a sentence is, the more you run the risk of inadvertently writing a fragment or a comma splice.

Test Tip

It is vital for you to practice integrating source material into your own writing. You want to achieve fluency. Study good models to see how effortlessly an excellent writer weaves in quotations, paraphrases, and summaries. The true danger in simply plopping in a quotation like a glob of mashed potatoes on your plate is that you may lose control of your writing. The essay is yours; it is your argument. Use direct and indirect references as evidence for your ideas. Your essay should not be a string of someone else's words, no matter how lovely.

SUMMARIZING AND PARAPHRASING SOURCES

Surely you already know that a summary is a shorter version of a passage and a paraphrase is similar in that it may also be shorter than the original, but in a paraphrase you've put the text into your own words. These are tools we've been taught to use in our writing since we were in grade school. In the context of this exam, it is important for you to remember that a summary or paraphrase is also a method of citing a resource in support of your argument.

Both are indirect references, which means your evidence from the text is not "word for word" as in a direct quotation. Besides imbuing your essay with a stronger sense of your voice, summaries and paraphrases are important for other reasons.

A summary is obviously used when the breadth of the information is too great to represent in a small space or the information is not portable. It might be necessary, for example, to summarize the main point of a graphic (such as a chart or other diagram) to make the information usable as evidence. Sometimes a paragraph is simply too long and needs to be compressed. When you write a summary, be careful not to interpret. Instead, shorten the work with precision, keeping the exact argument intact. You may even use some words and phrases from the original, but you will need to write your own statement. The trick to a good summary is finding the key facts and representing them exactly in your version.

When you write a paraphrase, you are doing so for two reasons. One reason is that the text you want to cite is complicated, perhaps too technical for your needs or the wording too sophisticated for your reader. In this case, you must read carefully to make sure you understand the original enough to reword it.

The second reason to paraphrase is to create a sentence or phrase that fits your essay and writing style. You want to create an idea that is a fluent companion to what you've written. Still, a paraphrase is not a different idea—you are not changing the writer's intentions or the facts. Keep in mind that since you are analyzing a provided text in Question 2, a quotation will often work better than a paraphrase.

Summaries and paraphrases require some skill. It's much easier to quote a source word for word. This is exactly why the AP® exam expects you to mix it up and use a combination of direct and indirect references. If you need practice, then you should practice. This is an easy goal to achieve.

When reviewing your sources for the synthesis essay, you may encounter a text that is too difficult to paraphrase. If so, you risk not understanding it and might use the information incorrectly. Avoid that source as evidence. You are expected to cite only three to four of the sources, so leaving something out isn't going to be a problem. However, remember that the point of choosing three to four sources from the group is to test your ability to support your point with the appropriate evidence. Do take some time to read and comprehend to the best of your ability each of the provided sources, so that you <u>do</u> have a choice.

PRIMARY AND SECONDARY SOURCES

Know the difference between primary and secondary sources. A **primary source** is created by the person with the vision, insight, or story to tell. A **secondary source** is a synthesis of primary sources or an analysis or interpretation of information garnered from primary sources.

Primary	Secondary
autobiographies, diaries, email, interviews, letters, minutes, news film footage, official records, photographs, raw research data, and speeches works of art, music, literature, etc., an original creation	literary criticism analyzing a play, poem, novel, or short story magazine or newspaper articles about events or people, commentary or analysis textbooks

GENERAL GUIDELINES

- Cite only what's needed, not more, not less. If you need only a phrase from a quotation, cite only that.

- On the other hand, if you need only a phrase, it may be best to paraphrase instead of using a direct quotation. Remember, you still must document a paraphrase. In general, use direct quotations when you cannot say something better (more eloquently or more succinctly) than the original.

- Use a paraphrase when an idea needs clarification or when integrating the original phrasing will be an awkward fit for your prose. If you have to [bracket] more than one word in a direct quotation, you may be much better off paraphrasing.

- In any paragraph, begin and end with your own sentence, not a quotation. The essay is yours, so it is your voice that must dominate. Even in the conclusion, if you use an engaging quotation, end with one more sentence of your own prose that puts your cherry on top.

TERMS TO KNOW

This brief list simply defines some key terms for you.

1. **Bibliography**: a list of sources consulted.

2. **Citation**: a reference used in evidence; also used to document a source in an essay.

3. **Direct quotation**: using another's words or a passage from a text as written, word for word. Direct quotations may be whole or partial. "Whole" means that an entire sentence or group of sentences is used. "Partial" means that only part of the text is used—whatever is most pertinent to the writer's needs.

4. **Endnotes**: notes, cross-references, or other pertinent information indicated in the text with superscript numbers showing that corresponding notes can be viewed at the end of the text.

5. **Footnotes**: notes, cross-references, or other pertinent information indicated in the text with superscript numbers showing that a corresponding note can be viewed at the bottom of the page.

6. **Paraphrase**: to put a source note into your own words.

7. **Parenthetical documentation**: inclusion of documentation information, such as an author's last name or a page number, in parentheses near its inclusion in the text.

8. **Plagiarism**: to intentionally or unintentionally use someone else's work or words without citing or crediting the source; intellectual dishonesty.

9. **Summary**: essentially a shortened version of an original text.

10. **Works cited**: a list of sources cited in the paper.

Free-Response Question 1:
The Synthesis Essay

The use of criticism, in periodical writing, is to sift,
not to stamp a work.—Margaret Fuller

OVERVIEW

The first prompt you'll encounter in the free-response section of the exam is the synthesis question. This question tests your ability to argue a point that is supported by references, which are provided as part of the exam. By the time you are a junior or senior in high school, you have most likely had at least one, if not several, experiences writing a traditional research paper. This part of the exam is not much different from that.

Consider what the word *synthesis* means for a moment. The simplest, most direct way to explain synthesis in this context is as a "blending" of disparate sources as evidence for one claim. Test-takers must deal with six sources for Question 1. You are expected to cite evidence from at least three of these sources in your entire essay. What AP® readers hope to see is your use of evidence from more than one source in a paragraph (in defense of one claim).

Keep in mind, AP® readers are looking for you to "enter the conversation." This means that in addition to effectively synthesizing evidence from the supplied sources, you must add your own examples and observations. What additional knowledge can you bring to the argument? The clearer you are, the better your score.

The College Board is fully committed to presenting issues and topics for the synthesis question that are relevant to your life and experiences. They hope that you will "genuinely want answers" for such topics. If you can engage ideas because you have a stake in the outcome, you will likely write a stronger argument because your position will be authentic and not just be an isolated exercise for an exam. For example, a recent synthesis question asked students to consider whether or not personal digital technologies (tablets, smartphones, computers, even television) have an adverse affect on our lives.

Even if the topic for Question 1 does not immediately appear to be relevant to you personally, keep an open mind. As you read the sources, surely you will encounter connecting points. Remember to be open and empathetic as well as critical as you read.

WHAT IS A SYNTHESIS ESSAY?

Think of a synthesis essay as a short research paper. You are given resources to use in support of a thesis that you develop after you read the prompt and the resources in the Bluebook digital testing app. This section will describe the process of writing this essay.

When you begin Part Two of the exam, you are provided with a collection of resources: excerpts from articles, books, and journals, photographs, charts and graphs, illustrations, or cartoons to read and consider. Extra time is added to this exam to allow for this reading. There will always be one or two visual texts for you to consider. You will typically have six resources to study. As you read each of these (even the graphics) you must make notations—*annotate* them using the Bluebook digital highlighting and annotation tools. See Chapter 11 for more on engaged and active reading.

Test Tip

> By the time you get to the third or fourth source, you will probably be seeing commonalities. You will want to make note of them, such as "A, D, and E all support the idea that _____." This will help you to know which sources to use, but could also help you decide on your own point of view.

Before you read the supplied resources, however, you need to understand the prompt. You will be given a clear, precise prompt. As with all of your essays for this exam, you must read it carefully to ensure you understand the subject and your task. Keep this consistent prompt wording in mind:

"The writer's argument should remain central. The sources should support the argument."

You are the writer. If you push ahead too quickly and don't develop your own position, you'll likely only end up summarizing the sources and will earn a low score.

Remember that the introduction to each source is also useful information. All information given to you is there for a reason and all of it can be helpful—even supplied MLA information. Such citations can help you determine relative reliability and/or validity of a source.

One strategy for the synthesis essay is to approach it like you would the argument essay. Formulate your position and thesis first. Then read the sources to gather sufficient evidence. You will also want to provide your own examples when valid. This strategy may help you guard against the dreaded "summary."

Write your thesis. This will be a clear but brief statement (generally one sentence) that expresses your position and may set up your line of reasoning. You should use the prompt to create your original thesis, but do not simply restate the prompt. Respond to the prompt by taking a coherent position. Be sure you can defend your thesis with evidence from at least three of the supplied references. By the time you actually write the thesis, you probably will have thought about your main supporting claims. Review Chapter 17 for more help with thesis statements.

Perhaps you're a person who can visualize a full argument in your head, but if you're not, make a quick list of your main claims. In fact, you can outline these claims on scratch paper furnished by the proctor. Doing so will keep you on task and help you stay organized. Spelling out your plan of attack will help reduce your anxiety level.

Realize that testing situations are inherently stressful, and stress produces cortisol, a brain chemical that can have a detrimental effect on short-term memory. Being organized is instrumental in reducing anxiety and setting the stage for strong performance on exam day.

You are expected to use three (or four) of the supplied resources to defend your position in this essay. You may be directed to make both direct and indirect references. See more on this below. DO NOT cite all of the sources, thinking it will make your paper stronger. It won't. First of all, not all of the sources will support your position. The true danger in citing too many sources is that you will be simply summarizing them and not using them to defend your argument.

As you read the supplied sources, be on the lookout for sources that stand in obvious contradiction to each other (or in contradiction to your position). Good thinkers will consider opposing views. Sometimes such an exercise will aid you in finding a weakness in your own argument. It is always best to at least acknowledge that some people hold an alternate view. When you point out this view in your essay, you can refute it while acknowledging valid parts of the argument, thereby increasing your own ethos. Review Chapter 6 on how to structure an argument.

Keep in mind that you are expected to synthesize. You must blend evidence from more than one source to defend or prove a claim. This should happen in more than one of your body paragraphs.

The rest is just writing! Of course, this implies a lot of things, including

- clear, precise word choice, particularly in your thesis statement and your topic sentences.

- concise but fully developed sentences and paragraphs

- logical organization and progression of your argument or line of reasoning. Never forget that it is your responsibility to connect your evidence to your claims through your commentary (explaining how and/or why the evidence fits). Don't forget to transition to the next idea, whether in the same paragraph or the next.

- correct use of source material to support your argument, both direct and indirect references

- correctly citing the sources you use

Test Tip

Make a mini-outline in the margin and try to stick to it. Don't think, however, that you can't veer off at the last minute if you happen to suddenly think of the perfect point to make. The outline, if it is a summary of your main points, as it should be, will help you keep your argument on track. It will also keep you from lapsing into summary, or worse, an irrelevant digression. Also, as a recordkeeping check, use the list of sources in the prompt as a checklist, making a tally mark each time you cite a particular source. Such a list may also keep you from relying too much on one source.

SUMMARIZING, EXPLAINING, AND ARGUING: WHAT IS THE DIFFERENCE AND WHY DOES IT MATTER?

To do well on this essay, you MUST take a position and argue it. This is not a paper in which you simply explain what the writers are saying. It is also not meant as a test of your ability to summarize the contents of the resources. Often, however, this is what students fall back on since it is quick and easy.

HOW TO KNOW IF YOU ARE . . .

Summarizing	Your paper will sound very much like the three or four sources you've chosen. You will be retelling what you learned from an article, excerpt, or a chart. Your reader will not be able to tell what you think. In a way, you are acting like a copying machine.
Explaining	Your paper will sound like you are trying to get your reader to understand the various sources. You are showing what you have learned, but you do not have a position. You may even cite parts of an article to show what you mean, but all you are doing is illuminating someone else's ideas. You are acting like a tutor or museum tour guide.
Arguing	Your thesis sets up your own position, one with which someone else might disagree. You have taken a stance. Your essay will have several (three or four) reasons why what you say is true. Your reader will be able to find these points easily. You are a critical thinker and persuasive writer. You are acting as an influential leader as you work to change your readers' minds.

The chart above shows the different aspects of an overall approach to the essay. You would never just summarize all of the sources and present that as an argument, nor would you just explain all of the sources. However, within your argument, you might summarize a section of Source A, or you might need to explain the ethical appeal of a photograph given as Source D.

COMMON PROBLEMS

The following list is a summary of the main problems AP® readers see in students' synthesis essays.

- Not taking a clear position or wavering between positions.

- Substituting a thesis-oriented expository essay for an argumentative essay.

- Being reluctant to engage in verbal combat because "everyone's entitled to his or her own opinion," so there's nothing to argue about.

- Slipping out of focus, digressing into a tangential topic that does not aid the writer's argument.

- Misreading sources.

- Alluding to sources instead of citing them. If your paragraph does not begin with your own topic sentence, you have lost control of your line of reasoning. Never begin by saying, for example, "According to. . . ." A source citation is not a claim.

- Lacking development or organization.

- Providing a weak link between argument and sources.

- Displaying immature control of writing, syntax, and mechanics.

- Offering vague generalizations.

- Simply summarizing the sources. The sources are there to support your argument, not to become your argument.

- Forgetting to combine (synthesize) evidence from multiple sources.

SAMPLE PROMPT AND ESSAY

Below you will find a sample synthesis prompt and a sample essay that responds to the prompt. You can use this material in a couple of ways:

1. You could simply read the material to understand the component parts of a synthesis prompt and a corresponding essay.

2. Without reading the sample essay, you could use this section as an opportunity to write your own synthesis essay, taking care to put into practice what you've learned. After you've written your own essay, compare it with the sample essay and see how your attempt measures up.

However you decide to use these materials, the prompt and sources replicate what you will find on your exam.

SAMPLE PROMPT

QUESTION 1

(Suggested time: 40 minutes.)

As technology has advanced, the curricula in American schools have changed. Schools increasingly use technology as a means of educating students today. Not only are schools focusing more on teaching computer skills, they also are including the use of such technology as video games, iPods, and podcasts as part of ordinary class work. Not surprisingly, school districts vary widely in their ability to provide technological aids for all students. Yet incorporating new technologies into the average classroom remains a priority for school districts across the country. What is the effect of this changing approach to education? Is it a clear improvement over traditional education, or is it merely a compromise?

Carefully read the following six sources, including the introductory information for each source. Then synthesize information from at least three of the sources and incorporate it into a coherent, well-developed essay taking a clear position that defends, refutes, or qualifies the claim that schools that are embracing the new technological approach to education are effectively teaching students the skills they need in today's world.

Make sure your argument is central; use the sources to illustrate and support your reasoning. Avoid merely summarizing the sources. Indicate clearly which sources you are drawing from, whether through direct quotation, paraphrase, or summary. You may cite the sources as Source A, Source B, etc., or by using the descriptions in parentheses.

Source A (Empire High School)

Source B (U.S. Department of Education)

Source C (Cartoon)

Source D (Johnson)

Source E (Miller)

Source F (National Education Association)

SOURCE A

"Arizona High School Chooses Laptops Over Textbooks." *VOANews.com.* Voice of America, 20 Oct. 2005. Web. 15 Oct. 2010.

The following passage is excerpted from an article about a new educational approach adopted by Empire High School in Vail, Arizona.

A new high school opened in Vail, Arizona, this past July with all the resources you would expect to find in classrooms these days—except textbooks. Instead, every student received an Apple laptop computer . . . making Empire High School a pioneer in the growing use of technology in American education.

. . . a committee visited classrooms that were making partial use of laptops, and came away with two distinct impressions. "One was that students in schools where laptops were being used were clearly more engaged," Mr. Baker says. "And the other impression was that we felt we could do more with laptops. Because we had the opportunity here of opening a new school, we could make them an integral part of what we do, and actually change the way we do things. And we sort of forced that issue by not buying any textbooks."

Teachers helped plan the school's wireless curriculum, often experimenting with different ideas in classrooms where they taught before. . . .

Michael Frank teaches a first-year biology course, where students use their laptops to access instructions for their lab work, organize data, and graph the results. . . . "[Students] will be putting together all the results from this experiment in a PowerPoint presentation for the class later. . . . And I know I can just give them an address for a website that has information and they can go look at it there. A lot of times with science, we use it because you can get immediate access to the most recent information. You don't have to wait 5 or 6 years for it to get into a textbook. So there's much more access to just a huge amount of data about things."

. . . There was a surprise once classes got underway as well. . . . "We thought the kids would be better at computing than they actually are. Being able to drive your Xbox or your iPod is not the same thing as being able to take a computer, use it, create a document, save it with a file name, put it in a particular location and retrieve it. And that has been a real challenge."

But administrators say the system is working well overall, and students seem to agree. . . .

Calvin Baker also stresses that he is not trying to make Empire High a technology school. And he says quality education still has to be about things like hard work, self-discipline and outstanding teaching—with laptops becoming a natural part of the classroom, just as they have become a natural part of workplaces across America.

SOURCE B

"Archived: Educational Technology Fact Sheet." *Ed.Gov.* U.S. Department of Education, 29 Mar. 2006. Web. 15 Oct. 2010.

The following information is excerpted from the Department of Education's "Educational Fact Sheet" regarding the availability of technology to students in the United States. Today's technology allows distance learning courses; in these courses, students work on their own from home or another off-site location, communicating with teachers and other students by using such technology as email, videoconferencing, and instant messaging.

Statistics:

- In 2003, the ratio of students to computers in all public schools was 4.4 to 1.

- 48 states included technology standards for students in 2004–2005.

- In 2003, 8% of public schools lent laptop computers to students. . . .

- Schools in rural areas (12%) were more likely than city schools (5%) and urban fringe schools (7%) to lend laptops.

- In 2003, 10% of public schools provided a handheld computer to students or teachers.

- 16 states had at least one cyber-charter school operating in 2004–2005.

- 22 states had established virtual schools in 2004–2005.

- 56% of two- and four-year degree-granting institutions offer distance education courses, with 90% of public institutions offering distance education courses. . . .

Distance Learning

- 36% of school districts and 9% of all public schools have students enrolled in distance education courses.

- There were an estimated 328,000 enrollments in distance education courses by K–12 students during the 2001–2002 school year.

- 68% of the enrollments were in high school with an additional 29% in combined or ungraded schools.

- 45,300 enrollments in distance education were Advanced Placement® or other college-level courses.

- A greater proportion of rural area districts had students enrolled in distance education courses than did urban and suburban districts.

- 42% of districts that have students enrolled in distance-education courses are high poverty districts.

- When small districts offer distance learning, they are more likely to involve a greater proportion of schools.

- 80% of public school districts offering online courses said that offering courses not otherwise available at their schools is one of the most important reasons for having distance education.

- 50% of public school districts offering online courses cited distance learning as very important in making Advanced Placement® or other college-level courses available to all students.

- 92% of districts enrolled in online distance education courses had students access online courses from school.

- 24% of districts with students accessing online courses from home provided or paid for a computer for all students, while an additional 8% did so for some students.

Friendship Through Education

- Using the internet to connect students in the U.S. and Arab nations to develop mutual understandings of one another's cultures.

SOURCE C

Rosandich, Dan. "EDUCATION CARTOONS." *Danscartoons.com.* Web. 16 Oct. 2010. *(Reprinted with permission.)*

"What a school day! The computers broke down and we had to LISTEN!"

SOURCE D

Johnson, Doug. "School Media Services for the 'Net Generation,' Part One." *Doug Johnson Website*. 1 Jan. 2007. Web. 15 Oct. 2010.

This passage is excerpted from an article by Doug Johnson, who has been director of media and technology for the Mankato (Minnesota) Public Schools since 1991.

. . . kids expect fast communication responses, tune out when things aren't interesting, and may be more visually than verbally literate. For them, technology is a tool for learning on any topic they choose. (Are you reading anything you don't already know from the media or from personal observation?)

. . . Our current crop of students believes "teachers are vital," "computers can't replace humans," and motivation is critical in learning. They like group activities, believing building social skills is a part of schooling. They identify with their parents' values. And they are achievement oriented, feeling it is "cool to be smart." And although they are fascinated with new technologies, their knowledge of them is often "shallow."

(Who actually maintains the computers in your home or school?)

Finally, the studies point to how this generation learns—or likes to learn. Our current crop of students with their hypertext minds like inductive discovery rather than being told what they should know. In other words, they want to learn by doing rather than simply listening or reading. They enjoy working in teams, on "things that matter," often informally, and not just during school hours. And given their quick response requirements, they need to be encouraged to reflect.

It is my firm belief that schools will be more productive if educators acknowledge the unique attributes and preferences of the Net Generation and adapt educational environments to suit students instead of trying to change their basic natures. So what are some implications for NG (Net Generation) library media centers?

To a large degree, media centers may be the most NG-oriented places in schools. . . . Given their preference to work in groups, the NG media center should provide spaces for collaboration on school projects and socialization. It should contain the tools necessary for the production of information, not just its consumption — computers with the processing power and software to edit digital movies and photographs, scanners, and high-quality printers and projection devices — and, of course, assistance in the use of these tools.

. . . It should have comfy chairs, and be a friendly atmosphere, low-stress, safe, and forgiving — and yes, in high schools, an in-house coffee shop. Spaces for story times, puppetry, plays, and games along with computer stations with age-appropriate software and websites are just as important in elementary schools. If the "room" is not a wonderful place to be, students and teachers will stay on the internet or in the classroom. Period. (And given the rise in online schools, is there a lesson here for classrooms as well?)

SOURCE E

Miller, Ed, and Joan Almon. "Child Advocates Challenge Current Ed Tech Standards" (press release). Alliance for Childhood. 30 Sept. 2004. Retrieved 21 Jan. 2011 at *http://drupal6.allianceforchildhood.org*. Reprinted by permission.

The following passage is excerpted from a press release from the Alliance for Childhood, a non-profit organization concerned with healthy child development.

The high-tech, screen-centered lifestyle of today's children — at home and at school — is a health hazard and the polar opposite of the education they need to take part in making ethical choices in a high-tech democracy, according to a new report released today by the Alliance for Childhood.

Tech Tonic: Towards a New Literacy of Technology challenges education standards and industry assertions that all teachers and children, from preschool up, should use computers in the classroom to develop technology literacy. That expensive agenda ignores evidence that high-tech classrooms have done little if anything to improve student achievement, the report says.

The report strongly criticizes the extensive financial and political connections between education officials and school technology vendors.

It urges citizens to wake up to the increasing influence of corporations in policymaking for public education.

"The lack of evidence or an expert consensus that computers will improve student achievement—despite years of efforts by high-tech companies and government agencies to demonstrate otherwise—is itself compelling evidence of the need for change," *Tech Tonic* states. "It's time to scrap . . . national, state, and local policies that require all students and all teachers to use computers in every grade, and that eliminate even the possibility of alternatives."

At the same time, the Alliance suggests, high-tech childhood is making children sick—promoting a sedentary life at a time when childhood obesity is at epidemic levels.

Today's children will inherit social and ecological crises that involve tough moral choices and awesome technological power, *Tech Tonic* warns. To confront problems like the proliferation of devastating weapons and global warming, children will need all the "wisdom, compassion, courage, and creative energy" they can muster, it adds. Blind faith in technology will not suffice.

"A new approach to technology literacy, calibrated for the 21st century, requires us to help children develop the habits of mind, heart, and action that can, over time, mature into the adult capacities for moral reflection, ethical restraint, and compassionate service," the report states.

The Alliance for Childhood is a nonprofit partnership of educators, researchers, health professionals, and other advocates for children, based in Maryland. *Tech Tonic* is a follow-up to the Alliance's widely noted 2000 report *Fool's Gold*. In *Tech Tonic* the Alliance proposes a new definition of technology literacy as "the mature capacity to participate creatively, critically, and responsibly in making technological choices that serve democracy, ecological sustainability, and a just society."

Tech Tonic proposes seven reforms in education and family life. These will free children from a passive attachment to screen-based entertainment and teach them about their "technological heritage" in a new way, rooted in the study and practice of technology "as social ethics in action" and in a renewed respect for nature.

The seven reforms:

- Make human relationships and a commitment to strong communities a top priority at home and school.

- Color childhood green to refocus education on children's relationships with the rest of the living world.

- Foster creativity every day, with time for the arts and play.

- Put community-based research and action at the heart of the science and technology curriculum.

- Declare one day a week an electronic entertainment-free zone.

- End marketing aimed at children.

- Shift spending from unproven high-tech products in the classroom to children's unmet basic needs.

"To expect our teachers, our schools, and our nation to strive to educate all of our children, leaving none behind, is a worthy goal," *Tech Tonic* says. "To insist that they must at the same time spend huge amounts of money and time trying to integrate unproven classroom technologies into their teaching, across the curriculum with preschoolers on up, is an unwise and costly diversion from that goal. It comes at the expense of our neediest children and schools, for whom the goal is most distant."

The report proposes 10 guiding principles for the new technology literacy and offers examples of each. It also includes suggestions for educators, parents, and other citizens to develop their own technology literacy, with a similar emphasis on social ethics in action.

"Today's children will face complex and daunting choices, in a future of biotechnology, robotics, and microchips, for which we are doing very little to prepare them," says Joan Almon, head of the Alliance. "We immerse them in a virtual, high-tech world and expect them to navigate the information superhighway with little guidance and few boundaries. It is time for a new definition of technology literacy that supports educational and family habits that are healthy both for children and for the survival of the Earth."

"It is within the context of relationships that children learn best," adds Dr. Marilyn Benoit, past president of the American Academy of Child and Adolescent Psychiatry and vice president of the Alliance Board of Trustees. "As we shift more towards the impersonal use of high technology as a major tool for teaching young children, we will lose that critical context of interactive relationship that so reinforces early learning."

SOURCE F

"NEA's policy recommendations" from "Technology in Schools: The Ongoing Challenge of Access, Adequacy and Equity," An NEA policy brief, 2008, *http://www.nea.org*.

The following information is excerpted from a policy brief released by the National Education Association.

1. Improve access to technology

Educators have been remarkably creative with limited computer access, but if technology is to be integrated into instruction, more computers must be made available for students' use, whether that is through stand-alone computers or portable and wireless technologies. States and school districts should pay more attention to building wireless infrastructures that can support increased access to technology.

2. Increase internet access, address software issues, and expand technical support

Programs designed to close the achievement gaps must begin addressing equity issues related to internet access, software, and technical support. Educators across the board should have greater access to computer software for planning and instruction. Educators in urban schools, in particular, need better instructional software, and more instructional staff should be involved in making decisions about software purchases for their schools. Educators in elementary schools should have more age-appropriate software for students, but, just as importantly, they need more high-speed internet services.

Maintenance support for computers must be adequate to ensure that computers function properly and reliably. Quality technical support for computers and other technologies should be available in every school. Particular attention should be given to senior high schools, as well as to schools located in urban areas, where maintenance and technical support are less likely to be provided. One option is for districts or schools to make use of their students' technical expertise by formally arranging for qualified students to provide technical assistance where needed. Another important point is separating the instructional support role of paraprofessionals from that of providing maintenance and technical support.

3. Expand professional development in technology

Technology training—most commonly offered for administration, communications, and research—should focus more on applications for instruction. And those entering the profession, as well as experienced educators, should have access to high-quality professional development in technology. Particular attention should be paid to training opportunities provided for educators working in schools located in urban and rural areas, where educators believe the technology training in their schools has not been adequate.

4. Capitalize on teachers' and students' enthusiasm about technology

Schools should seek more ways to use technology for the greatest gain in student achievement, particularly in urban and rural/small-town schools. State and district leaders should encourage schools to use technology in more creative ways by permitting more flexibility in instruction and by providing incentives that support technology-enriched programs. More ways should be found to motivate the most experienced educators to use technology through better training and more curriculum-related opportunities.

5. Involve educators as advocates

Teacher organizations, such as NEA and its state affiliates, can be a valuable ally in the goal of fully integrating technology into education.

State and local associations can also help educate parents and the business community about the benefits of better integrating technology into teaching and learning. They can actively support district and state efforts to secure more funding for school technology by lobbying state legislatures, establishing partnerships with commercial and private enterprises, and seeking federal and private grants.

SAMPLE ESSAY RESPONSE

Anyone who has ever been issued a dog-eared or graffiti-filled[1] ten-year-old textbook for a class would certainly agree that being provided with an iPad or a laptop would be a huge improvement in educational tools. Even if the textbook were brand new, it is still a finite resource, whereas an internet-connected device is a potentially limitless resource that encompasses all subject areas. As more and more schools turn to technology and tools like iPads, opponents have expressed concern that plugged-in students are at a disadvantage compared with their pre-internet peers. While a tech-driven curricula might carry some dangers, the educational benefits to students, rich and poor, far outweigh the risks.[2]

No student will learn anything if his or her attention is not focused on the lesson. A student must be engaged in the learning process to benefit.[3] According to Source A[4] "students in schools where laptops were being used were clearly more engaged." Part of that engagement comes from the way today's students consume information.[5] Johnson points out that the Net Generation (NG) expects

[1] Writer uses imagery to engage readers as well as appeal to their common experience as students.

[2] The thesis is complex. That is, it addresses opposing views, allowing for movement/growth/development of an idea along a line of reasoning—rather than a static single idea to be proven repeatedly throughout.

[3] The first two sentences in this first body paragraph state a claim: students must be engaged to learn. Paraphrasing the first sentence doubles the effect of the claim.

[4] The writer makes an attribution statement ("according to") to integrate evidence from a source.

[5] The writer uses a transition sentence to help explain the evidence and link the two pieces of evidence. Note that this writer has synthesized evidence from more than one source to defend an assertion.

information to be fast. What's more, he says students "tune out when things aren't interesting" (Source D). Because technology can entice and maintain student interest, it may, for the NG generation particularly, be an educational necessity.[6] In addition, since internet[7]-connected devices provide students with "immediate access to the most recent information" (Source A), that information is potentially more relevant and more interesting to students.

Internet connected devices don't only provide access to information, such devices also provide something potentially more important, especially to schools in rural areas or to schools with a high percentage of students in poverty. Internet connected devices effectively break down the walls of a school and give students the ability to learn from home (distance learning), to take advanced classes, or even engage with students from other countries.[8] The U.S. Department of Education reports that in 2004, 22 states had established virtual schools and that 36 percent of school districts have students enrolled in distance education programs (Source B). Online courses would allow students to learn from home, if necessary, but these programs are also a benefit to those going on to one of the many colleges that also provide similar online courses (Source B).

Distance education is beneficial in other ways as well. In such cases where a school cannot afford to offer higher-level courses, its students can join more than 45,000 other students enrolled in online Advanced Placement courses (Source B).[9] Perhaps the greatest impact that technology can have in schools is to give all students equal learning opportunities. Source B points out that "42% of districts that have students enrolled in distance-

---

[6] In this sentence, the writer is clarifying the argument by drawing a conclusion.
[7] Finally, the writer concludes this paragraph by using a partial quote that supports one last point.
[8] In the second body paragraph, the writer advances the argument by listing several advantages to giving students internet-connected devices. The advantages listed were part of available information in the sources, but this writer focuses on the advantages of distance learning and defends assertions with evidence.
[9] While all of the evidence for claims in this paragraph comes from one source, there are multiple uses of the source, and the writer uses only what is necessary in support.

education courses are high poverty districts," which implies[10] these schools have found a way to offer their students more despite limited resources. Just like their peers in wealthier schools, these students will leave high school or college and enter a workplace where computers have become commonplace (Source A).[11] To fail to integrate similar technologies into all schools seems to ignore a real world educational need.

Nevertheless,[12] there are those who argue that a strong, singular focus on technology could actually be harmful to children. Miller and Almon point out "a lack of evidence or an expert consensus that computers will improve student achievement" (Source E). They also say that since using computers is a sedentary activity, high technology use might be "making children sick" and be exacerbating the childhood obesity problem (Source E). However, it seems the technology trend is here to stay and once schools have fully embraced digital learning, no doubt convincing evidence for its effectiveness will emerge. As for the health claim, surely no school would chain its students to their computers all day. As always, striking a balance between bookwork and physical activity is important. The fact that the book is a computer makes no difference.

Today's world[13] is information driven, and business and commerce rely on computers or other devices to access this information. While there is still great value in traditional styles of learning,

---

[10] In this paragraph, the writer is clearly drawing an inference about the data given in Source B. In a clear ethical appeal, the writer suggests that technology will provide equal education opportunities for all students. The final sentence in this paragraph reinforces the ethical appeal.

[11] To explain why access to technology is important, the writer uses information from a second source in this paragraph.

[12] In the third body paragraph, the writer transitions to the counterargument, and acknowledges that some believe technology in schools is harmful. The writer presents two of the opponents' claims: 1) lack of evidence that technology is effective and 2) a sedentary learning style is harmful to children's health. Rather than offer solid evidence to refute these claims, the writer of this essay appeals to common-sense alternatives.

[13] The conclusion to this essay is short, but it furthers the writer's ethical appeal by suggesting that to deny students access to computers is a disservice.

schools that do not allow students to learn using the tools of their future are doing them a great disservice.

ADDITIONAL COMMENTARY

Take note of how well organized this essay is. The writer's claim is clearly stated in the introduction. The argument progresses logically and evidence is used convincingly. This writer makes use of direct quotations, summaries, and paraphrases, but is careful to document the source of all evidence. It is easy to see how this writer has synthesized evidence to support the central argument. This writer has not strung together a summary of the sources, but instead has clearly shown independent thought throughout the essay. Ethical appeals enhance this writer's ethos. As for the writer's syntax, sentences are varied and effective. The writer's choice of words (*encompasses* and *exacerbates*, for example) shows an ability to use sophisticated language. As you read this essay, you may be thinking that the writer could have made other points or could have taken an entirely different approach. You're right. There is always more than one way to respond to the synthesis prompt, and your observation shows your engagement in these ideas.

Free-Response Question 2:
Rhetorical Analysis

*Get the habit of analysis—analysis will in time enable synthesis
to become your habit of mind.*—Frank Lloyd Wright

OVERVIEW

The purpose of this chapter is to give you a closer look at the particulars of Free-Response Question 2: Rhetorical Analysis. However, you will need to study more than just this chapter to be successful with this essay. While the entire book aims to help you be a stronger reader, writer, and thinker, please also review the following chapters in combination with this one:

- Chapter 6 on rhetorical strategies;

- Chapter 7 on logical fallacies;

- Chapter 11 on engaged and active reading;

- Chapter 15 on satire;

- Chapter 16 on prompts (focusing on those for Question 2).

REVIEWING QUESTION 2

Question 2 is an analysis exercise, where you are by definition analyzing the component parts of a writer's argument. By component parts, I mean rhetorical strategies and stylistic elements. Your main task will be to analyze how a writer's choices function in accomplishing his or her purpose.

In the **rhetorical analysis essay**, your thesis should clearly state which of the writer's rhetorical choices you will analyze. It must also convey your basic claim as to how and why he or she made those choices, focusing on the effect or function of those choices.

You will need to assess the rhetorical situation. Refer to the ETCEAS points. By now you should have ETCEAS memorized and be able to quickly make a mental list of an author's purpose and the context in which the argument was created.

Chapter 16 contains the stable prompt wording for Question 2. Review it carefully.

GUIDING YOUR ANALYSIS

To *analyze* is to examine the parts of something in order to understand how they function in the whole. So, to analyze an effective satirical essay, for example, you'll first need to recognize that the text is satire. Next, you need to ask the right questions as you read, such as "Who or what is the satirical target?" and "Which techniques are employed and where?" Reading so you have a sophisticated understanding of the text is necessary for your success with this essay.

As you read the text, annotate. Mark anything you see regarding appeals, rhetorical strategies, and stylistic choices (diction, syntax, figurative language, etc.). Make comments on the rhetorical situation.

No matter what text you're provided, you must isolate the author's thesis and the rhetorical strategies and stylistic techniques he or she uses to achieve their desired effect.

DETERMINE THE PATTERN OF EXPOSITION

It may be helpful to identify the genre or expository pattern of the passage. While it won't be necessary to actually present this information in your essay, being able to identify the genre may help you know what to look for. Keep in mind that patterns of exposition can be combined for effect. A direct logical argument may contain a short anecdote (narrative), a definition of a complex term, a comparative (or contrasting) analogy, or make use of figurative language.

Making a determination regarding pattern should take you only seconds. Do not labor over this aspect of the text.

Remember that no matter what, the text will contain a clear and dominant argument. It would not be on the exam if it didn't. The point here is simply to remind you that there is no one standard method of expressing an argument.

1. A simple persuasive **argument**?

   - Look for types of appeals.
   - Watch for logical fallacies.
   - What is it the writer wants you to believe or do?

2. An **expository** essay (one that explains or explores a topic using a variety of methods):

   - Description
     - — Used commonly by nature and environmental writers, description relies on imagery to get the reader to "see" the subject.
   - Narrative
     - — The writer will explore a topic using the framework of a story, perhaps a look at one person's life as a model or example of the main subject.
   - Cause-and-Effect
     - — Look for a problem or a current issue and the writer's theories about the underlying causes.
   - Problem/Solution
     - — An obvious problem, in policy usually, will be presented along with one or more viable solutions.
   - Process Analysis
     - — The writer shows how something is done or how something works.
   - Definition
     - — This pattern is used when an idea is too abstract for people to grasp or when there are conflicting explanations for a term. For example, many people might benefit from having "supply-side economics" defined more fully. The writer is, of course, giving their point of view.
   - Compare/Contrast
     - — The writer shows how two issues are alike (or different) in a way that illustrates a position.

3. **Satire**?

- Who or what is the satirical target?

- What aspect of the social contract is flawed or broken?

- What specific method does the writer use to criticize the target?

- What does the satirist want the reader to understand, know, or do?

RHETORICAL TRIANGLE REVISITED

Review Chapter 6 for a detailed explanation of rhetoric and rhetorical strategies. Briefly, Aristotle defined three components of rhetoric:

- Logos (appeal to reason, using facts, verifiable evidence, expert opinion, etc.)

- Ethos (the credibility of the writer, the tone or spirit in which the writer presents the argument)

- Pathos (appeals to emotion)

Take caution: NEVER simply say "the writer uses pathos in line three" or the like. Logos, Ethos, and Pathos come to us, the audience, through a writer's rhetorical choices. Through their appeals, they ask us to consider, to agree, and to feel. Be sure you understand Aristotle's framework in a holistic way.

ORGANIZING THE ESSAY

You will need to present a defensible thesis that takes a position in response to the prompt. **DO NOT simply proceed to answer a question.** You will earn few, if any, points if you do. Your essay must be well organized, with an introduction, body paragraphs—with subordinate claims and evidence from the text in support—and a conclusion.

Create a mini-outline or concept map to guide your general explanation or argument. Such an outline will help you stay focused. If you follow it, you should be less likely to repeat yourself or leave out cogent points.

The evidence for your rhetorical analysis essay will come from the text itself. If you state, for example, that the author makes an ethical appeal, you will need to be specific and explain in your commentary how the appeal functions in achieving the writer's purpose.

MORE TIPS FOR QUESTION 2

The following tips come from AP® readers' commentaries on Question 2.

DO:

- Read the text carefully, first (if you fail to do this, you run a high risk of misunderstanding not only the text, but also the prompt).

- Provide specific examples, rather than general.

- Offer cogent insights.

- Provide convincing analysis.

DO NOT:

- Drop in quotations from the passage without providing any meaningful commentary or explanation.

- Do not mistake identifying rhetorical terms you memorized in class for a clear analysis of *how* they work and *why* the writer chose them. An essay that merely points out the rhetorical devices employed earns a very low score or no score at all.

- Write personal comments (asides) about the content of the passage. Note: You may feel compelled to do this if the subject of the text conflicts with your views or values. Please remember that your job is to analyze, not necessarily agree. Control biases that prevent you from objectively managing your task.

- Paraphrase or summarize instead of analyze.

- Identify features of the text without explanation.

SAMPLE RHETORICAL ANALYSIS PROMPT

QUESTION 2

(Suggested time: 40 minutes.)

The essay below, "Should We Ban Cigarettes?," written in 2011 by Peter Singer, bioethics professor at Princeton University, examines the ethical nature of legal access to cigarettes. Read the essay carefully and write an essay in which you analyze how Singer crafts the text to express his view that cigarettes should be banned.

PRINCETON—U.S. President Barack Obama's doctor confirmed last month that the president no longer smokes. At the urging of his wife, Michelle Obama, the president first resolved to stop smoking in 2006, and has used nicotine replacement therapy to help him. If it took Obama, a
5   man strong-willed enough to aspire to and achieve the U.S. presidency, five years to kick the habit, it is not surprising that hundreds of millions of smokers find themselves unable to quit.

Although smoking has fallen sharply in the U.S., from about 40% of the population in 1970 to only 20% today, the proportion of smokers
10 stopped dropping around 2004. There are still 46 million American adult smokers, and smoking kills about 443,000 Americans each year. Worldwide, the number of cigarettes sold—six trillion a year, enough to reach the sun and back—is at an all-time high. Six million people die each year from smoking—more than from AIDS, malaria, and traffic accidents
15 combined. Of the 1.3 billion Chinese, more than one in ten will die from smoking.

Earlier this month, the U.S. Food and Drug Administration announced that it would spend $600 million over five years to educate the public about the dangers of tobacco use. But Robert Proctor, a historian
20 of science at Stanford University and the author of a forthcoming blockbuster entitled *Golden Holocaust: Origins of the Cigarette Catastrophe and the Case for Abolition,* argues that to use education as one's only weapon against a highly addictive and often lethal drug is unpardonably insufficient.

25 "Tobacco control policy," Proctor says, "too often centers on educating the public, when it should be focused on fixing or eliminating the product." He points out that we don't just educate parents to keep toys painted with lead-based paints away from their children's mouths; we ban the use of lead-based paint. Similarly, when thalidomide was found to
30 cause major birth defects, we did not just educate women to avoid using the drug when pregnant.

Proctor calls on the FDA to use its new powers to regulate the contents of cigarette smoke to do two things. First, because cigarettes are designed to create and maintain addiction, the FDA should limit the amount of
35 nicotine that they contain to a level at which they would cease to be addictive. Smokers who want to quit would then find it easier to do so.

Second, the FDA should bear history in mind. The first smokers did not inhale tobacco smoke; that became possible only in the nineteenth century, when a new way of curing tobacco made the smoke less alkaline. That tragic discovery is already responsible for about 150 million deaths,
40 with many times that toll still to come, unless something drastic is done. The FDA should therefore require that cigarette smoke be more alkaline, which would make it less easily inhaled, and so make it harder for cigarette smoke to reach the lungs.

Much of Proctor's book, which will be published in January, is based on
45 a vast archive of tobacco-industry documents, released during litigation. More than 70 million pages of industry documents are now available online.

The documents show that, as early as the 1940s, the industry had evidence suggesting that smoking causes cancer. In 1953, however, a
50 meeting of the chief executives of major American tobacco companies took a joint decision to deny that cigarettes are harmful. Moreover, once the scientific evidence that smoking causes cancer became public, the industry tried to create the impression that the science was inconclusive, in much the same way that those who deny that human activities are
55 causing climate change deliberately distort the science today.

As Proctor says, cigarettes, not guns or bombs, are the deadliest artifacts in the history of civilization. If we want to save lives and improve health, nothing else that is readily achievable would be as effective as an international ban on the sale of cigarettes. (Eliminating extreme poverty
60 worldwide is about the only strategy that might save more lives, but it would be far more difficult to accomplish.)

For those who recognize the state's right to ban recreational drugs like marijuana and ecstasy, a ban on cigarettes should be easy to accept. Tobacco kills far more people than these drugs.

65 Some argue that as long as a drug harms only those who choose to use it, the state should let individuals make their own decisions, limiting its role to ensuring that users are informed of the risks that they are running. But tobacco is not such a drug, given the dangers posed by secondhand smoke, especially when adults smoke in a home with young children.

70 Even setting aside the harm that smokers inflict on nonsmokers, the free-to-choose argument is unconvincing with a drug as highly addictive as tobacco, and it becomes even more dubious when we consider that

most smokers take up the habit as teenagers and later want to quit. Reducing the amount of nicotine in cigarette smoke to a level that was
75 not addictive might meet this objection.

The other argument for the *status quo* is that a ban on tobacco might result in the same kind of fiasco as occurred during Prohibition in the U.S. That is, like the effort to ban alcohol, prohibiting the sale of tobacco would funnel billions of dollars into organized crime and fuel corruption in
80 law-enforcement agencies, while doing little to reduce smoking.

But that may well be a false comparison. After all, many smokers would actually like to see cigarettes banned because, like Obama, they want to quit.

Peter Singer is a professor of bioethics at Princeton University and Laureate Professor at the University of Melbourne. His books include Animal Liberation, Practical Ethics, *and* The Life You Can Save.

Copyright © 2011 by Project Syndicate. *www.project-syndicate.org.*

SAMPLE ESSAY RESPONSE

In "Should We Ban Cigarettes?," Peter Singer's[1] main claim is that since smoking kills nearly a half million citizens each year, the United States government should prohibit the sale of cigarettes as the only way to solve the problem.[2] However, until that time, he argues specifically that the U.S. Food and Drug Administration (FDA) should use its powers to make cigarettes less powerful and addictive. Singer targets his message[3] to all citizens, as everyone is affected in one way or another by the problem, but perhaps most particularly to smokers, since without their willingness to accept a ban, it would not likely come to pass. To convince his audience that the government should ban the sale of cigarettes, Singer relies

---

[1] The introduction includes the title of the article and the author's full name. All subsequent mentions of the author use only his last name.

[2] In this statement, the writer references Singer's main claim. Since this essay is an analysis, you should be able to isolate the author's thesis, which becomes your starting point for showing how the writer (in this case, Singer) defended his thesis.

[3] The writer acknowledges Singer's potential audience.

on factual evidence, ethical appeals, and a reference to a popular president in order to humanize the situation.

In order to point out the magnitude of the problem, Singer provides a sharp visual representation of a fact by describing how the six trillion cigarettes sold each year would be enough "to reach to the sun and back" (Lines 12–13).[4] However, Singer somewhat inflates the danger to US citizens since the six trillion represents the number of cigarettes sold worldwide, not just in the U.S.[5]

In support of his claim, Singer gives evidence of the extensive problem. He says that smoking kills more people each year than "AIDS, malaria, and traffic accidents combined" (14). He does not, however, cite the source for this statistic. In addition to pointing out that smoking is a killer, Singer says the fight against smoking is expensive. He cites an announcement by the FDA (from November 2011) that the agency "would spend $600 million over five years to educate the public about the dangers of tobacco use." And yet, as Singer explains, education doesn't work, despite the money spent on it.[6]

Singer provides expert testimony[7] for his argument that education is ineffective by citing Stanford University's Robert Proctor, whose book *Golden Holocaust: Origins of the Cigarette Catastrophe and the Case for Abolition* details the failure of previous attempts to educate the public about the dangers of smoking and the need for a federal ban. Singer uses Proctor's analogy[8] to suggest it is ridiculous to try to save people from the dangers of smoking through education, just as we would not "educate parents to keep toys painted with lead-based paints away

---

[4] In the first line citation in the essay, the writer uses the word "Lines," but in all further line citations, the numbers only are used.

[5] Here the writer is seen to be a critical reader and thinker by pointing out a discrepancy in Singer's illustration.

[6] This sentence serves as a transition to the next paragraph, which will further analyze the education aspect of Singer's argument.

[7] The writer clarifies the type of evidence Singer uses.

[8] The writer of this essay clearly understands the source of the analogy, but acknowledges its effectiveness in Singer's argument.

from their children's mouths" (26–28). Instead, we banned the dangerous element and saved countless children from devastating effects. In an ethical appeal, Singer implies through this comparison that it is immoral to simply let people become ill or die from smoking cigarettes, which the tobacco industry has known since the 1940s "causes cancer" (49).

While Singer[9] would like an overall ban on cigarettes, he realizes an all-out ban might be too difficult to achieve. Therefore, he argues that the FDA must make two important policy changes to make cigarettes less harmful: make them more alkaline so that people are less likely to inhale (to replicate pre-19th century tobacco before technology existed to reduce harsh alkalinity) and limit nicotine to make cigarettes less addictive (33–34). Singer does not provide proof of the addictive nature of cigarettes, but references Proctor, whose book includes documentation that proves the tobacco industry knew "as early as the 1940s . . . that smoking causes cancer," underscoring the fact that smoking is a deadly habit (48–49).

Singer concedes[10] that these days fewer people smoke, about 20% of the population versus 40% in 1970, but in his view, there are still far too many deaths to discount the importance of the issue. In a clear emotional appeal, Singer refers to the "tragic" fact that historically, 150 million people have died from cigarettes (39).

Singer acknowledges the opposition's argument.[11] He realizes that some believe that "as long as a drug harms only those who use it, the state should let individuals make their own decisions" regarding its use (65–66). This logic is flawed, says Singer, who points out that most smokers begin their habit as teenagers

---

[9] This paragraph analyzes complex aspects of Singer's argument and synthesizes a couple of key points. Singer wants the FDA to make cigarettes less harmful and addictive, which is important because cigarettes cause cancer.

[10] The writer recognizes that Singer makes a concession to the fact that the issue is not as dire as it once was, but shows that Singer refutes that stance through emotional appeal by saying that too many still die needlessly.

[11] In this paragraph, the writer shows how Singer acknowledges another opposing view and refutes it.

"and later want to quit" (73). His implication is that people begin smoking when they're least likely to be able to make reasonable judgments regarding their health, and before they realize it, teens are addicted. The smoking habit, as Singer points out in a logical appeal in paragraph one,[12] is even difficult for an adult like President Obama, "a man strong-willed enough to aspire to and achieve the U.S. presidency" (5), so then how much harder for ordinary people, particularly teens.

To support his notion that a ban would be acceptable to U.S. citizens, Singer says in his conclusion, many smokers "want to quit." However, he fails to say that there are also many smokers who enjoy smoking and do not want the government to control their access to cigarettes.[13]

To conclude,[14] the author could have made an appeal to ethics by pointing out the known fact that second-hand smoke inflicts damage on nonsmokers or how unfair it is for healthy nonsmokers to have to share in the growing health care costs that result from the unwillingness (or inability) of smokers to quit a habit they know is harmful to themselves and others. Nevertheless, Singer effectively adds to an important discussion about what can be done to reduce smoking deaths, since education is not an effective option in combatting a known health hazard to U.S. citizens.

---

[12] The writer cites the source of the information from the paragraph, not the specific line. This is also an acceptable method if the paragraph is easily located, such as the first, second, or last. Never make someone count to find the seventh paragraph, for example. Take note also that reference is made to the kind of appeal Singer uses.

[13] The writer points out that Singer makes a generalization.

[14] While not required, this writer signals the conclusion. In this conclusion, the student points out other arguments Singer could have made, which shows critical thinking. Finally, the essay wraps up by tying back to the essence of Singer's thesis.

Free-Response Question 3:
The Argument Essay

*Writing, to me, is simply thinking through
my fingers.*—Isaac Asimov

OVERVIEW

Question 3 is where you show off your own rhetorical skills by creating an argument of your own. This is not to say that your other essays lack an argument. That's not what I mean. For each essay you write on the exam, you will establish a position to defend. But this essay is different. There is no safety net—all your evidence must come from your head: from your reading, from your experiences, and from your observations.

This chapter focuses on the key elements of Question 3. Be sure to study other chapters in this book so you are fully prepared to write this essay.

REVIEWING QUESTION 3

For Question 3, you will be presented with a question or an idea and asked to take a position. Sometimes the question or idea is paired with a brief quotation or passage from a text to help activate your thinking. You're not meant to cite or quote the provided text.

Evidence for your claims for this essay come from your reading, your general knowledge, your experience, and your observations. See Chapter 16 for the stable prompt wording for this question.

PROVIDE APPROPRIATE EVIDENCE

For Question 3, evidence is a bit different. You won't be quoting or citing the prompt. Your evidence is constructed from the reasons and examples you provide in defense of your position. These reasons and examples will come from your reading, your general knowledge, your observations, and your own life experiences. In other words, your proof will come from everything you know. Nevertheless, the evidence you use must be relevant, current, credible, and reliable.

EXAMPLES:

1. Real life: these examples come from what you've experienced or observed.

2. Specific: referring to particular people or events.

3. General: referring to types of people or events.

ABOUT PERSONAL EXAMPLES

A personal example differs from a real-life example in that it is from your own personal experience. Be cautious when using personal examples and avoid using private examples. Any information that should not be publicly shared is inappropriate in this context.

Personal examples are more limited in their universal value. In other words, your proof will come from everything that you know. On the other hand, an example from real life that involves significant events or large numbers of people is going to carry more weight.

If your personal example is compelling and unique, it might be excellent evidence.

STATISTICS

You will not have access to any resources, so you won't be able to look up any information. But that doesn't mean that you can't cite some facts if you know them. A good strategy for citing facts, especially if you're not

100 percent sure of the numbers, is to qualify your statements with terms such as "approximately," "about," "in general," etc. For example, you might remember that you heard on a news broadcast that one in three middle- and high-school students reported being bullied. If you're not sure, you can say "approximately one in three." Don't forget to mention the source. If you can't remember which network broadcast the story, refer in general, by saying, "In a recent television news broadcast, it was reported that . . . "

OTHER RHETORICAL STRATEGIES

- Appeals to values, needs, emotions: review Chapter 6.

- Effective syntax: review Chapter 9.

- Effective diction and language: review Chapter 17.

Prepare for Question 3 by being well read. Read not only nonfiction works from your English course, but also from your other courses. For example, maybe you will read *A Sand County Almanac* in your environmental studies class. Don't think of that as just a science-oriented text. Everything you read is potentially valuable to you on this exam. See Chapter 4 for a list of authors and texts. In addition to reading books, articles, editorials, etc., as you read, contemplate the various ways the ideas in these works connect with your life. Try to engage personally with everything you read. What do YOU THINK?

MAKE YOUR THINKING TRANSPARENT

One weakness of immature, nervous, or hurried writers is that they sometimes assume that their ideas, arguments, and connections are self-evident. They may think that if they get it, everyone will get it. Confusion occurs if your understanding of an idea lies in unstated connections, or in conclusions that you have only thought about but not shown in writing. DO NOT forget to explain. If you have not explicitly stated your interpretations and conclusions, you are hiding your thinking, not showing it. Again, if you haven't put your thinking on paper, you haven't made it transparent. Your commentary must link your evidence to your thesis (and other claims).

TRANSITIONAL WORDS AND PHRASES

By using transitional words and phrases in your writing, you will be less likely to write confusing or woolly prose. Chapter 17 gives you a list of common transitional words and phrases. Do not disregard their importance. Transitions not only lead your reader through your thinking, they also help you maintain a fluent and consistent line of reasoning.

TRANSITIONS IN ACTION

1. They bridge paragraph changes.

2. They signal new ideas.

3. They establish logical relationships.

4. They make it easy for you to reiterate a previous idea.

POINT OF VIEW

BLENDING FIRST AND THIRD PERSON

You know that writing in the third person gives you an authoritative voice, but there are times when you need to use the first person. It would be impossible to relate a personal example without it. Think about your essay as a blending of the two. Default to the third person; use the first person when relaying truly first hand experience as evidence; then, go back to third person authoritative.

UNIVERSAL FIRST PERSON

When you include yourself in the community of human beings, whether a small society such as your high school student population or the entire population of the globe, you will use the pronouns "we," "us," and "our." This is appropriate and necessary if you desire to take a stance from such a point of view. But, as with any deviation from authoritative third person, do not go overboard.

AUTHORITATIVE VOICE

Do not express opinions with qualifiers. If you do, you lessen the strength of your statement. An opinion, expressed in your essay, unless attributed to someone else, is obviously your opinion. It's your essay. Notice in the examples below how the statements on the right sound more authoritative.

No	Yes
I think the general population is experiencing ennui when it comes to the Green Movement.	The general population is experiencing ennui when it comes to the Green Movement.
It is my opinion that students should be allowed to use computers to write all exams, even AP® exams.	Students should be allowed to use computers to write all exams, even AP® exams.

If you are an avid gamer, maybe it's time to leave the dusky shadows of your virtual environment for awhile and play the game of life by talking with your parents, grandparents, neighbors, teachers, coaches, and friends about the issues of the day. Does your family "get into it" at dinner about politics or religion? Instead of skulking away, use those heated moments as opportunities for analysis and reflection. If your family tends toward the left in their views, read what those on the right are thinking. In other words, add to your perspective by actively thinking about and studying those opinions right under your nose.

ABOUT YOUR AUDIENCE

Your audience is a well-read, experienced adult who is accustomed to engaging with intelligent and sophisticated texts. Therefore, your ethos as a writer is very important. You must believe in the ideas you present in this essay. If you don't, everything about your essay will ring false or seem insincere. This exam is not a place for you to charm your reader with platitudes and flowery phrases. AP® readers will see this tactic immediately for what it is, which is an evasion of your task. Instead, wow them with your honest exploration of ideas.

Your ethos is evident in the following ways:

- Level of knowledge (your credibility);

- Truthfulness (honesty);

- Sincere intentions;

- Level of detail; concrete facts or deep understanding of an issue versus superficial references

GENERAL QUALITIES OF GOOD WRITING

STRIVE FOR:

- Varied and effective sentence structure.

- Rich, but standard vocabulary.

  — Avoid specialized terms or jargon, unless their use is warranted and you clarify their meanings.

- More than a few examples or other details in support.

- Explain evidence.

- Present a coherent, compelling argument.

- Provide context for references, particularly personal or contemporary cultural references your AP® reader won't automatically be familiar with. For example, most people over a certain age have no idea who current pop icons are or why they're important to know. Providing context will bridge that gap in understanding.

AVOID:

- Unnecessary repetition or redundancy. This is generally a result of getting your thinking tires stuck in the mud. Avoid this situation by referring often to your mini-outline or concept map.

- Overly short paragraphs (one or two sentences). If a claim is worth stating, it is worth exploring and supporting fully.

- Stating generalizations as claims. Claims must be specific and supported.

- Discursive and overly general introductions that "talk" around the subject.

- Repeating the prompt, either directly or in paraphrase.

- Summary conclusions. Instead, strive to present an insightful idea in your conclusion that originates logically from your argument.

SAMPLE PERSUASIVE PROMPT

QUESTION 3

(Suggested time: 40 minutes.)

Consider the distinct perspectives expressed in the following statements.

> Advice is seldom welcome; and those who want it the most always like it the least.

> *Philip Dormer Stanhope, Earl of Chesterfield (1694–1773)*

> I have lived some thirty years on this planet, and I have yet to hear the first syllable of valuable or even earnest advice from my seniors.

> *Henry David Thoreau (1817–1862)*

In a well-organized essay, take a position on the importance of advice, using the above quotes as a starting point. Support your argument with appropriate examples.

SAMPLE ESSAY RESPONSE

"Take my advice." You hear it from your elders from childhood on. The idea that you are in dire need of their wisdom and experience can be irritating, particularly if you are an independent, headstrong person. However, it is best to listen closely to the advice you are given. If experience is the best teacher, certainly you can learn from someone else's experience and the advice that comes out of it.

Most people like to think for themselves, make their own decisions, learn from their own mistakes. As Chesterfield asserts, "advice is seldom welcome." Young people in particular tend to believe that they know what is best for themselves, and they chafe at following the advice of some busybody or know-it-all. Yet as Chesterfield also observes, the people who need advice the most like it the least. It is precisely the headstrong, overconfident person who could use a bit of wise counsel, who blunders ahead despite what anyone advises. A moment's reflection on some helpful advice might lead that person to make a life-improving decision. In junior high, I had my heart set on making the basketball team, but my uncle suggested that my small size and agility were better suited to soccer. After some long nights of thinking (and some choice words for my uncle's unwanted advice), I finally decided to give soccer a try. The result was a fun career in a sport I still enjoy.

Thoreau's quote is the perfect encapsulation of the headstrong attitude many young people have. Thoreau claims to have never heard "the first syllable of valuable or earnest advice" from his elders. In this way, he seems to be one of the very people that Chesterfield is describing in his quote. And apparently Thoreau still held his view about advice at the relatively advanced age of thirty. Nevertheless, most young people, lacking the genius of Thoreau, could surely benefit from the advice of older, wiser people. Even Thoreau must have learned something from reading older writers or following the example of some admired person. You could say that much classical literature is a form of advice from the past, from our "seniors."

Human nature being what it is, young people will doubtless go on ignoring or despising advice from their elders. But that doesn't mean that advice isn't necessary. Like a dose of bitter medicine, a piece of helpful advice can prevent much worse consequences in the future.

NOTES ON THIS ESSAY

The student's response to the prompt makes good use of the opposed quotes on advice from Chesterfield and Thoreau. First, the student sets out a viewpoint on the importance of advice in the first paragraph: "However, it is best to listen closely to the advice you are given." Next, the student organizes the second paragraph around the two parts of Chesterfield's quote — that "advice is seldom welcome" and that the people who need it the most like it the least. The student points out that helpful advice can lead to a life-changing decision for the better, and then the student offers an example from their own experience that reinforces the point. In the third paragraph, the student examines the Thoreau quote and criticizes the idea that advice from elders is not valuable. The student makes the canny point that "much classical literature is a form of advice from the past, from our 'seniors.'" In the final paragraph, the student briefly summarizes the main idea that advice can be helpful. Overall the essay is forcefully argued and well organized.

Aim High: Tips and Tools for Success

Excellence is the gradual result of always striving to do better.—Pat Riley

OVERVIEW

Included in this chapter are general tips for success, an analysis of each of the three scoring rubrics, and a study method that uses samples of student essays from previous years.

Knowing the pitfalls to avoid and what AP® readers are looking for should help you compose high-scoring essays. Do engage your study group to make the most of this chapter.

TIPS FOR SUCCESSFUL ESSAYS

General Reminders

- Master the prompt by underlining key verbs and words and paraphrasing your task. If you do not understand the prompt or the rhetorical situation, your response essay will most likely be off task and could earn no points. Stay focused on the question, but do not simply restate the prompt. Respond instead by taking a position.

- Make sure your thesis contains your position—that is, your take on the issue or what *you* think. You must be able to defend your thesis with evidence.

- Introductions are important, so be sure you are not using vague, empty language that says nothing. Don't say, for example, "Throughout history people have striven for peace and freedom." That may be true, but so what? Every sentence you write in your short 40 minutes needs to have a purpose. Review Chapter 17.

- Demonstrate that you understand the rhetorical situation. Review the ETCEAS organizer in Chapter 4.

- For the synthesis essay, be sure to select apt and sufficient evidence to defend your thesis and supporting claims. Be sure to combine (synthesize) evidence from multiple sources. Don't forget to add your own examples when possible.

- Explain, through fluent commentary, the relationship between the evidence and your thesis (and supporting claims).

- If you struggle to keep ideas straight in your head, create a mini-outline, semantic web, or other graphic organizer to guide your writing. There will be space in your green booklet (which you are given for Section II of the exam) to do this step.

- One quality of high-scoring essays is that they are clear and concise. They aren't redundant or discursive. Keep CECT in mind: Claim, Evidence, Commentary, and Transition. Lead your reader logically and purposefully in your line of reasoning.

- If possible, in Questions 1 and 3 acknowledge a counterargument and provide a concession or refutation. Don't forget to provide evidence.

- Go beyond: Why is the issue important? Who is affected? What are the implications? Remember to add your voice to the ongoing conversation about an issue.

- Remember to leave readers with something to think about. Avoid merely restating your thesis in your conclusion.

COMPOSITION EXCELLENCE

This exam is the place for you to show off your composition skills. AP® readers expect to be reading college-level essays. This is what they want to see:

- **Mastery of Conventions:** You must know how to use punctuation properly, how to write complete sentences, how to write primarily in active voice, how to weave in textual evidence, and more. See Chapters 9, 10, and 17.

- **Advanced Vocabulary:** One primary attribute of essays that score well is the sophistication of the writer's word choice. You not only need to be able to understand the words you use, but you also need to be able to use them effectively. However, don't waste time artificially inflating your language. That is, if you just plop in a word you don't know because you think it will score you points, an AP® reader will recognize the weak strategy in a second and your ethos will be shot. See Chapter 12.

- **Sentence Variety:** You are expected to be able to vary your sentence structure to match your purpose. One of the key elements of syntax is emphasis. Learn how writers use devices like repetition, parallel structure, and other patterns for effect. Learning sentence fluency and variety takes time. This is something you can study and practice, however, and it will be worth your time. See Chapters 9 and 10.

- **Control of Tone and Diction:** Chapter 6 explains that ethos is the character of the writer that convinces the reader to believe him or her. One way to control your tone is to actually believe in what you are writing. If you are just "answering a question" on a test instead of writing an essay, your lack of commitment will be revealed in your tone and word choice.

A STUDY METHOD USING ONLINE SAMPLES

Sample student essays found online at AP® Central are excellent study tools. Each year, the College Board posts sample essays for each of the three free-response questions, as well as related commentaries and scoring rubrics.

The sample essays are chosen because they represent a range of success, from poor to excellent. The commentaries specifically explain why an essay was scored the way it was. You can learn from a poor essay as well as a good essay. Use these student samples as one more opportunity to learn what it takes to score well on the free-response section.

Three strategies for using these resources follow. Strategy 1 is the least time consuming, but also less beneficial than Strategy 3, which takes the most time and effort but is also the most enlightening of the three strategies.

ACCESSING THE MATERIALS YOU NEED

Go to *https://apcentral.collegeboard.org/courses/ap-english-language-and-composition/exam/past-exam-questions*. You will find a table that contains information that looks similar to what is shown below.

	Samples	**Commentaries**	**Scoring Guidelines**
The year the questions and samples are from.	Links to sample essays for each question.	Links to readers' commentaries for each sample.	Link to the rubrics used to score the essays.

You may need to search for the question prompts and related materials separately. Ongoing AP® Central website updates may present these resources a bit differently than what is shown here.

Strategy 1:

Simply read all the materials online, taking notes about what you're learning. Think about how your insightful reading reinforces what you've learned in this book. Make note of any particular "aha" moments.

Strategy 2:

Do this if you have time. For maximum benefit, ask your study group to do this with you.

1. Download and print:

- The question prompts and related materials
- The sample essays
- The commentaries
- Scoring rubrics

2. Seal up the commentaries for later use.

3. Read the question prompts and related materials.

4. Read the rubrics, so you are clear about how the essays were scored.

5. Read the essays.

6. Have a discussion about the strengths and weaknesses of each essay.

7. Finally, read the commentaries and talk about how your impressions matched those of the AP® readers or if you missed important points.

Strategy 3:

At step three listed above in Strategy 2, prepare to write your own essays, using the skills you have learned in this book. Review Chapters 19, 20, and 21 first. (Set a timer for a real exam experience, 135 minutes). As you read each prompt and related materials, put your close reading skills to work and annotate.

Then, write. Be true to the experience and put forth your best effort.

When you're done with your essays, take a break. Then, read the rubrics and assign yourself a score for each essay. It's a good idea to write down your justification for each score.

Continue with step 5 listed in Strategy 2. Take notes. My students were amazed at the insightful moments that occurred through this process.

Rubric Analysis
for Essays

The College Board scoring rubrics are customized for each of the three free-response essays on the English Language exam. Each essay is worth six points and the points are divided into three sections. Each of the three rubrics is summarized and explained below.

The analysis that follows is not meant to replicate the actual rubrics (or how they are visually structured) but to impart to you the key components of each rubric. As you study the following summaries, you may think they all state identical expectations. However, a closer look will reveal that each set of expectations is customized for its essay.

The overall weight of the free-response section accounts for 55% of the total exam score. Each essay makes up an equal third of that 55%.

If you used one of the study methods above, you are already acquainted with the new rubrics, so what follows will be an even stronger reinforcement of the new rubric expectations.

SYNTHESIS ESSAY (QUESTION 1)

Rows	Rubric Focus	Explanation
Row A 0–1 point	Thesis	You are expected to respond to the prompt in a defensible thesis. Your position must be evident in your thesis. Remember, the synthesis essay is the one where you will establish a claim and from the supplied sources provide apt and sufficient evidence in your defense.
Row B 0–4 points	Evidence and Commentary	You are scored based on several factors: • How many of the supplied sources you cite or reference (and how effectively). • How well you synthesize your selection of evidence. • How apt your choice of evidence is in defense of your thesis • How cohesive your commentary is and how clearly you connect your evidence to your claims.
Row C 0–1 point	Sophistication	In general, *sophistication* means complexity of thought and understanding, but also your ability to express yourself. To earn this point, one *or more* of the following must be apparent in your work: • Nuanced or multifaceted thesis • Argument situated in the broader context of the issue • Effective rhetorical choices • Effective and complex prose style

RHETORICAL ANALYSIS ESSAY (QUESTION 2)

Rows	Rubric Focus	Explanation
Row A 0–1 point	Thesis	You are expected to respond to the prompt with a defensible thesis that analyzes the writer's rhetorical choices.
Row B 0–4 points	Evidence and Commentary	You are scored based on several factors: The number of and quality of your references to the text (these references are your evidence) in defense of your argument. • You provide evidence to support all claims in a line of reasoning. • Your commentary consistently explains how evidence supports a line of reasoning.
Row C 0–1 point	Sophistication	In general, *sophistication* means the complexity of understanding of the rhetorical situation, but also your ability to express yourself. To earn this point, one *or more* of the following must be apparent in your work and be part of your argument: • Explanation of the relevance of the writer's key ideas in a broader context. What are the implications given the rhetorical situation? • Explanation of a purpose or function of the passage's complexities or tensions. • Effective and complex prose style

ARGUMENT ESSAY (QUESTION 3)

Rows	Rubric Focus	Explanation
Row A 0–1 point	Thesis	You are expected to respond to the prompt with a defensible thesis that establishes your line of reasoning (sets up your argument).
Row B 0–4 points	Evidence and Commentary	You are scored based on several factors: Providing sufficient evidence as well as the relevance and quality of your evidence in defense of your argument. • Your commentary is well-developed (not superficial) and clarifies the relationship between your thesis and your evidence. • Your evidence and commentary advance a coherent argument and establish a clear line of reasoning.
Row C 0–1 point	Sophistication	In general, *sophistication* means the complexity of your understanding of the rhetorical situation, but also your ability to express yourself. To earn this point, one *or more* of the following must be apparent in your work and be part of your argument: • Developing a nuanced argument by consistently exploring tensions or complexities. • Articulating the implications or limitations of the argument in the broader context. • Effective rhetorical choices that strengthen your argument. • Vivid and effective prose style.

FURTHER EXPLANATION OF RUBRICS

A. THESIS

You either do or do not earn the thesis point. There is no in-between. Because the thesis point is isolated, you can tell how important it is. Be sure to memorize this little rule: **"respond, don't restate."** Restating the prompt is the lowest level of recognizing your task. Responding means that you have considered the scope of the prompt and you have written a thesis that expresses your own view clearly as well as guides your argument. See more about thesis statements in Chapter 17.

You will earn zero points in this section for the following reasons:

- No defensible thesis

- Thesis summarizes the topic, but does not present a coherent claim.

- The thesis does not respond to the prompt (is off topic completely).

The thesis does not have to sit at the end of the introduction, but that is the most logical place and may be easiest. There is no value in trying to be creative with your thesis placement.

It may seem ironic, but you can earn your thesis point even if you fail to argue as you intend to from that point on. However, if all you have is a good thesis and you fail to provide evidence and commentary, you will likely only score one point overall, which is obviously not what you should aim for.

In the **synthesis essay,** your thesis must express a clear position that you will be able to defend by citing evidence from several of the supplied sources. Take care to not merely reference the topic, but to explicitly state your position.

In the **rhetorical analysis essay,** your thesis should clearly state which of the writer's rhetorical choices you will analyze and it must convey your basic claim as to how and why he or she made those choices, focusing on the effect or function of those choices.

In the **argument essay,** your thesis should reveal that you have taken a position and are not merely riding the pro and con fence. In other words, you need to commit to a defensible stance on an issue. *Defensible* simply means you are able to defend your claim with apt and sufficient evidence—that you are able to prove your claim.

B.   EVIDENCE AND COMMENTARY

This section is scored by how well you met the criteria and points are awarded over a range—from 0–4. Zero represents the absence of the criteria or work so poorly done as to negate credit. A 4 means the opposite, of course.

To earn a high score, no matter which essay you're writing, you must provide well-developed commentary that explains in explicit and coherent terms the relationship between your evidence and your thesis. Evidence can never stand on its own without commentary.

Keep in mind that AP® readers are looking for you to "enter the conversation." This means that, in addition to effectively synthesizing evidence from the supplied sources, you add your own examples and observations. What additional knowledge can you bring to the argument? Students who go to this level are those who earn higher scores.

In addition, it is important to sustain a logical line of reasoning. Creating a mini-outline in the margin of your test document will help you stay focused on your main claims and supporting evidence and avoid straying off topic.

In the **synthesis essay**, using only two of the supplied sources is automatically going to place you in the lower range earning only one point. However, don't think you can earn a higher score by citing all of the sources. That is just as bad. Your ability to select an apt amount of appropriate evidence to prove your claims is what you need to demonstrate.

Even if you cite more than two sources, you can earn a low score if

- your commentary is superficial or somehow incoherent.

- you fail to use commentary (expect the source citation to stand on its own).

- you fail to synthesize (integrate) material from more than one source in specific commentary.

In the **rhetorical analysis essay**, evidence for your claims about a writer's rhetorical choices will come from the provided passage itself. Commentary for this essay is crucial in helping your reader understand your argument. Keep in mind, evidence is not self-explanatory. If you cite a portion of a metaphor, you will have to explain how the metaphor functions. Providing but not explaining evidence will earn you low or no points. *Important:* You will earn a zero if you merely summarize the writer's argument instead of providing an analysis of his or her rhetorical choices.

In the **argument essay**, your commentary must clarify the relationship between your key claims and your evidence. Always remember, commentary makes your thinking transparent.

C. SOPHISTICATION

Here is where skillful writers will shine. While each rubric specifies its own set of criteria for sophistication, the following list is good to remember overall. Pushing yourself to implement one or more of the things in this list, you can ensure that this point is earned, which may offset a weaker performance in evidence and commentary. Instead of considering these aspects of an argument as "add ons," think of them instead as constant indicators of high quality.

1. Nuanced thesis: You do not restate the prompt and your thesis leads readers to consider a unique or complex perspective. In other words, your thesis goes beyond the ordinary. To position yourself to do well here, it is crucial that you are well-read and have an open and engaging mind.

2. Situating or placing your argument in the broader context of the issue means that you consider other ramifications or implications of your argument. Too narrow a focus will blind you to what lies beyond or underneath the obvious. Again, being well-read is an aid to you here. Keep in mind that by offering your own informed insight, you can take an argument beyond a narrow focus. What examples or evidence of your own can you provide?

3. Perhaps the easiest of these "extras" is to acknowledge a counterargument (questions 1 and 3 only). Keep in mind that it will not be enough to simply state the counterargument; you will also be expected to concede, rebut, or refute.

   • In the **synthesis essay**, a counterargument should be readily apparent via one or more of the supplied sources.

   • In the **argument essay**, don't think you have to give more than one side to each of the points you make in your argument, but it might be good to acknowledge, in at least one area of your argument, that a counterargument exists, then concede, rebut, or refute it.

4. How will you establish your skill at making effective rhetorical choices? First, you must understand the rhetorical strategies available to you (see Part II of this book). Then, through practice, it will be easier for you to employ various appeals and strategies.

5. To maintain a consistent line of reasoning, be sure your paragraphs begin with a claim (that directly supports your thesis) and that the evidence you provide for this claim is sufficient. Keep each paragraph unified. Use transitions effectively.

6. Judging sophistication of your prose style may seem unfair, but you were always judged this way. Avoid clumsy syntax and diction, ambiguous or incoherent expression, confusing organization, and casual or imprecise word choice. Instead, remember that you are in control of expressing your thoughts. It's the writer's job to be clear—not the reader's job to guess or interpret what you meant to say.

Does grammar matter? Yes. According to the College Board, "writing that suffers from grammatical and/or mechanical errors that interfere with communication cannot earn the fourth point."

PART V

MASTERING THE MULTIPLE-CHOICE SECTION

General Test-Taking Strategies

*The beginning of knowledge is the discovery of something
we do not understand.*—Frank Herbert

OVERVIEW

You've been taking standardized tests since you were in elementary
school. No one knows more about test-taking than a high school student.
However, this is a high-stakes exam, so it's appropriate to review the skills
and strategies needed to answer multiple-choice questions. Some of what
you find in this chapter will seem familiar, as if you've read it in other
chapters. But these tips bear repeating.

You will want to have these strategies ingrained in your brain. Test
day presents its own stresses. You should not have to worry, for example,
about a guessing strategy. Use this chapter in combination with Chapter
25 to ensure your best possible score for Part One of the exam.

STRATEGIC READING

Strategic reading on exam day means you should read with a pen in
hand, making notes on your scratch paper about key ideas. Be prepared
to use the digital annotation tools in the Bluebook digital testing app.

WHAT TO NOTE/MARK:

- Highlight and link related words. Five words or phrases with a
  sarcastic tone in a passage are worth noting, for example.

- Underline key statements (anything that seems to be significant).

- Any shift in speaker, point of view, tone, or purpose is important to note on scratch paper or by using the exam annotation tools in the Bluebook app. Also comment on what you think is happening because of this shift.

- Isolate and identify thesis, claims, and important evidence.

- If a concession exists, note it.

- Don't forget **ETCEAS**. It's important you grasp the rhetorical situation.

- Write your own questions in the margin, even questions as simple as "Why?" or "What does this mean?" Your questions show you are thinking and may be answered as you read further, which will provide a logical link for you.

- For the writing questions, the texts provided are likely to be drafts, so don't be alarmed if as you read, something seems confusing or incomplete. This is purposeful. The questions engage you in a process of making the draft better.

USE THE QUESTIONS TO SHARPEN YOUR FOCUS

- Regard the questions as sources of information. They may provide insight into the passage and improve your reading comprehension. In other words, the questions themselves could provide hints as to the author's purpose, the speaker's point of view, etc.

- Skimming the questions before you read each text can give you a stronger purpose for reading and will help you know how to annotate as you read.

TIPS ON ANSWERING QUESTIONS

- While it sounds like common sense, be sure to read the questions carefully. Ascertain what a question is asking for. Cursory reading leads to careless errors. See Chapter 25 for an analysis of what may be asked.

- As a matter of procedure, cross out answers that you know right away are wrong. If you automatically do this, you are not adding extra work, and you are likely to achieve a higher level of accuracy.

- For the "EXCEPT" questions, it may work to circle similar answers, crossing out the one that doesn't belong. That is then your correct answer.

- If you really don't know the answer but can eliminate two or more answers, taking a 50–50 guess might be better than skipping the question. Points are not deducted for wrong answers. Your score for Part One is based only on what you answer correctly. Making an educated guess is still a good strategy.

- Many of the really tough questions provide two similar answers that you think are correct. In this case, you must choose *the most correct* answer. "Most correct" means the answer is more precise or more detailed. If another answer is only "sort of" right, then that is most likely not the one to choose.

- Don't overthink a question. Some questions are really, really easy. Most students think they couldn't possibly put such an easy question on the exam, so they overthink it and get it wrong.

- If the question asks you to analyze ironic elements, the statement in the answer will reveal the irony. In other words, the answer itself will sound ironic.

- Many questions are going to require a *rereading* of lines or paragraphs from the text. **Do not skip this step.** Your notes and markings of the text should help you navigate quickly as you reread.

PRACTICE FOR REAL

Find sample questions in Chapter 26 of this book. Work carefully through this practice exercise using the tips above.

When you finish, analyze your results. Look back at your answers and ask yourself two questions:

1. Why did I get it wrong?

2. Why did I get it right?

It is as important to figure out what you understood as what you did not. Your careful analysis of your results is as important to your learning as actually taking the practice test.

A full-length practice exam accompanies this book. Go to *www.rea.com/studycenter* for access to the exam.

Types of Questions
in the Multiple-Choice Section

You must train your intuition—you must trust the small voice inside you which tells you exactly what to say, what to decide.—Ingrid Bergman

OVERVIEW

The following information comes from an analysis of the latest instructional goals set out by the College Board. You will be presented with a total of 45 questions in the 60-minute multiple-choice section. You will have five selected texts to read. (See Chapter 1 for this breakdown.)

Approximately one-half of the 45 multiple-choice questions will ask you to think like a reader and answer analytically about writers' rhetorical choices and the function and effect of those choices in the text. You will still need to base your inferences and conclusions on specific aspects of the text, but you will be guided to relative sections and phrases with line numbers.

The remaining questions will ask you to think like a writer to determine the most effective stylistic or rhetorical approach. In other words, these questions will ask you to decide which of four composition strategies will work best for a particular effect. The writing questions require more reading, as each answer choice can be lengthy.

In all, the exam will test your knowledge and skill on the four Big Ideas: (1) rhetorical situation, (2) claims and evidence, (3) reasoning and organization, and (4) style. See Chapter 1 for more details and exam weights of each of these ideas.

Additionally, you will no longer be expected to simply identify or determine the meaning of rhetorical terms or strategies. This is because you are expected to possess a functional knowledge of such terms and strategies prior to exam day.

BASIC QUESTION TYPES

1. **Reading Questions**: As a reader, you'll analyze rhetorical choices and aspects of an argument in a given text.

2. **Writing Questions**: From a writer's perspective, choose the most effective composition strategies.

3. **Double Answers:** Answer choices are given in pairs, such as "civil but angry" or "genial yet self-interested." Often the pairs contain one element that cannot be correct. Tip: If one part of a double answer is wrong, the entire thing is wrong.

4. **All of the following EXCEPT. . .** Be sure to recognize this type of question and carefully consider which answer is *not* like the others.

MULTIPLE-CHOICE QUESTION FOCUS AREAS

The list below includes some of the most frequent tasks and skills entailed with the exam's multiple-choice questions.

BASIC QUESTION STEMS:

What is the effect of. . . ?

How does ___ function. . . ?

Why (or How) does the writer. . . ?

How do ___ contribute to. . . ?

Which choice best exemplifies. . . ?

How does the writer use. . . ?

How does the argument. . . ?

What is the relationship between. . . ?

Which of the following best restates the author's purpose?

RHETORICAL SITUATION (READING):

1. Determine the message, audience, purpose, or context.

2. Decide what provoked or inspired the writer.

3. How do the writer's rhetorical choices in the introduction and conclusion reveal his or her purpose?

4. How do the writer's rhetorical choices show his or her awareness of the audience's values, beliefs, or needs?

5. How does the writer's choice in diction and syntax engage the audience and/or advance the argument?

6. How does the writer's word choice affect his or her ethos or reveal a bias? To what extent might such choices impact the effect of the argument?

RHETORICAL SITUATION (WRITING):

1. What rhetorical choices should be made to improve the introduction or conclusion in order to better engage the audience?

2. What word choices should be made to bolster a writer's credibility with an audience?

3. What revisions should be made to eliminate bias?

CLAIMS AND EVIDENCE (READING):

1. How does the writer's selection of evidence advance his or her purpose?

2. How does the writer acknowledge another's ideas (cite the source of information)?

3. How does the author acknowledge a counterargument?

CLAIMS AND EVIDENCE (WRITING):

1. How can the writer effectively establish a claim?

2. What is the most effective use of evidence?

3. What is the function of a particular type of evidence?

4. How might the thesis be revised once new evidence is revealed?

5. How might specific words, phrases, or clauses modify or qualify a claim?

6. What best strategy is used to concede, rebut, or refute a counterargument? How might such a strategy limit or undermine your argument?

REASONING AND ORGANIZATION (READING):

1. How does the writer's commentary link the evidence to his or her thesis or subordinate claims (or establish a logical relationship)?

2. How does the sequence of paragraphs reveal the line of reasoning?

3. What is the effect of a particular method of organization or pattern of exposition?

4. What is the effect of the writer's appeals?

REASONING AND ORGANIZATION (WRITING):

1. Determine a more logical order or organization.

2. Suggest a more effective transition.

3. Determine how or why the argument requires additional evidence or examples?

4. What clauses or phrases could be added, reordered, or removed to improve coherence?

6. Which rhetorical mode is best suited for the writer's purpose?

STYLE (READING):

1. How effective is the writer's word choice (connotation and denotation) in the rhetorical situation?

2. How does the writer's syntax contribute to his or her style?

3. What is the effect of the writer's tone? Irony? Satire?

4. What is the value of any stylistic choice in complementing or enhancing the writer's purpose?

5. How does the arrangement of words and ideas in clauses and phrases affect the tone, purpose, or other aspect of the text?

STYLE (WRITING):

1. Which word choices will improve clarity or reduce confusion in the text?

2. What is the best arrangement of sentences in a text to emphasize ideas?

3. Which sentence construction best communicates a key idea?

Practice Multiple-Choice Questions

In May, when you take your actual exam, you will have five passages to read and 45 questions to answer in 60 minutes. Each question will present four answer choices. As stated earlier, there are two major types of questions: questions that ask you to consider a passage from the perspective of a reader and questions that ask you to consider a passage from the perspective of a writer. This chapter provides you with practice in both areas.

For a complete experience, visit the REA Study Center (*www.rea.com/ studycenter*) to access a timed, full-length practice exam.

READING: QUESTIONS 1–16

Read the following excerpt from "Night and Moonlight" by Henry David Thoreau. Then use it to answer questions 1–9.

I complain of Arctic voyagers that they do not enough remind us of the constant peculiar dreariness of the scenery, and the perpetual twilight of the Arctic night. So he whose theme is moonlight, though he may find it difficult, must, as it were, illustrate it with the light of the moon alone.

5 Many men walk by day; few walk by night. It is a very different season. Take a July night, for instance. About ten o'clock—when man is asleep, and day fairly forgotten—the beauty of moonlight is seen over lonely pastures where cattle are silently feeding. On all sides novelties present themselves. Instead of the sun there are the moon and stars, instead of the wood-
10 thrush there is the whip-poor-will—instead of butterflies in the meadows, fire-flies, winged sparks of fire! Who would have believed it? What kind of cool deliberate life dwells in those dewy abodes associated with a spark of fire? So man has fire in his eyes, or blood, or brain. Instead of singing birds,

the half-throttled note of a cuckoo flying over, the croaking of frogs, and
15 the intenser dream of crickets. But above all, the wonderful trump of the
bullfrog, ringing from Maine to Georgia. The potato-vines stand upright,
the corn grows apace, the bushes loom, the grain-fields are boundless.
On our open river terraces once cultivated by the Indian, they appear to
occupy the ground like an army—their heads nodding in the breeze. Small
20 trees and shrubs are seen in the midst overwhelmed as by an inundation.
The shadows of rocks and trees, and shrubs and hills, are more conspicuous
than the objects themselves. The slightest irregularities in the ground are
revealed by the shadows, and what the feet find comparatively smooth
appears rough and diversified in consequence. For the same reason the
25 whole landscape is more variegated and picturesque than by day. The
smallest recesses in the rocks are dim and cavernous; the ferns in the wood
appear of tropical size. The sweet fern and indigo in overgrown wood-
paths wet you with dew up to your middle. The leaves of the shrub-oak
are shining as if a liquid were flowing over them. The pools seen through
30 the trees are as full of light as the sky. "The light of the day takes refuge in
their bosoms," as the Purana says of the ocean. All white objects are more
remarkable than by day. A distant cliff looks like a phosphorescent space
on a hillside. The woods are heavy and dark. Nature slumbers. You see the
moonlight reflected from particular stumps in the recesses of the forest, as
35 if she selected what to shine on. These small fractions of her light remind
one of the plant called moon-seed—as if the moon were sowing it in such
places. . . .

It does not concern men who are asleep in their beds, but it is
very important to the traveler, whether the moon shines brightly or is
40 obscured. It is not easy to realize the serene joy of all the earth, when she
commences to shine unobstructedly, unless you have often been abroad
alone in moonlight nights. She seems to be waging continual war with
the clouds in your behalf. Yet we fancy the clouds to be her foes also. She
comes on magnifying her dangers by her light, revealing, displaying them
45 in all their hugeness and blackness, then suddenly casts them behind into
the light concealed, and goes her way triumphant through a small space
of clear sky.

1. What rhetorical task does the author set for himself in the first paragraph?

   (A) To list and analyze all the facts he knows about the moon

   (B) To present the theme of moonlight by describing the effects of moonlight at night

   (C) To compare the dreariness of an Arctic night to a moonlit night in a forest

   (D) To walk through an unfamiliar landscape at night guided only by the moonlight

2. In line 8, the word "novelties" refers to

   (A) the moon and stars

   (B) tricks of the light

   (C) birds and animals that look like toys

   (D) wonders rarely seen

3. Which of the following best conveys the main idea in lines 21–28?

   (A) The moonlight reduces every feature of the landscape to a rough and shadowy sameness.

   (B) The landscape is easier to negotiate in the moonlight than by day.

   (C) Shadows take on frightening shapes in the moonlight.

   (D) The moonlight serves to exaggerate the features of the landscape.

4. The details Thoreau presents in lines 25–30 function as examples or illustrations for which of the following statements?

   (A) "On all sides novelties present themselves" (line 8)

   (B) "But above all, the wonderful trump of the bullfrog, ringing from Maine to Georgia" (lines 15–16)

   (C) "On our open river terraces once cultivated by the Indian" (line 18)

   (D) "The slightest irregularities in the ground are revealed by the shadows" (lines 23–24)

5. Evidence for a claim that Thoreau has personified the moon can be found in

   (A) lines 7–8

   (B) lines 9–11

   (C) lines 21–24

   (D) lines 34–35

6. Thoreau's rhetorical purpose in lines 21–28 is accomplished through

   (A) analogy

   (B) anecdote

   (C) exemplification

   (D) allusion

7. What is the function of the quoted material from the Purana (lines 30–31)?

    (A) To add credibility to the author's claim in the previous sentence

    (B) To deepen the overall argument by use of a biblical allusion

    (C) To expand the argument by including facts about the ocean

    (D) To illustrate that ancient poets also considered natural subjects

8. Which of the following best describes the author's exigence in this passage?

    (A) Recognition of the dangers of exploring the effects of the moon at night

    (B) Concern over the desire to awaken his fellows to the marvels of the world at night

    (C) The need for citizens to protect nocturnal species

    (D) Concern over the fact that most explorers, particularly arctic explorers, fail to describe landscapes sufficiently

9. The style of the passage as a whole is most accurately characterized as

    (A) clever and satirical

    (B) disjointed and querulous

    (C) lyrical and descriptive

    (D) complex and scholarly

Read the following speech delivered by President Kennedy before the American Society of Newspaper Editors in Washington, D.C., April 20, 1961. Then use it to answer questions 10–16.

The President of a great democracy such as ours, and the editors of great newspapers such as yours, owe a common obligation to the people: an obligation to present the facts, to present them with candor, and to present them in perspective. It is with that obligation in mind
5   that I have decided in the last 24 hours to discuss briefly at this time the recent events in Cuba. On that unhappy island, as in so many other areas of the contest for freedom, the news has grown worse instead of better. I have emphasized before that this was a struggle of Cuban patriots against a Cuban dictator. While we could not be expected to
10 lend our sympathies, we made it repeatedly clear that the armed forces of this country would not intervene in any way. It is not the first time that Communist tanks have rolled over gallant men and women fighting to redeem the independence of their homeland. Nor is it by any means the final episode in the eternal struggle of liberty against tyranny, anywhere
15 on the face of the globe, including Cuba itself. Mr. Castro has said that these were mercenaries.[1] According to press reports, the final message to be relayed from the refugee forces on the beach came from the rebel commander when asked if he wished to be evacuated. His answer was: "I will never leave this country." That is not the reply of a mercenary. The
20 Cuban people have not yet spoken their final piece, and I have no doubt that they and their Revolutionary Council, led by Dr. Míro Cardona and members of the families of the Revolutionary Council, I am informed by the Doctor yesterday, are involved themselves in the islands—will continue to speak up for a free and independent Cuba. Meanwhile we
25 will not accept Mr. Castro's attempts to blame this Nation for the hatred with which his onetime supporters now regard his repression. But there are from this sobering episode useful lessons for all to learn. Some may be still obscure and await further information. Some are clear today. First, it is clear that the forces of communism are not to be underestimated; in
30 Cuba or anywhere else in the world. The advantages of a police state—its use of mass terror and arrests to prevent the spread of free dissent—cannot be overlooked by those who expect the fall of every fanatic tyrant. Secondly, it is clear that this Nation, in concert with all the free nations of this hemisphere, must take an even closer and more realistic look at the
35 menace of external Communist intervention and domination in Cuba. The American people are not complacent about Iron Curtain tanks and

---

[1] A mercenary is a soldier who is paid to fight.

planes less than 90 miles from our shores. The evidence is clear—and
the hour is late. We and our Latin friends will have to face the fact that
we cannot postpone any longer the real issue of the survival of freedom

40   in the hemisphere itself. Third, and finally, it is clearer than ever that
we face a relentless struggle in every corner of the globe that goes far
beyond the clash of armies or even nuclear armaments. The armies are
there, and in large number. The nuclear armaments are there. But they
serve primarily as the shield behind which subversion, infiltration, and a

45   host of other tactics steadily advance, picking off vulnerable areas one
by one in situations which do not permit our own armed intervention.
Power is the hallmark of this offensive—power and discipline and deceit.
The legitimate discontent of yearning peoples is exploited. The legitimate
trappings of self-determination are employed. But once in power, all

50   talk of discontent is repressed—all self-determination disappears—and
the promise of a revolution of hope is betrayed, as in Cuba, into a reign
of terror. The message of Cuba, of Laos, of the rising din of Communist
voices in Asia and Latin America—these messages are all the same. The
complacent, the self-indulgent, the soft societies are about to be swept

55   away with the debris of history. Only the strong, only the industrious, only
the determined, only the courageous, only the visionary who determine
the real nature of our struggle can possibly survive.

10. Which of the following is the best restatement of the speaker's main
    idea in lines 4–9?

    (A) The people of Cuba are so unhappy that we cannot help but feel
        sympathetic.

    (B) We owe the patriots in Cuba the advantage of our military
        intervention.

    (C) Cuba isn't the only place in the world where people yearn for
        freedom.

    (D) It is up to the press as well as the president to present the facts
        about the Cuban threat to the American people.

11. What is the primary rhetorical function of the quotation in line 19?

   (A) To suggest the rebel commander will not be a good faith negotiator for peace

   (B) To underscore Kennedy's rebuttal of Castro's claim that his enemies are mercenaries

   (C) To provide an emotional appeal to a Cuban-American audience

   (D) To concede to Castro's assertion that his enemies are only paid puppets

12. All of the following accentuate the urgent tone of Kennedy's speech EXCEPT

   (A) "owe a common obligation to the people: an obligation to present the facts, to present them with candor, and to present them in perspective" (lines 2–4)

   (B) "forces of Communism are not to be underestimated" (line 29)

   (C) "menace of external Communist intervention and domination" (line 35)

   (D) "Iron Curtain tanks and planes less than 90 miles from our shores" (lines 36–37)

13. Which of the following supports Kennedy's assertion that Castro has exploited the "legitimate discontent of yearning peoples"? (line 48)

   (A) Stating that Castro is "picking off vulnerable areas one by one" (line 45)

   (B) Pointing out that Castro has "nuclear armaments" (line 43)

   (C) Alluding to Castro's earlier "promise of a revolution of hope" (line 51)

   (D) Calling Castro's regime a "reign of terror" (line 51)

14. Which of the following appeals is not apparent in this speech?

    (A) Appeal to reason

    (B) Appeal to tradition

    (C) Appeal to fear

    (D) Appeal to caution

15. How does Kennedy characterize dictators in general?

    (A) As terrorists

    (B) As revolutionaries

    (C) As visionaries

    (D) As mercenaries

16. Which of the following best expresses Kennedy's primary purpose in this speech?

    (A) Make clear to the press that they have an equal obligation to fight the threat of Communism.

    (B) Urge the press to warn the public about Castro's threat.

    (C) Make sure the press is fully aware of how dangerous Castro is.

    (D) Explain to Cuban citizens that Castro is a threat to their self-determination.

WRITING: QUESTIONS 17–25

The following is a draft of an essay written (as you would see for Question 3) in response to the prompt that follows. Read the prompt and the essay. Then, thinking as a writer looking to improve a draft, answer questions 17–25.

Everyone, it seems, has a mobile phone. Such devices connect us with others in an instant and can reassure us that help is not far away in an emergency. Just as quickly, we can use our phones to photograph special moments and share them as well as our impressions of life in general with friends and family through social media. And yet, some would argue that such ubiquitous access to cell phone technology is not benign.

In a well-organized essay, argue your own position about the relative benefits of always having a cellphone with us.

(1) Just as the world will never return to the horse-and-buggy days, so will there be no going back to a single corded telephone per household. (2) When your grandmother texts you a popular gif, you know the world has fully adapted to instant, digital communication. (3) However, as we are now learning, the overuse of cellphones causes harmful effects: physically, socially, and mentally. (4) Apple has confirmed that a select group of employees "listen" to what Siri hears in order to improve their AI's ability to comprehend and respond to human language. (5) Implementing laws that restrict mobile phone use (and other handheld internet devices) to people age 18 and older may reduce instances of depression, anxiety, and physical harm due to accidents involving distraction.

(6) It's one thing to be quietly texting; it's quite another to talk out loud. (7) The problem isn't just the noise, though overhearing someone else's private conversation can be awkward. (8) The problem is that a person on the phone has become oblivious to his or her surroundings, and as a result, fails to take into account the needs and feelings of those around them.

(9) Socially, we are more disconnected than ever. (10) A group of friends who gathers and texts each other instead of talking face to face is losing the ability to converse. (11) And it's not just that. (12) It

seems people are finding it harder than ever to put their phone aside for a moment just to engage with another person, whether it's a child answering a parent's question or a classroom of students tuning out of a presentation. (13) When a person you're with is drawn into their phone, they may as well be a hundred miles away. (14) Just try getting their attention to prove the point.

(15) A phone is a portal to an online world where we look to others—sometimes our real friends, but often people we've never met—to affirm our feelings. (16) Others "like" our post or add a smiley emoji to a photo we've shared. (17) These positive digital engagements produce dopamine—our feel-good brain chemical, and the more we get, the more we want, so we go back to our phones, often to the point of being addicted. (18) While not everyone's phone use is at the point of addiction, reports say that people who are forced to give up their phones (even temporarily) feel increased levels of stress and anxiety.

(19) There are also physical detriments. (20) Holding a phone and operating it with one hand can cause damage to the structure of the thumb and ligaments. (21) Those who continually look down at their phone are developing humps at the base of the neck, due to a change to the cervical spine. (22) Even worse is the potential and irreversible harm blue light causes the eyes. (23) Still, none of these effects are fatal. (24) Government statistics report that "distracted walking" accidents outnumber distracted driving accidents.

(25) Social isolation also occurs due to the wide variety of media we consume. (26) Whereas in the past we could talk with each other about our one or two favorite television shows because we were all limited by the same choices, today our media consumption is almost as individual as we are. (27) It takes a "viral" media event to link us together. (28) Even then, social media memes or binge-watched shows are blips in time and have a limited impact on bringing us together.

(29) The group most at risk for harmful effects is children. (30) While it would be best to deny children under a certain age their own phones, if parents feel a phone is a necessity for their child, then screen time limits should be implemented. (31) Going further, for the betterment of all, some places should be designated device-free areas or limited-use areas: restaurants, museums, and other public places; public transportation

(silent use only), the car (hands-free only), school classrooms (except as educational tools), playgrounds and other recreational venues. (32) And in the home, the dinner table and the bedroom. (33) To show we care, we should put our phones away in any place where it is logical or desirable to place one's attention on those you're with at the moment instead of those connected through bytes.

(34) We can benefit tremendously from using our cellphones—satellite messages bounce to us in seconds, and we can ask Siri or Alexa to send us an ambulance, order us a pizza, or simply answer our nagging trivia questions. (35) But what they cannot do is look into our faces and see that we need them. (36) They cannot hear in our voices the fact that we've had a bad day and just need to talk. (37) Only another person can do that.

17. Of the following statements regarding Sentence 4, which one is INCORRECT?

   (A) It is a statement of verifiable evidence.

   (B) It would be best used as evidence in a paragraph on loss of privacy.

   (C) The sentence is not logically connected to the introduction and should be removed.

   (D) The sentence is too controversial to be included in any thoughtful argument.

18. If placed before Sentence 6, which of the following statements would provide a smoother and more logical transition to Paragraph 2?

    (A) Furthermore, using a phone in public is no more annoying than other public noise, such as traffic.

    (B) Anyone who has ever been annoyed by another's loud phone conversation in a public place has probably wished there were a law against using a cellphone in public.

    (C) While there's no law against using a cellphone in public, it would be a law that some would welcome.

    (D) My main point in this paragraph is that cellphone use makes users unaware of their surroundings.

19. In Sentence 3, reproduced below, which is a better wording of the underlined section?

    However, as we are now learning, the overuse of cellphones causes harmful effects: physically, socially, and mentally.

    (A) causes physical, social, and mental harm.

    (B) causes a myriad of problems.

    (C) causes a lot of effects: both physical as well as mental.

    (D) causes people to suffer needless harm.

20. Paragraph 6 (beginning at Sentence 25 with "Social isolation also occurs") would be more effective at developing the established line of reasoning if it were

    (A) placed after the introduction

    (B) placed after Paragraph 3

    (C) placed after Paragraph 4

    (D) removed entirely

21. The following sentence, reproduced below, would improve the coherence and logical progression of the argument if placed after which of the following in Paragraph 5 (beginning with Sentence 19)?

    > Walking into traffic or driving across the center line because you've been responding to a text or social media post can be deadly to oneself or others.

    (A) It is best placed after Sentence 23 as an illustration of the point.

    (B) It would work best as the main claim of the paragraph and should go first.

    (C) This sentence would work equally well at the beginning or the end.

    (D) The sentence serves no purpose and should not be added.

22. Which of the following edits would best improve the logical coherence of Paragraph 7 (sentences 29–33)?

    (A) Delete sentences 29 and 30.

    (B) Combine sentences 29 and 30.

    (C) Eliminate the examples given in Sentence 31.

    (D) Add a sentence at the end to tie back into the claim made in Sentence 29.

23. Which of the following is the best revision of the underlined section of Sentence 35, reproduced below, in order to remove the ambiguous pronoun they?

    > But what they cannot do is look into our faces and see that we need them.

    (A) But what our phones cannot do. . . .

    (B) But what technology cannot do. . . .

    (C) But what Siri and Alexa cannot do. . . .

    (D) But what was missing even in the old phones was the ability to. . . .

24. Which of the following is the best replacement for Sentence 19 (reproduced below) to reduce ambiguity, but also to create a more effective transition to the topic explored in Paragraph 5?

    "There are also physical detriments."

    (A) Stress and anxiety are just two examples.

    (B) There are also harmful physical detriments.

    (C) Harmful physical effects have also been tied to excessive cellphone use.

    (D) Some effects of excessive cellphone use can be fatal.

25. Which of the following is a more effective thesis for this argument (replacing Sentence 5)?

    (A) While it is unlikely any laws would be passed to prohibit cellphone use among minors, parents should implement common sense rules to ensure no harm comes to their children.

    (B) As a society, we need to accept and adhere to common sense rules to minimize the negative effects of cellphone use.

    (C) Cellphones should never have been invented they're just causing us to be less and less engaged with each other.

    (D) The old days were far simpler times and we would be better off if we returned to less technology-driven ways of life.

ANSWERS TO PRACTICE QUESTIONS

1. (B)

    The author "complains" at the beginning of the passage about Arctic voyagers who do not focus enough on the "peculiar dreariness" of the Arctic landscape. He then declares that "he whose theme is moonlight"—i.e., himself—must show that theme "with the light of the moon alone." The author then proceeds to "present the theme of moonlight" by describing in detail a moonlit July night. Answer choice (B) is correct. The author doesn't list all the facts he knows about the moon (A), and he is not comparing an Arctic night to a moonlit night in a forest (C). He does seem to be walking through a strange landscape at night guided only by moonlight, but this is not the task related to the ideas in the first paragraph (D).

2. (D)

    The author says, "On all sides novelties present themselves," referring to the different sights a person walking on a moonlit night might see. He then describes some of the unusual things—"wonders rarely seen" (D). These wonders include, but are not limited to, the moon and the stars (A) and tricks of the moonlight (B). He does not compare birds and animals to toys (C).

3. (D)

    The author shows that the shadows of things in the moonlight "are more conspicuous than the objects themselves," and that the smooth ground "appears rough and diversified." The whole landscape looks different, and the "smallest recesses in rocks are dim and cavernous," and thus exaggerated in size and effect. So answer choice (D) is correct. The moonlight does the opposite of reducing features to a sameness (A). With the exaggerated shadows, the landscape is probably harder, not easier, to negotiate at night (B). The idea is not that the shadowy shapes are frightening (C).

4. (D)

    The correct answer is choice (D). Lines 25 through 30 provide details that show exaggerated or incongruous detail: The smallest are cavernous, the ferns are tropical in size, the plants wet the walker up to his middle, and pools are said to contain the light of the sky, none of which seem slight, but magnified, and are therefore "irregular." Although lines 25–30 detail "novelties," the examples in those lines function as more than a simple list, so the statement in answer choice (A) is less specific than the correct answer (D). Answer choice (B) is incorrect because that line presents details unrelated to the cited passage. In line 18, Thoreau presents a factual detail by recognizing the land he now observes was once farmed by Indigenous people (C), but the details in lines 25–30 are not examples of this.

5. (D)

The author simply describes the moonlight as beautiful in lines 7–8 (A). In lines 9–11 (B), the author mentions the moon, but only as a factual aspect of night. In lines 21–24 (C), Thoreau describes the shadows, which are caused by the moonlight, but nothing indicates the moon willfully directs the shadows. The correct answer is (D). The phrase "as if she selected" indicates a human trait, the ability to choose.

6. (C)

Thoreau's purpose in this section is to show how the moonlight reveals even "the slightest irregularities" in the night's landscape. He offers several supporting examples. Answer choice (C) is thus correct. There is no little story or anecdote (B) nor comparative situation or analogy (A). An allusion would require a reference to mythology or other literary or cultural comparison, so (D) is incorrect.

7. (A)

The reference in line 30–31 is to ancient Sanskrit texts, not the Bible (B). The language is figurative, but Thoreau is not concerned with the exigencies of ancient poets (D). The quote does not cite any scientific facts (C). The correct answer is (A). The author's ability to draw on ancient texts to illustrate his claim in the previous sentence deepens his credibility. We are more likely to believe claims with rich, broad-based support.

8. (B)

Nowhere in the passage does the author describe hazards or things to fear (A). While some nocturnal species are mentioned, the writer is not compelled to advocate for their care (C). Although Thoreau refers to his complaint that northern voyagers do not remind him enough of the peculiarities of the "perpetual twilight of the Arctic night," the passage mentions no other explorers or similar failures (D). The correct answer is

(B). While he does not state explicitly that he wishes others could observe what he observed, the reverent tone with which Thoreau reveals what he has witnessed implies that the landscape at night is worthy of everyone's notice.

9. (C)

The author employs many lyrical, or poetic, images and comparisons in his portrayal of a moonlit night: "You see the moonlight reflected from particular stumps in the recesses of the forest, as if she selected what to shine on. These small fractions of her light remind one of the plant called moon-seed—as if the moon were sowing it in such places." He also provides such descriptive details as "The potato-vines stand upright, the corn grows apace, the bushes loom, the grain-fields are boundless." Answer choice (C) is correct.

10. (D)

Although Kennedy sympathizes with the Cuban people (A), his speech goes far beyond Castro's effect on Cuban citizens. He refers to tyrannical threats elsewhere (C), but only to underscore the seriousness of the current situation. Kennedy clearly states there can be no military intervention (B). The main point is contained in choice (D): The president as well as the press have "a common obligation" to tell the true story of the communist threat in Cuba.

11. (B)

In line 15, Kennedy presents Castro's claim. Then he provides commentary to set up his evidence (the quotation) in the next lines. Lastly, he clarifies through commentary the validity of his evidence by saying, "That is not the reply of a mercenary." No evidence supports the other answers.

12. (A)

Answer choice (A) is correct because it represents a worthy goal for all time, not only for the current critical moment. In that line, Kennedy reminds his audience of their shared responsibility. The remaining answers, particularly choice (D), add to the urgent tone.

13. (C)

Kennedy suggests that by giving people hope, he gains their trust (C), which he later exploits for his own political goals. The other choices reveal a general or specific threat from a communist regime, but they do not suggest exploitation.

14. (D)

Appeal to caution (D) is not technically a rhetorical claim. Further, Kennedy does the opposite by telling newspaper editors that the situation in Cuba is urgent and dire. He does so by using solid logic (A) throughout, by reminding his audience in the opening lines of America's long-standing tradition (B) to present the truth, but is most effective in relaying the real and present danger so close to our southern shores (C).

15. (A)

Choice (A) is correct. In lines 30–31, Kennedy says dictators turn their countries into police states and use "mass terror and arrests to prevent the spread of free dissent." Further in line 51, Kennedy calls the Cuban dictator's government "a reign of terror." No evidence supports the other choices.

16. (A)

In this speech, Kennedy goes beyond mere information (C). Cuban citizens (D) are not the immediate audience for this speech and would likely not have had access to it. Kennedy acknowledges the press as a partner in the fight against communism, even saying they share a "common obligation" (A), and he does provide a clear warning (B). So the correct answer is (A).

17. (D)

The only answer choice that does not fit is (D) because it contains a specious claim. All thoughtful arguments are valid. Controversy is not a disqualifying aspect of any argument. The evidence can indeed be verified (A). Sentence 4 does not support introductory statements or claims made in the body of this essay, so it should be removed (C). However, if the writer had included a paragraph about loss of privacy, this sentence would work well there (B).

18. (B)

Answer choice (B) is correct because it sets up the context needed to understand Sentence 6. Although (A) might be true, it is not connected logically to the following paragraph about how cellphone users become disengaged with their surroundings. Even if the writer had provided evidence for the claim in answer choice (C), it is logically intangible. The direct, first-person strategy used in answer choice (D) also would never be acceptable in an AP®-level essay. If a writer has to tell readers what the main point is, the main point is likely not coherent otherwise.

19. (A)

"Physically, socially, and mentally" are adverbs that would be used to modify a verb, such as "overuse." Adjectives are needed instead to modify the noun "effects." But then the construction would be awkward. The best revision is (A), which states the main aspects of the claim in simple, direct language. Answer choice (B) is too vague. Answer choice (C) ignores social effects, which the writer addresses in depth in the essay. Answer choice (D) is also too vague and makes an unhelpful value judgment by injecting the notion of needless suffering.

20. (B)

Though not the strongest paragraph in the essay, Paragraph 6 still has value, and answer choice (D) is thus incorrect. The content of Paragraph 6 aligns best with paragraphs 3 and 4, but works best of all after Paragraph 3 (B) because it links to the last two sentences in Paragraph 3. Paragraph 4 provides a logical transition to Paragraph 5, so you wouldn't want to interrupt the line of reasoning by placing it after Paragraph 4 (C). Moving the paragraph after the introduction would make no logical sense (A).

21. (A)

The sentence is clearly an illustrative example of the point that some effects can be fatal. Sentence 23 is a transition to the example, and Sentence 24 provides evidence for the example. No other placement option is logical.

22. (A)

Answer choice (A) is correct. The desire for device-free or limited-use areas is the main idea in this paragraph, and the first two sentences are unrelated, so they should be deleted. Combining sentences 29 and 30 (B) does not solve the problem, nor does making a further reference to sentences 29 and 30 (D). Eliminating examples in Sentence 31 (C) would weaken the argument.

23. (A)

The correct answer is (A), because "phones" is the specific topic of the piece, not the more general "technology" (B). "Siri" and "Alexa" (C) are even narrower references and would not clarify the writer's intention. "Old phones" (D) is off-topic.

24. (C)

Although answer choice (A) links to the previous paragraph, it begs the question, "examples of what," and is still vague. By itself, answer choice (A) also does not set up the topic of the paragraph. By adding the adjective "harmful," choice (B) has a more urgent tone, but that addition does not create a stronger transition. Choice (D) doesn't work because the paragraph is not just about fatal effects. Choicer (C) is correct. It states the topic clearly and uses the simple word "also" as a linking transition.

25. (B)

The essay never supports an argument about the need to enact laws, so answer choice (A) is incorrect. The writer engages readers by referring to the past in the first sentence, the reference only shows how far removed we are from pre-high-tech days. There is no claim that we should return, so answer choice (D) is incorrect. Choice (C) is incorrect because the assertion is logically unsound. Cellphones have been invented, and it gains nothing to argue they shouldn't have been. Only answer choice (B) is correct. The statement contained in this response tells readers there are problems, which will be addressed in the essay, and that "common-sense rules," which the writer later lists, will help "minimize the negative effects."

Reiteration: Advice Worth Restating

Chapter

27

The purpose of this section is to summarize some of the best advice I can leave with you. Most of these points you have already read in this book, but sometimes what we read last we remember best. The starred items (★) refer to reminders for the exam itself.

RHETORICAL READING

Prepare for your exam by reading complex texts from various writers and perspectives. Challenge yourself with pre-20th-century texts. There will always be several such texts on the exam. These older texts typically feature more difficult syntax and vocabulary. If you are jumping into this challenge at the last minute, find the Essential Reading list in Chapter 4. While it is best to read more than what is on that list, if you literally do not have time for more, those texts are excellent "last-minute" choices.

★ Do not skip over introductions to any selection given in the exam. Introductory material, as well as footnotes, are added purposefully and often provide important comprehension clues.

★ Do not forget to annotate. By making even just a few quick notes to underscore key points and the author's strategies, you'll make your analysis task easier. Annotating also helps you stay focused on the text, which will help you block out any distractions in the room.

Consider that everything you read is an argument in one way or another. As you "read" your world, consider the following for each genre you encounter: audience, author's purpose (main point), and the rhetorical tools/strategies he or she uses to create the effect.

RHETORICAL ANALYSIS

★ An analysis is not a listing of rhetorical elements or strategies, but requires students to describe how the writer's rhetorical tools accomplish his or her overall purpose and/or how or why the writer chose them.

Bolster your ability to develop your analysis by improving your vocabulary—and not just general vocabulary. For this exam it is crucial that you have a working knowledge of terms one uses to write about effective rhetoric. Review Chapter 5, as well as all key terms found throughout this book.

★ All the texts you encounter were created within a context: historical as well as cultural. Do not make the mistake of layering your own culture and history over the text and expect it to conform. The more you read, the more you will improve your ability to comprehend diverse perspectives.

WRITING PERSUASIVELY

★ AP® readers are looking for students to construct clear, rhetorically valid arguments that support an assertion. Evidence in support should be detailed, specific, and convincing.

★ Avoid broad generalized conclusions. Words like *all, none, always, never,* or other absolute terms are typically not effective.

★ Any example (or citation of evidence) in your argument is not automatically self-evident. You must always provide an explanation that shows "why" or "how." When necessary, provide context for references an older audience (an AP® reader for example) may be unfamiliar with.

★ Don't forget to synthesize evidence for the synthesis essay. In the simplest terms, this means to use evidence from more than one source as you argue a claim.

GENERAL REMINDERS

★ Take enough time to read and understand the expectations of a prompt. You will always be given explicit or implicit guidance in the prompt. If you veer from the expectations set forth in the prompt, you risk writing an essay considered "off topic," which would rarely score higher than a 1.

In many ways, since the AP® English Language and Composition exam is a test of one's ability to think, it is by default a test of your ability to use (or at least regard as valuable) everything you learn in every class in school. In math, you learn to read and infer the consequence of data presented in graphs. That's a perfect skill necessary in the synthesis prompt. In your civics or social studies classes, you learn about world events and leaders of consequence. Often, such people will be featured in passages on the AP® English Language exam.

Your ability to draw on all your school and other learning experiences and to see your education as one integrated experience is at the heart of your ability to do well on this exam. This exam does not test something separate and detached from your full experience, which makes it a challenge, but also a wonderful opportunity for you to show what you know and what you can do.

Finally, the AP® English Language and Composition exam is only one test of what you know and can do at this particular point in your life. It does not define you or what you will be capable of in the future. Relax and bring your best to the experience.

Best of luck to you!

References

Chrisomalis, Stephen. "Philosophical Isms" *The Phrontistery*. 2007, accessed August 5, 2010, *http://phrontistery.info/isms.html*.

Decker, Randall E. *Patterns of Exposition 10*. Boston: Little, Brown and Company, 1986.

Donovan, M. *A Philosophical Timeline of Lives and Texts*, accessed July 24, 2010, *http://www.santarosa.edu/~mdonovan/whatis/line.htm*.

Fowler, H. Ramsey, ed., *The Little Brown Handbook*. Boston: Little, Brown and Company, 1980.

Gaarder, Jostein. *Sophie's World: A Novel About the History of Philosophy*. New York: Berkley, 1994.

Harris, Robert. "The Purpose and Method of Satire" *VirtualSalt*, 2004, accessed August 14, 2010, *http://www.virtualsalt.com/satire.htm*.

Marvin, Christopher. "The Window: Philosophy on the Internet" *Timeline*, 2000, accessed July 24, 2010, *http://www.trincoll.edu/depts/phil/philo/timeline.html*.

Miller, Robert K. *The Informed Argument*. San Diego: Harcourt Brace Jovanovich, 1986.

Rottenberg, Annette T. *Elements of Argument*. Boston: Bedford/St. Martin's, 2000.

Purdue OWL: Verb Tenses. Purdue University, 2018. Web. 18 Apr. 2018. *https://owl.english.purdue.edu/owl/resource/601/04/*

Shertzer, M., ed. *The Elements of Grammar*. New York: Macmillan Publishing Company, 1986.

Notes

Notes

Notes

Notes

Notes

Notes

Notes